WORLD ECONOMIC AND FINANCIAL SURVEYS

Exchange Rate Arrangements and Currency Convertibility
Developments and Issues

Prepared by a Staff Team led by R. Barry Johnston

with
Mark Swinburne
Alexander Kyei
Bernard Laurens
David Mitchem
Inci Otker
Susana Sosa
Natalia Tamirisa

INTERNATIONAL MONETARY FUND
Washington, DC
1999

Production: IMF Graphics Section
Figures: Theodore F. Peters, Jr.
Typesetting: Joseph Ashok Kumar

ISBN 1-55775-795-X
ISSN 0258-7440

Price: US$25.00
(US$20.00 to full-time faculty members and
students at universities and colleges)

Please send orders to:
International Monetary Fund, Publication Services
700 19th Street, N.W., Washington, D.C. 20431, U.S.A.
Tel.: (202) 623-7430   Telefax: (202) 623-7201
E-mail: publications@imf.org
Internet:http://www.imf.org

recycled paper

Contents

Figures

Section

The following symbols have been used throughout this volume:

. . . to indicate that data are not available;

— to indicate that the figure is zero or less than half the final digit shown, or that the item does not exist;

– between years or months (for example, 1995–96 or January–June) to indicate the years or months covered, including the beginning and ending years or months;

/ between years (for example, 1995/96) to indicate a fiscal or financial year.

"Billion" means a thousand million; "trillion" means a thousand billion.

"Basis points" refer to hundredths of 1 percentage point (for example, 25 basis points are equivalent to ¼ of 1 percentage point).

"n.a." means not applicable.

Minor discrepancies between constituent figures and totals are due to rounding.

As used in this volume the term "country" does not in all cases refer to a territorial entity that is a state as understood by international law and practice. As used here, the term also covers some territorial entities that are not states but for which statistical data are maintained on a separate and independent basis.

Preface

This study is the latest in a series reviewing developments and issues in the exchange arrangements and currency convertibility of IMF members. The last report on this topic was published in April 1995 as *Issues in International Exchange and Payments Systems*. The present report was completed in July 1997, and outlines developments on the basis of information available at that time. The principal information source is the *Annual Report on Exchange Arrangements and Exchange Restrictions (AREAER)* prepared in consultation with national authorities. Beginning in 1996, the coverage of the *AREAER* was significantly expanded to cover the regulations that affect cross-border capital transactions in a more comprehensive manner. The format of the *AREAER* report was also changed to present the information in a standardized tabular format. These modifications are reflected in the coverage and content of this study.

The study was prepared in the Exchange Regime and Market Operations Division, Monetary and Exchange Affairs Department, under the direction of R. Barry Johnston, Division Chief. The division is also responsible for the preparation of the *AREAER*. Coauthors of the study are Mark Swinburne, Deputy Division Chief; Alexander Kyei, Bernard Laurens, and Susana Sosa, Senior Economists; Inci Otker and Natalia Tamirisa, Economists; and David Mitchem, Consultant. Virgilio Sandoval and Melissa Weiss provided the research assistance. Francine Koch provided excellent secretarial assistance. Juanita Roushdy of the External Relations Department edited the manuscript and coordinated production of the publication.

The study has benefited from comments and suggestions from staff of other IMF departments, as well as from Executive Directors; however, the analysis and policy considerations are those of the contributing staffs and should not be attributed to Executive Directors, or their national authorities.

List of Abbreviations

AFR	African Department (Angola, Benin, Botswana, Burkina Faso, Burundi, Cameroon, Cape Verde, Central African Republic, Chad, Comoros, Côte d'Ivoire, Democratic Republic of the Congo, Republic of Congo, Equatorial Guinea, Eritrea, Ethiopia, Gabon, The Gambia, Ghana, Guinea, Guinea-Bissau, Kenya, Lesotho, Liberia, Madagascar, Malawi, Mali, Mauritius, Mozambique, Namibia, Niger, Nigeria, Rwanda, São Tomé and Príncipe, Senegal, Seychelles, Sierra Leone, South Africa, Swaziland, Tanzania, Togo, Uganda, Zambia, and Zimbabwe)
APD	Asia and Pacific Department (Australia, Bangladesh, Bhutan, Brunei, Cambodia, China, Fiji, Hong Kong SAR, India, Indonesia, Japan, Kiribati, Korea, Lao People's Democratic Republic, New Zealand, Macao, Malaysia, Maldives, Marshall Islands, Micronesia, Mongolia, Myanmar, Nepal, Palau, Papua New Guinea, Philippines, Samoa, Singapore, Solomon Islands, Sri Lanka, Taiwan Province of China, Thailand, Tonga, Vanuatu, and Vietnam)
AREAER	*Annual Report on Exchange Arrangements and Exchange Restrictions*
BIBF	Bangkok International Banking Facility
BIS	Bank for International Settlements
BPA	Bilateral payment arrangement
BSRD	Bangko Sentral Registration Document
CBA	Currency board arrangement
CCI	Controls on current payments and transfers indices
CFETS	China's Foreign Exchange Trading System
CLS	Continuous linked settlement
CLSS	Continuous Linked Settlement Services
CMEA	Council for Mutual Economic Assistance
CPSS	Committee on Payment and Settlement Systems
EBS	Electronic Brokering System
ECB	European Central Bank
ECHO	Exchange Clearing House
ECI	Exchange and capital controls indices
ECU	European currency unit
EMS	European Monetary System
EMU	European Economic and Monetary Union
ERM	Exchange rate mechanism
ESAF	Enhanced Structural Adjustment Facility

EUI	European I Department (Albania, Aruba, Austria, Belgium, Bosnia and Herzegovina, Bulgaria, Croatia, Cyprus, Czech Republic, Denmark, Finland, France, Germany, Greece, Hungary, Iceland, Ireland, Israel, Italy, Luxembourg, Malta, the Netherlands, the Netherlands Antilles, Norway, Poland, Portugal, Romania, San Marino, Slovak Republic, Slovenia, Spain, Sweden, Switzerland, Turkey, United Kingdom, and former Yugoslav Republic of Macedonia
EUII	European II Department (Armenia, Azerbaijan, Belarus, Estonia, Georgia, Kazakhstan, Kyrgyz Republic, Latvia, Lithuania, Moldova, Russia, Tajikistan, Turkmenistan, Ukraine, and Uzbekistan)
FCDU	Foreign currency deposit unit
FEAC	Foreign exchange adjustment center
FFE	Foreign-funded enterprises
FTC	Foreign trading company
GDP	Gross domestic product
GNP	Gross national product
IOSCO	International Organization of Securities Commissions
KCI	Capital controls indices
LAIA-RPCA	Latin American Integration Association Reciprocal Payments and Credit Agreement
LIFFE	London International Financial Futures Exchange
MAI	Multilateral Agreement on Investment
MCP	Multiple currency practices
MED	Middle Eastern Department (Islamic State of Afghanistan, Algeria, Bahrain, Djibouti, Egypt, Islamic Republic of Iran, Iraq, Jordan, Kuwait, Lebanon, Libyan Arab Jamahiriya, Mauritania, Morocco, Oman, Pakistan, Qatar, Saudi Arabia, Somalia, Syrian Arab Republic, Sudan, Tunisia, United Arab Emirates, and Republic of Yemen)
MICEX	Moscow Interbank Foreign Currency Exchange
MIGA	Multilateral Investment Guarantee Agency
NDF	Nondeliverable forward
NDFC	Nondeliverable forward contract
OECD	Organization for Economic Cooperation and Development
SAEC	State Administration of Exchange Control
SEC	Security and Exchange Commission
SIL	Special import license
WHD	Western Hemisphere Department (Antigua and Barbuda, Argentina, The Bahamas, Barbados, Belize, Bolivia, Brazil, Canada, Chile, Colombia, Costa Rica, Dominica, Dominican Republic, Ecuador, El Salvador, Grenada, Guatemala, Guyana, Haiti, Honduras, Jamaica, Mexico, Nicaragua, Panama, Paraguay, Peru, St. Kitts and Nevis, St. Lucia, Suriname, St. Vincent and the Grenadines, Trinidad and Tobago, the United States, Uruguay, and Venezuela)
WTO	World Trade Organization

Part I

I

Overview

During the past decade, most economies have become more open, as evidenced by the increase in world exports of goods and services as a share of GDP from about 18 percent in 1987 to about 23 percent in 1997. Likewise, international flows of direct and portfolio investments expanded substantially. In developing countries, net direct and portfolio investment inflows as a share of GDP increased from about 2 percent in 1987 to 5 percent in 1997. The daily turnover in major foreign exchange markets more than doubled between 1989 and 1995 to reach $1.26 trillion.

One of the principal forces driving the growth of international trade and investment was the liberalization of financial transactions, including the deregulation of financial markets, the removal of controls on international capital movements, and the liberalization of trade and exchange controls. A review of trends through July 1997 in the use of controls on payments and transfers for current international transactions and capital movements (Sections II and III) indicates that most IMF member countries continued to liberalize these controls, and that the process has accelerated since 1990. A key indicator of the progress is the number of IMF members that have accepted Article VIII, Sections 2, 3, and 4 of the IMF's Articles of Agreement (71 since the beginning of 1993) bringing the total to 145 in June 1998. Although some exchange and capital controls were reintroduced in the context of the Asian crisis, such controls concerned a few countries and were mostly short-lived.

The trends in trade and investments and the liberalization of exchange restrictions and capital controls are compared in Figure 1. During the 1990s, a relatively rapid liberalization of exchange controls on invisible transactions and liberalization of controls on capital movements coincided with the rapid growth of capital flows, which outstripped the growth of international trade. For industrial countries, cross-border transactions in bonds and equities now far exceed total international trade. For developing countries, net foreign capital inflows exceed the annual increase in exports.[1]

Technological and financial innovation has also shaped the evolution of the international exchange and payments systems. Advances in computers, communications, and electronically based payment technologies have reduced the costs of collecting, processing, and executing transactions, and thus fostered the development and integration of financial markets. Furthermore, advanced computer technologies have been instrumental in devising complex pricing strategies for new financial products (especially options) that have expanded hedging and investment opportunities and broken down barriers between financial instruments and markets. Investment strategies have increasingly included an international dimension aimed at diversifying portfolio risks and increasing rates of return, while corporate strategies have evolved toward relying more on foreign investment, exports, "outsourcing," and international alliances.

Technological and financial innovation has, in turn, created a demand for a more liberal and sophisticated international exchange and payments system. It has also increasingly rendered obsolete distinctions between various types of financial institutions, instruments, and transactions and weakened the effectiveness of administrative controls (Section II). As a consequence, the focus has shifted from the authorization of exchange transactions to broader surveillance and supervision of markets. Greater emphasis has been given to fostering the development of sound financial institutions and to promoting transparency as a basis for informed private market decision making. Likewise, in prudential regulation, the tendency is to rely less on quantitative limits for controlling risks and more on oversight of the internal capacity for risk management and public disclosure.

The forces of globalization, liberalization, and innovation have also exerted an important influence on the exchange rate arrangements of member countries (Section IV). There has been a trend by member countries to adopt more flexible market-based exchange rate arrangements. In part, this has reflected moves toward currency convertibility and tensions between economic objectives. The increasing volumes of capital movements, which may respond to interest rate and exchange rate policies, have required greater coordination of monetary and exchange rate policies. In most cases, the policy response to capital inflows has in-

---

[1]The comparison between the contribution of net foreign capital inflows and export growth is based on the empirical evidence that economic development is positively related to foreign financial investment and to increased access to foreign markets as measured by export growth.

Figure 1. Trends in Trade, Capital Flows, and
Exchange and Capital Controls

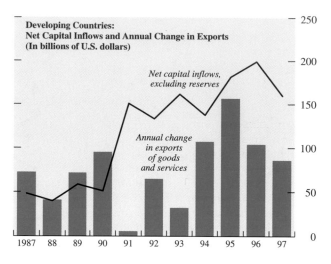

Developing Countries:
Net Capital Inflows and Annual Change in Exports
(In billions of U.S. dollars)

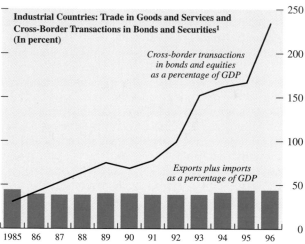

Industrial Countries: Trade in Goods and Services and
Cross-Border Transactions in Bonds and Securities[1]
(In percent)

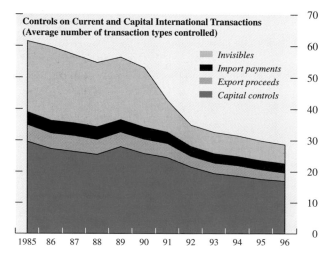

Controls on Current and Capital International Transactions
(Average number of transaction types controlled)

[1]Average for selected industrial economies, including Canada,
France, Germany, Italy, and the United States.

volved allowing more flexibility in exchange arrangements. Nevertheless, some countries have subordinated monetary policies to the maintenance of exchange rate pegs as part of their programs of stabilization and structural reform, or in the context of regional integration initiatives. More rigid forms of pegged arrangements that require the strongest commitment to the exchange rate peg (such as currency unions and currency boards) have been more resilient in the face of increased capital flows than, for example, conventional pegs to single or baskets of currencies.

Exchange rate arrangements have generally become more market based, with much greater reliance on interbank markets to coordinate the supply and demand for foreign exchange (Section IV). In the major markets, the relative importance of traditional dealing in spot and forward exchange is, if anything, declining, as other markets, not least in derivatives, have grown rapidly. The adoption of electronic matching systems in the major markets and moves toward a single currency in Europe has resulted in some refocusing of exchange trading toward emerging currencies. This has reinforced the trends in emerging foreign exchange markets toward more market-based exchange arrangements. Among developing countries, there has also been a continued decline in reliance on multiple exchange rate systems and significant progress with the development of forward exchange markets.

Overall, further progress toward the establishment of a multilateral exchange and payments system consistent with the purposes of the IMF has been significant.[2] This continuing progress has required the IMF, in its turn, to review and update its monitoring techniques and the advice it provides to members on exchange systems, particularly in the context of assisting members on the liberalization of their capital accounts (Section III). The IMF has expanded its information on international exchange and payments systems to include the regulations affecting capital movements, and proposals are being developed to make the database available on the Internet. In advising on reforms of exchange systems and the liberalization of the capital account, the IMF has increasingly adopted an integrated approach that emphasizes the linkages between liberalization and the need for sound financial markets and institutions, the implementation of indirect monetary control, the adoption of appropriate macroeconomic and exchange rate policies, and the development of prudential safeguards to address the specific risks involved in capital flows. Work has been intensified on designing the precise operational se-

[2]Under Article I, Section (iv) of the Articles of Agreement, one of the purposes of the IMF is "To assist in the establishment of a multilateral system of payments in respect of current transactions between members and in the elimination of foreign exchange restrictions which hamper the growth of world trade."

quencing of reforms to the capital account and coordinating it with broader financial sector reforms.

The IMF classifies members' exchange rate arrangements on the basis of countries' official descriptions of the arrangements; however, considerable ambiguity exists in the present classification scheme. In many cases, the actual exchange arrangement practice differs from the official classification, raising issues for transparency, as well as for analysis and research. This has become a more critical issue in an environment where consistency of monetary and exchange rate policies are a key concern in avoiding excessive short-term capital flows. As a consequence, IMF staff have developed additional indicators of exchange rate arrangements (Section IV), and this study presents a revised classification scheme that combines monetary and exchange rate indicators and takes account of members' actual exchange rate policies.

II

Convertibility of Currencies for Current International Payments and Transfers

Developments in the convertibility of members' currencies for current payments and transfers over the period 1993–97 have clearly been toward more liberal exchange systems for payments and transfers for current international transactions. A measure of such a trend is the increasing number of IMF members that have accepted, since 1993, the obligations of the Article VIII, Sections 2, 3, and 4 of the Articles of Agreement, which provides for freedom of payments and transfers for current international transactions (see Figure 2).

A member country normally accepts the obligations of Article VIII only after eliminating all exchange restrictions, as defined by the IMF's Articles of Agreement. Although the concept of restriction under the IMF's jurisdiction is narrower than the concept of exchange control, the acceptance of such obligations is usually an important part of broader liberalization.[3] In addition, countries that have not formally accepted the obligations of Article VIII, Sections 2, 3, and 4 are more liberal today than some years ago, as they have continued to liberalize their exchange system by improving the functioning of their exchange and financial markets and by removing restrictions on capital movements (see Section III). The IMF has been active in promoting such liberalization, by exercising its jurisdiction, providing technical assistance and training, and exercising surveillance, and through the design of its adjustment programs.

The IMF's Jurisdictional View of Exchange Restrictions

At the end of 1997, 131 countries, or about 70 percent of the membership, were free of restrictions on payments and transfers for current international transactions compared with 119 at the end of 1993. Fifty member countries maintained exchange restrictions compared with 60 countries at the end of 1993. Of

these, 20 had accepted the obligations of Article VIII, Sections 2, 3, and 4; of the remainder that were availing themselves of the transitional arrangements of Article XIV, 25 maintained Article VIII restrictions (i.e., restrictions introduced after accession to the IMF), and 5 maintained only restrictions under Article XIV. Under the provisions of Article XIV, a member may maintain and adapt to changing circumstances the restrictions on payments and transfers for current international transactions that were in effect on the date on which it became a member; the IMF is required to make annual reports on these restrictions.

Eighty percent of the members maintaining restrictions under Article VIII did so without IMF approval (see Tables 1 and 2). The Articles of Agreement do not stipulate the conditions for approval by the IMF of exchange measures subject to Article VIII. The Executive Board, however, has adopted several decisions over time governing the approval of exchange restrictions. To be approved, restrictions have to be temporary, maintained for balance of payments reasons, and nondiscriminatory. Restrictions for reasons of national or international security are not objected to. While restrictions can be approved only if they are imposed for

Figure 2. Number of Countries That Have Accepted the Obligations of Article VIII, Sections 2, 3, and 4
(Cumulative as of October 31, 1998)

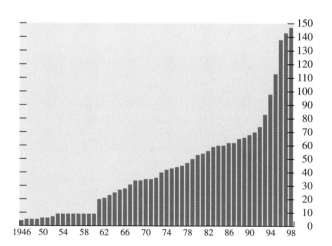

---

[3]In contrast to a restriction, an exchange control may apply to any transaction in foreign exchange, either a receipt or a payment, or to the acquisition or holding of assets denominated in foreign currencies, and to transactions by nonresidents in the local market and by residents in foreign markets or by various monetary instruments.

Table 1. IMF Members with Article XIV Status at the End of 1997[1]

	Number of Years Under Article XIV	Fund Quota (in percent)	Without Restrictions	Maintaining Restrictions		
				Under Article VIII		Under Article XIV
				Approved	Unapproved	
Afghanistan, Islamic State of	42	0.08			x	x
Albania	6	0.02			x	
Angola	8	0.14			x	x
Azerbaijan	5	0.08			x	x
Belarus	5	0.19			x	x
Bhutan	16	0.00				x
Bosnia and Herzegovina[2]	5	0.08			x	
Brazil	32	1.49			x	
Bulgaria[3]	7	0.32				x
Burundi	34	0.04	x			
Cambodia	28	0.04	x			
Cape Verde	19	0.00				x
Colombia	52	0.39			x	
Congo, Dem. Rep. of the	34	0.20			x	
Egypt	52	0.47			x	
Eritrea	5	0.01				x
Ethiopia	52	0.07			x	x
Iran, Islamic Republic of	52	0.74			x	
Iraq[4]	52	0.35				
Lao People's Dem. Rep.	36	0.03	x			
Liberia	35	0.05			x	
Libya	39	0.56			x	
Macedonia, former Yugoslav Republic of[3]	5	0.03	x			
Maldives	19	0.00	x			
Mauritania	34	0.03		x		
Mozambique	13	0.06				x
Myanmar	45	0.13			x	
Nigeria	36	0.88			x	
Romania[3]	25	0.52			x	
Rwanda[3]	34	0.04	x			
São Tomé and Príncipe	20	0.00			x	x
Somalia	35	0.03			x	
Sudan	40	0.12			x	
Syrian Arab Rep.	50	0.14			x	x
Tajikistan	4	0.04	x			
Turkmenistan	5	0.03			x	
Uzbekistan	5	0.14			x	
Vietnam	41	0.17			x	x
Zambia	32	0.25	x			

[1]In some instances, restrictions or practices may have been removed subsequent to the cut-off date.
[2]On December 14, 1992, Bosnia succeeded to the membership of the Socialist Federal Republic of Yugoslavia.
[3]The country has subsequently accepted the obligations of Article VIII, Sections 2, 3, and 4.
[4]No Article IV consultation has been held with Iraq since 1980.

balance of payments reasons, multiple currency practices can be approved when they have been introduced for non-balance of payments reasons "provided that such practices do not materially impede the member's balance of payments adjustment, do not harm the interests of others, and do not discriminate among members."[4]

Member countries availing themselves of the transitional arrangements under Article XIV numbered 39 at the end of 1997; 60 percent of which had been members for at least 20 years. In total, 31 of those members maintained restrictions, with 8 maintaining both Article VIII and Article XIV restrictions (Table 1). The restrictions consisted mainly of binding foreign exchange allowances for current invisible payments and transfers, and multiple currency practices (MCPs) mostly arising from the existence of exchange rate guarantees or forward exchange contracts. More extreme forms of restrictions, such as foreign ex-

[4]Executive Board Decision No. 6790-(81/43), paragraph 4 in IMF (1997c) p. 442.

Table 2. Members with Article VIII Status Maintaining Exchange Restrictions or Practices Subject to Approval by the IMF[1]

1993		1994		1995		1997	
Approved	Unapproved	Approved	Unapproved	Approved	Unapproved	Approved	Unapproved
Bangladesh[2]	Dominican Republic	Bangladesh[2]	Dominican Republic	Chile[3]	Dominican Republic	Botswana	Belize
Guatemala[4]	Haiti	Guatemala[4]	Haiti	Ecuador[5]	Honduras	Guinea[6]	Dominican Republic
Kenya	Honduras[7]	Kenya	Honduras[7]	Guatemala[8]	India	India[9]	Honduras
Mauritius	India	Mauritius	India	Kenya	Malta	Jordan[10]	India
Nicaragua	Malta	Nicaragua	Malta	Mauritius	Seychelles	Kenya	Malta[11]
Pakistan	Nicaragua	Pakistan[12]	Seychelles	Nicaragua[13]	South Africa[15]	Kyrgyz Republic	Mongolia
	Seychelles		South Africa	Papua New Guinea[14]	Suriname	Philippines[16]	Seychelles
	South Africa		Suriname		Tunisia	Russia[17]	Suriname
	Suriname		Tunisia			Sierra Leone	Thailand
	Tunisia					Zimbabwe	Tunisia
							Ukraine[19]

[1]In some instances, restrictions or practices may have been removed or newly introduced, and therefore, the table may not necessarily reflect the position as of end of the year. The following countries maintain optional bilateral payments agreements that provide for settlement periods longer than three months: Argentina, Bolivia, Brazil, Chile, Colombia, Ecuador, Mexico, Paraguay, Peru, Uruguay, and Venezuela. Pending a forthcoming review of the jurisdictional aspect of such arrangements, the IMF does not object to the maintenance in existing official or clearing arrangements of settlement provisions that do not require the settlement of balances at least as frequently as every three months, if such provisions were in force before July 1, 1994.

[2]Bangladesh was granted approval for two multiple currency practices until the end of September 1994; these practices ceased to exist as of September 1994.

[3]Limitations on certain profit remittances were removed in August 1995.

[4]Exchange restrictions evidenced by external payments arrears approved until March/June 1994.

[5]Board approval of multiple currency practices (MCP) was given through June 30, 1995.

[6]Arrears approved until January 31, 1998.

[7]Honduras maintained a multiple currency practice and a restriction on the size of allowable bids in the foreign exchange auction, both subject to approval under Article VIII.

[8]Arrears approved until mid-September 1995.

[9]The MCP arising from exchange rate guarantees on nonresident deposits was approved until August 1997.

[10]Arrears approved until the end of September 1997.

[11]The MCP arising from a forward exchange rate guarantee scheme for U.K. and Irish tour operators was eliminated in November 1997.

[12]Restrictions and MCP were approved until June 30, 1994.

[13]The Executive Board of the IMF approved exchange restrictions on payments for invisibles until the end of February 1995, and restrictions on payments for private debts and an MCP until the end of June 1995.

[14]Restriction approved until July 31, 1995.

[15]Restrictions were eliminated on March 13, 1995 with the unification of the exchange rates by means of the abolition of the financial rand.

[16]Restrictions arise from forward cover provided to oil importers. Approval expired along with contracts by March 1997.

[17]At the time of accepting the obligations of Article VIII the authorities were dismantling one remaining restriction.

[18]Restriction eliminated on May 31, 1997.

Table 3. Exchange Controls on Payments and Transfers for Current International Transactions

	1993	1994	1995	1996	1997
Number of controls[1]					
On import payments	404	387	377	375	368
On invisible transactions	1,217	1,186	1,141	1,098	1,069
Memorandum items					
Total external payment arrears[2]					
(in billions of SDRs)	58.47	63.95	53.01	57.68	58.51
Number of IMF member countries	179	180	181	181	182

Source: International Monetary Fund, *Annual Report on Exchange Arrangements and Exchange Restrictions* (various years).

[1]In compiling the table, "not available" data is treated by averaging two series: in one, data that is "not available" is treated as representing the existence of a control and in the other, data that is "not available" is treated as not representing the existence of a control.

[2]It includes official and private arrears.

change budgets, advance import deposits, bilateral payment arrangements (BPAs) with restrictive features, and restrictions evidenced by the existence of external payments arrears, were in place in very few countries (see Part III, Table A1).

In 1997, 20 Article VIII countries maintained exchange restrictions; of these, 11 maintained unapproved restrictions. This compared with 15 countries, of which 10 were maintaining unapproved restrictions, in 1993 (see Table 2). The restrictions maintained were predominantly MCPs (see Part III, Table A2). Most of the 18 countries with unapproved restrictions have maintained such unapproved restrictions for a number of years. These included restrictions and a multiple currency practice resulting from the operation of a foreign exchange auction in Honduras; temporary restrictions in India; and restrictions arising from the administrative allocation of foreign exchange for current payments and transfers and those evidenced by the existence of arrears in the Seychelles. In some other cases, the nature of the unapproved restrictions varied over the period (see Table 2).

Trends in Exchange Controls on Payments for Current Account Transactions and Current Transfers

Exchange controls on payments and transfers for current international transactions have followed a similar trend to restrictions subject to IMF jurisdiction and have been reduced during the period 1993–97 (Table 3). Following the trend of earlier years, the number of liberalization measures has generally continued to exceed the incidence of tightening of exchange controls, with a particularly marked reduction in controls on invisibles. The volume of external payments arrears after falling sharply in the early 1990s has fluctuated in recent years (Figure 3).

As of the end of 1997, 107 countries reported some form of control over payments for imports. In most of these countries, documentation requirements for the release of foreign exchange were in effect, usually to limit capital flight. Those requirements normally consist of an obligation to open letters of credit, the pre-shipment inspection of the goods imported, a domiciliation requirement for the transactions related to the import, the need to present an import license, or prior approvals to make payments in excess of set limits. Import financing requirements were in effect in about a third of the countries with controls on import payments, and consisted mostly of regulations on the type of imports affected and amount and timing of advanced payments, but also included in a few cases advance import deposits requirements, and restrictions on the sources of funds. Only 35 countries (or less than 20 percent of the membership) had three or more controls on import payments, and the strictest form of control—that is, rationing of foreign exchange resources, mainly through foreign exchange budgets, was present in only 11 countries. The number of countries adopting quantitative import controls implemented through the exchange system remained about 10 percent of the membership during 1994–97. Most quantitative restrictions on imports are now in the form of trade restrictions.

Up to 1990, the liberalization of exchange controls on invisibles had been less extensive than that on controls on import payments. In most cases, controls were either in the form of quantitative limits on the amounts for specific transactions (such as travel) or in the provision of foreign exchange on a case-by-case basis. Controls on transfers of profits and dividends earned on foreign direct investments generally took the form of a maximum amount that could be transferred either as an annual percentage of the original investment or in the form of the phasing of transfers. Controls were intended, inter alia, to avoid capital transfers and to ensure that required tax payments were made.

Figure 3. Exchange Measures on Current Account Transactions, 1985–97
(Number of measures)

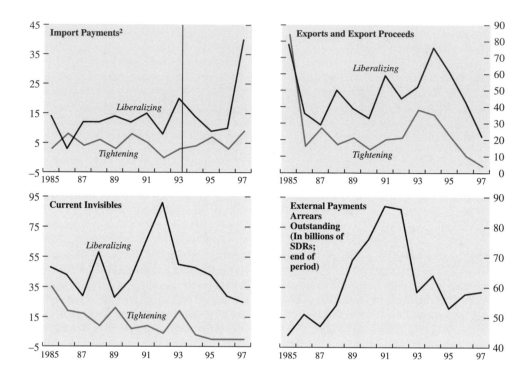

Sources: IMF, *Annual Report on Exchange Arrangements and Exchange Restrictions,* various issues.
[1]These trends depict the number of measures taken, irrespective of their economic significance.
[2]During 1985–92, only import deposits are taken into account. During 1993–97, all controls on import payments are included.

During the 1990s, liberalization of controls on payments and transfers for current invisible transactions has been extensive and the number of controls has fallen significantly (Table 3 and Figure 3). By the end of 1997, only eight countries maintained strict controls on a broad range of invisible transactions, in the form of prior approval requirements or the existence of absolute quantitative limits, or both (Angola, Bhutan, Cape Verde, Myanmar, Somalia, Syrian Arab Republic, Turkmenistan, and Vietnam maintained 10 or more controls on invisible transactions). In these cases, the categories of payment more strictly controlled included remittances of foreign workers' earnings, of profits, interest, and dividend payments; and transfers for the payment of medical expenses and study costs abroad. The elimination of controls on invisibles and current transfers often took place simultaneously with the opening of the capital account (e.g., in Botswana, Fiji, India, Israel, Jordan, Kenya, Namibia, Nepal, the Slovak Republic, South Africa, Zambia, and Zimbabwe), or as part of the completion of the liberalization of payments and transfers for current international transactions in the context of the acceptance of Article VIII, Sections 2, 3, and 4 obligations (e.g., in Bangladesh, Hungary, Malta, Pakistan, the Philippines, Poland, Sri Lanka, and Tunisia). One hundred and one countries (or 55 percent of the membership) retained some type of control on the payments for invisibles; however, in most of these countries, the controls took the form of bona fide tests to avoid the transfer of capital abroad rather than to restrict the current payment and transfer, that is, requests for foreign exchange are granted, if it can be documented that the payment is for a legitimate purpose and not for transferring capital abroad.

The total amount of external payments arrears remained around SDR 60 billion during 1993–97, with over 75 percent of the stock in 1997 accounted for by only nine countries: Angola, the Democratic Republic of the Congo, Côte d'Ivoire, the Kyrgyz Republic, Myanmar, Nicaragua, Nigeria, Sudan, and the Republic of Yemen (see Part III, Table A3). The number of countries reporting arrears at the end of 1997 was 54, of which only 21 had private arrears (Vietnam only in convertible currencies).

Coordinating Exchange and Trade Liberalization

Exchange liberalization tends to start prior to, or concurrently with, trade reform, and to proceed in parallel with, but completed earlier than, trade reform. This conclusion emerges from the review of the experience with exchange and trade liberalization in five countries—China, India, Korea, Mexico, and Russia (see Part II, Section V). These countries eliminated binding exchange controls and promoted the development of a market-based exchange system either in advance of, or in tandem with, the liberalization of trade barriers. Most restrictive exchange controls were decisively abolished first, while trade liberalization was generally implemented more gradually. It is quite often easier to start with the exchange system rather than trade reforms since exchange barriers are not specific to individual products, firms, or sectors, and such reforms often do not face the same resistance from powerful lobbies in protected sectors.

Exchange controls and particularly controls on capital movements are also found to represent an important nontariff barrier to international trade for developing countries, and thus, further exchange and capital control liberalization could stimulate trade. By reducing distortions and costs, the liberalization of exchange and capital controls enhances competition in traded goods and services, and allocative and productive efficiency. Exchange liberalization also lowers transaction costs through promoting the development of foreign exchange markets and modern international payment instruments. By reducing disequilibrium in the foreign exchange market, exchange liberalization can also reduce reliance on trade restrictions for balance of payments reasons.

Bilateralism and Regionalism

The IMF has long discouraged members from adopting bilateral and regional payments arrangements that involve discriminatory and restrictive features. In an early discussion, the Executive Board urged "the full collaboration of all its members to reduce and to eliminate as rapidly as practicable reliance on bilateralism." The "persistence of bilateralism may impede the attainment and maintenance of convertibility," thereby hampering the establishment of a multilateral payments system.[5]

In some cases, bilateral payment arrangements were adopted as transitional arrangements while foreign exchange markets and multilateral payments mechanisms were being developed. Such arrangements can

interfere with the development of conventional payment instruments; delay the development of deeper and more efficient foreign exchange markets and participation in private payments systems; and expose central banks to credit and exchange rate risks. Bilateral and regional payment arrangements may also involve exchange restrictions subject to the Fund's jurisdiction—the IMF has based this determination on the length of the settlement period of balances in the arrangement, with settlement periods longer than three months being treated as a restriction—or multiple currency practices. Pending a forthcoming review, the IMF does "not object to the maintenance in existing official or clearing arrangements of settlement provisions that do not require the settlement of balances at least as frequently as every three months, if such provisions were in force before July 1, 1994."[6]

At the end of 1997, it is estimated that 96 members maintained 269 bilateral payment arrangements,[7] of which 156 were operative. This represents an 18 percent reduction in the number of total agreements and of 27 percent in the number of operative agreements since the end of 1993. Only a very few countries maintained bilateral payments arrangements with restrictive features at the end of 1997: Islamic State of Afghanistan, Albania, Cape Verde, Egypt, India, Sudan, and the Syrian Arab Republic. About 20 percent of members (most are formerly centrally planned economies) maintained more than 10 agreements each; more than half the agreements were inoperative. The most common obstacle to the prompt elimination of bilateral payments arrangements has been the difficulties in reaching agreement between the parties on the clearing of the outstanding balances.

The number of members that are involved in regional payment agreements has also declined since 1990 following the collapse of the CMEA (see Table 4). As of December 1997, there were six regional arrangements that included a payments clearance agreement involving 61 countries. In a number of cases, member countries of the regional arrangements have made efforts to increase the use of the facilities, and most have succeeded in attracting new participants and expanding the coverage of the facility. In several cases, clearinghouse arrangements have

---

[5]Executive Board Decision No. 433-(55/42), paragraph 3 in IMF (1997c) pp. 422–23.

[6]Executive Board Decision No. 10749 (94/67) in IMF (1997c), pp. 423.

[7]The number of agreements was estimated by adding all agreements reported for the 1998 *AREAER* by the authorities of at least one party to the agreement; in those cases where a member reported agreements with countries of the former Soviet Union, or other former multilateral clearing system of the former Council for Mutual Economic Assistance (CMEA), it was assumed that there were agreements with all those countries. In the case where one party reported the agreement as operative and the other party as inoperative, the agreement was classified as operative. As a result of the methodology used, both the number of operative agreements and the number of total agreement may be overestimated.

Table 4. Developments in Regional Payment Arrangements[1]

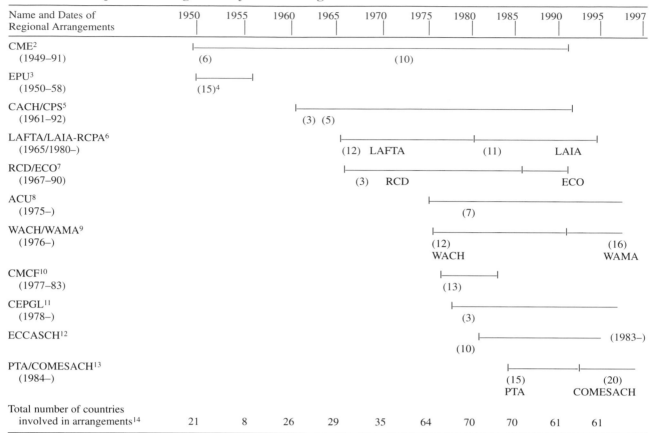

Name and Dates of Regional Arrangements	1950	1955	1960	1965	1970	1975	1980	1985	1990	1995	1997
CME[2] (1949–91)	(6)				(10)						
EPU[3] (1950–58)	(15)[4]										
CACH/CPS[5] (1961–92)			(3) (5)								
LAFTA/LAIA-RCPA[6] (1965/1980–)				(12) LAFTA			(11)		LAIA		
RCD/ECO[7] (1967–90)				(3) RCD					ECO		
ACU[8] (1975–)						(7)					
WACH/WAMA[9] (1976–)						(12) WACH				(16) WAMA	
CMCF[10] (1977–83)						(13)					
CEPGL[11] (1978–)							(3)				
ECCASCH[12]							(10)			(1983–)	
PTA/COMESACH[13] (1984–)								(15) PTA		(20) COMESACH	
Total number of countries involved in arrangements[14]	21	8	26	29	35	64	70	70	61	61	

[1]Figures in parentheses show the number of member countries.
[2]Multilateral clearing system of the former Council for Mutual Economic Assistance.
[3]European Payments Union.
[4]Excluding Sterling Area other than the United Kingdom and Ireland.
[5]Central American Clearing House/ Central American Payments System.
[6]Latin American Free Trade Association/Latin American Integration Association—Reciprocal Payments and Credits Agreement.
[7]Regional Cooperation for Development/Economic Cooperation Organization.
[8]Asian Clearing Union.
[9]West African Clearing House/West African Monetary Agency.
[10]Caribbean Multilateral Clearing Facility.
[11]Clearing House of the Economic Community of the Great Lakes Countries.
[12]Economic Community of the Central African States Clearing House.
[13]Preferential Trading Area for Eastern and Southern Africa/Community of Eastern and Southern African States Clearing House.
[14]These figures do not add to the sum of members in the arrangements, because some members participate in more than one arrangement, including Burundi, Rwanda, and the Democratic Republic of the Congo.

been organized within major regional integration initiatives.

The main features of the regional payment arrangements in effect in December 1997 are presented in Part III, Table A4. The arrangements do not have features that give rise to a restriction subject to the IMF's jurisdiction except for the Latin American Integration Association Reciprocal Payments and Credit Agreement (LAIA-RPCA), whose settlement period is four months. However, pending completion of a review of the jurisdictional aspects of official clearing and payments arrangements, the Executive Board decided in July 1994 that the IMF shall not object to the maintenance in those arrangements of longer settlement periods if such provisions were in force before July 1, 1994.

Procedures for Acceptance of Obligations of Article VIII, Sections 2, 3, and 4

In early 1993 and in recognition of the need to ensure further progress in developing the international monetary system, the IMF staff adopted enhanced procedures to encourage members to accept the obligations of Article VIII. As of January 1993 while only 75, or less than half of the members, had accepted the obligations of Article VIII, many other members maintained exchange systems that were either free of restrictions or had restrictions of minor significance. The guidelines thus requested the staff to discuss exchange restrictions maintained under Article XIV or subject to approval under Article VIII, and their elimination and the move toward acceptance of Article VIII status during Article IV consultations. The staff would point out the benefits associated with convertibility and press for the removal of exchange restrictions, paying due regard to the strength of the members' balance of payments. In addition, staff reports would contain a brief description of the exchange system and the prospects for the elimination of outstanding restrictions and the acceptance of Article VIII, Sections 2, 3, and 4 obligations.

Although a member country may accept the obligations of Article VIII at any time, the IMF normally encourages doing so only after all restrictive measures have been eliminated, whether they are maintained under Article XIV or subject to approval under Article VIII [8] This is in line with the significance of the acceptance, that is, that the member is committed to maintaining an exchange system that is free of restrictions on payments and transfers for current international transactions. As part of the process of acceptance, the IMF staff undertakes an in-depth examination of the exchange system to identify any remaining impediments to the adoption of current account convertibility. Generally, these procedures have ensured that all outstanding exchange restrictions are identified and discussed with the member before Executive Board notification. Where restrictions were identified, the member in many cases elected to eliminate these before Executive Board notification; in other cases the member provided a timetable for the elimination of the restrictions so that staff could recommend approval for the retention of the restrictions as part of the notification to the Executive Board. Part III, Table A5 reviews the nature of restrictions maintained by members accepting the obligations of Article VIII, Sections 2, 3, and 4, and whether they were approved.

The intensified efforts by the IMF staff, the growing recognition that exchange restrictions are inefficient and largely ineffective in achieving their intended results, and the greater flexibility of exchange rate policies have encouraged members to eliminate exchange restrictions on current international payments and transfers and to accept the obligations of Article VIII, Sections 2, 3, and 4. Thus, between early 1993 and June 1998, 71 members had accepted these obligations. Nevertheless, a number have continued to avail themselves of the transitional arrangements, in some cases for periods up to 50 years, even in cases where they no longer maintain restrictions that are covered by the transitional arrangements (see Table 1). The list of countries maintaining Article XIV restrictions at the end of 1997, and the nature of these restrictions, is provided in Part III, Table A1. Under Article XIV, Section 3, the IMF could make representation to a member that conditions are favorable for the elimination of any restriction under Article XIV; however, it has never done so.

---

[8] Executive Board Decision No. 1034-(60/27) states that "members may at any time notify the Fund that they accept the obligations of Article VIII, Sections 2, 3, and 4, and no longer avail themselves of the transitional provisions of Article XIV. Before members give notice that they are accepting the obligations of Article VIII, Sections 2, 3, and 4, it would be desirable that, as far as possible, they eliminate measures that would require the approval of the Fund, and that they satisfy themselves that they are not likely to need recourse to such measures in the foreseeable future."

III

Controls on Capital Movements

This section reviews the structure of and trends in controls on capital movements and some of the issues and approaches the IMF has adopted to address capital account issues in the context of its technical assistance. It begins by reviewing the information the IMF maintains on capital controls.

Information on Capital Controls

The IMF has traditionally maintained and published information on members' exchange systems in the context of the *AREAER,* which traditionally focused on the regulations affecting current international transactions. Major improvements to the information systems on exchange systems were made starting in 1996 with the aim of expanding the coverage to the capital account at the same time as increasing the accessibility of the information.

In December 1995, a questionnaire was sent to 52 member countries as part of a pilot project to gain experience with the collection and assessment of information on the regulatory framework of external capital account transactions. The questionnaire was developed after consultation with staff of the Organization for Economic Cooperation and Development (OECD) staff experienced with the OECD Code of Liberalization of Capital Movements. The information thus gathered was compiled, together with the data published annually on current international transactions, in a new electronic database with a revised, and more accessible format. In April 1997, a Supplement to the 1996 *AREAER* was published for the sample of 52 countries. The Supplement was well received by members and users who found the changes convenient and adding to the usefulness of the publication. The 1997 *AREAER* was published in August 1997 in the same tabular format and expanded the coverage on the regulation of capital movements to all IMF members.

The information now available on capital account controls covers measures affecting capital inflows and outflows, both for the underlying capital transactions as well as the related exchange transactions (payments, transfers, and receipts). The distinction between an underlying capital transaction and the payment and transfer for such a transaction is frequently not meaningful, and to a large extent controls on capital movements are exercised at the level of the underlying transactions rather than the associated payment and transfer. The extended data on capital controls classify measures into 20 broad categories (10 each for inflows and outflows), with associated subcategories (20 for inflows and 24 for outflows). These are summarized in Table 5.

Data on the number of transaction types controlled are intended to provide an indicator of the overall degree of openness of the economy to capital movements. The formalization of the measures of openness through the development of more inclusive restrictiveness indices is discussed in Part II, Section VII, which also reviews alternative measures used in the literature, and some of the shortcomings of these types of measures. The precise impact of the controls is the subject of considerable and ongoing research (see below for some examples). Data on transaction types controlled also are not intended to distinguish the purposes of different types of controls, but rather to identify regulations that discriminate between international and purely domestic capital transactions and, more specifically, between transactions involving nonresidents and those involving residents only. For the provisions specific to commercial banks, the information also covers regulations that result in differential treatment by the currency of transaction, since such differential treatment can also have an impact on capital movements. The database does not attempt to distinguish controls that are maintained for prudential reasons from capital restrictions. See Part III, Table A6 for a listing of the countries in each group discussed in the text.

Structure of Capital Controls

The use of capital controls has declined significantly over the 1990s as measured by the larger number of liberalization than tightening measures (see Figure 4). For industrial countries, controls now exist, on average, for four out of the 44 main types of transactions listed in Table 5, on which the IMF compiles data. Nonindustrial countries as a whole now control on average about 16 main transaction types.

The structure of controls on capital inflows and capital outflows as at the end of 1997 is reviewed in

14

Table 5. Types of Capital Transactions Possibly Subject to Controls[1]

Inflows	Outflows
Controls on capital market instruments	
Shares or other securities of a participatory nature	
Purchase locally by nonresidents	Sale or issue locally by nonresidents
Sale or issue abroad by residents	Purchase abroad by residents
Bonds or other debt securities	
Purchase locally by nonresidents	Sale or issue locally by nonresidents
Sale or issue abroad by residents	Purchase abroad by residents
Controls on money market instruments	
Purchase locally by nonresidents	Sale or issue locally by nonresidents
Sale or issue abroad by residents	Purchase abroad by residents
Controls on collective investment securities	
Purchase locally by nonresidents	Sale or issue locally by nonresidents
Sale or issue abroad by residents	Purchase abroad by residents
Controls on derivatives and other instruments	
Purchase locally by nonresidents	Sale or issue locally by nonresidents
Sale or issue abroad by residents	Purchase abroad by residents
Controls on credit operations	
Commercial credits	
To residents from nonresidents	By residents to nonresidents
Financial credits	
To residents from nonresidents	By residents to nonresidents
Guarantees, sureties, and financial backup facilities	
To residents from nonresidents	By residents to nonresidents
Controls on direct investment	
Inward direct investment	Outward direct investment
	Controls on liquidation of direct investment
Controls on real estate transactions	
Purchase locally by nonresidents	Purchase abroad by residents
	Sale locally by nonresidents
Controls on personal capital movements	
Loans	
To residents from nonresidents	By residents to nonresidents
Gifts, endowments, inheritances, and legacies	
To residents from nonresidents	By residents to nonresidents
Settlements of debts abroad by immigrants; transfer of assets	
Transfer into the country by immigrants	Transfer abroad by emigrants
Provisions specific to banks and other credit institutions	
Borrowing abroad	Maintenance of accounts abroad
	Lending to nonresidents
Provisions specific to institutional investors	
None	Limits (maximum) on securities issued by nonresidents and on portfolio invested abroad
	Limits (maximum) on portfolio invested locally

[1]This listing excludes certain other measures shown in the *AREAER* that cannot be conveniently summarized as controls over inflows or outflows since, depending on the exact details, they could be either, or they might discriminate in favor of international capital flows rather than against them. Examples are the *AREAER* information for differential treatment of foreign currency lending or deposits, or open position limits, within the provisions specific to banks; and other measures imposed by securities laws. For a full listing of the *AREAER* capital account categories, see Box 7.

Figure 4. Capital Account Measures by Country Group[1]

(Number of measures)[2]

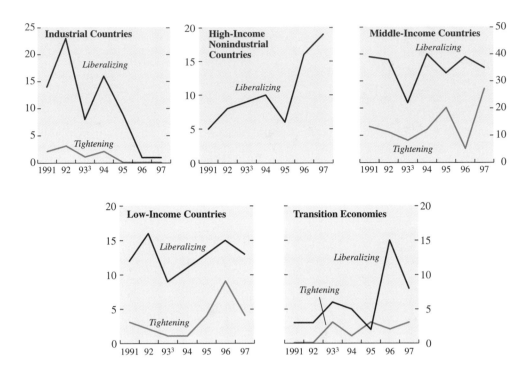

Sources: IMF, *Annual Report on Exchange Arrangements and Exchange Restrictions,* various issues.

[1]These trends depict the number of measures taken, irrespective of their economic significance.

[2]The measures during 1991–93 differ from those during 1993–97.

[3]To be consistent with past years, the figures for liberalization and tightening measures for 1997 do not include measures for personal capital movements.

Table 6. In industrial countries, controls on direct investment, capital market securities, and real estate investment account for over 85 percent of the remaining capital inflow controls. Inward direct investment is normally controlled because of social, sectoral, or strategic considerations rather than for macroeconomic or balance of payments reasons; inward direct investment is controlled to some degree by 16 of the industrial countries, mainly in sectors sometimes considered sensitive (such as banking and financial services, broadcasting, air and maritime transport, commercial fishing, energy, or telecommunications). Controls on inflows into capital market securities that are participatory in nature (either sales and issues abroad by residents or purchases locally by nonresidents) also reflect such concerns. Inward real estate investment is quite often also considered sensitive. With regard to outflows, controls over capital market securities mainly reflect restrictions on the sale or issue locally by nonresidents and have frequently been motivated by prudential and investor protection concerns. Controls on outflows through institutional investors have also sometimes reflected prudential concerns.

For nonindustrial countries, controls over capital outflows were somewhat more extensive than on capital inflows, in contrast to the industrial countries. This may reflect partly the concern, at lower-income levels, to limit capital outflows, and partly the fact that, for a number of countries, the domestic instruments and markets are not sufficiently developed to attract significant capital inflows.

Among the high-income nonindustrial countries, inflow controls relating to credit operations, money market, collective investment, and derivative instruments are considerably more common than for industrial countries, and the same applies in varying degrees to the transition and other nonindustrial countries. This may reflect an attempt to insulate monetary policy and to protect underdeveloped financial markets. For the low- and middle-income countries (and to some extent also for the transition economies), within the more liquid inflow categories, there is some tendency for relatively more weight on controls on credit operations, and relatively less on money market, collective investment, derivative, and other instruments, possibly reflecting the less common occurrence of such financial

Table 6. Structure of Controls by Country Group, End of 1997

(In percentage of total controls for each group, unless otherwise stated)

	Industrial Countries	High-Income Non-industrial Countries	Middle-Income Countries	Low-Income Countries	Transition Countries
Inflows					
Capital market securities	30.6	20.5	18.5	17.3	21.0
Money market instruments	6.1	8.4	8.1	9.9	13.4
Collective investment securities	0.0	14.5	7.3	8.6	9.8
Derivatives and other instruments	0.0	12.0	7.3	6.3	11.2
Credit operations	4.1	13.3	23.6	25.4	17.4
Direct investment	32.7	9.6	10.7	9.9	4.5
Real estate transactions	22.4	9.6	7.9	6.3	8.5
Personal capital movements	0.0	7.2	6.5	8.9	5.4
Commercial banks and other credit institutions	2.0	2.4	7.6	6.3	6.3
Institutional investors	2.0	2.4	2.5	1.0	2.7
Total	100	100	100	100	100
Memorandum item:					
Average number of controlled transaction types (in number of transaction types controlled, maximum of 20)	2.0	6.9	5.4	6.9	8.3
Outflows					
Capital market securities	29.8	19.0	18.1	16.4	19.2
Money market instruments	12.8	8.6	8.1	10.5	11.0
Collective investment securities	10.6	11.4	8.9	9.4	9.8
Derivatives and other instruments	6.4	9.5	6.7	6.1	9.5
Credit operations	6.4	12.4	16.1	16.0	16.4
Direct investment	4.3	5.7	10.3	11.6	6.6
Real estate transactions	4.3	10.5	7.3	9.4	7.3
Personal capital movements	2.1	12.4	9.9	9.9	6.6
Commercial banks and other credit institutions	8.5	5.7	8.9	8.8	9.1
Institutional investors	14.9	4.8	5.6	1.8	4.4
Total	100	100	100	100	100
Memorandum item:					
Average number of controlled transaction types (in number of transaction types controlled, maximum of 24)	2.0	8.8	7.6	9.9	11.7

Source: IMF, *Annual Report on Exchange Arrangements and Exchange Restrictions* (various years).
Note: Totals may not add because of rounding.

instruments. With respect to capital outflows, controls on the more liquid types of transactions were more common in all the nonindustrial country groups than for the industrial countries. There is some tendency toward relatively more weight on credit controls, and relatively less weight on money market, collective investment, and derivative and other instruments, in the low- and middle-income countries and transition economies compared with high-income nonindustrial countries.

Trends in Controls on Capital Movements

The trend toward more liberal capital accounts is reflected in the greater number of measures easing or eliminating capital controls, rather than introducing or tightening them in all country groups (Figure 4). For industrial countries, the number of measures taken recently is now very low, reflecting the fact that the bulk of the liberalization process in most of these countries is now complete. For nonindustrial countries, the num-

ber of liberalizing measures fell during 1997, probably reflecting a response to the Asian crisis. However, 1997 did not see much of a resurgence of tightening measures beyond a couple of individual countries in Asia (see below). For high-income nonindustrial countries, the pace of liberalization seems to have quickened in recent years prior to 1997, in part reflecting the initial high level of controls in some of these countries. For middle- and low-income countries too, the trend toward liberalization had been notable over the 1990s, notwithstanding increases in tightening measures in some recent years. For transition economies, the pace of capital account liberalization had accelerated significantly as the countries tackled major structural and macroeconomic reforms and liberalized exchange systems for current international transactions.

Trend Toward Liberalization of Capital Flows

The trend toward liberalization of capital movements has reflected a variety of motivations, including

17

the benefits from increased access to, and a lower cost of, investable funds. The liberalization of controls on capital outflows has in part been a response to stronger net capital inflows. Liberalization has also reflected a wish to avoid the potential distortionary effects of the controls and concerns about their overall effectiveness.

Research to test the effectiveness of capital controls generally concludes that controls may have some effectiveness in the short run but that it can be eroded quite quickly.[9] Thus, the longer that capital controls are in place, the more important becomes the issue of their effectiveness and their potential costs and distortions on the economy. Such costs may include more expensive borrowing and less diversified wealth portfolios. The channeling of capital to avoid the controls can result in less-developed financial markets and can distort financial intermediation and even damage the financial sector by encouraging the use of channels and instruments that are less well managed and supervised. The circumvention of capital controls also distorts the balance of payments statistics, which, therefore, become a less reliable guide for policy formulation and informed market decision making. Combating the circumvention typically requires new controls, involving mounting administrative and broader economic costs. The inevitable "investment" in circumvention techniques by market participants is privately profitable, but represents a socially inefficient allocation of resources. It is likely, too, that the costs of circumvention mean that the largest, wealthiest, and most sophisticated players are able to find ways of circumventing controls, while others carry more of the direct costs of the controls.

It is likely that growing doubts about the cost effectiveness of capital controls have been an important consideration in the general trend toward capital account liberalization in the nonindustrial countries, as it was in the industrial countries previously. In particular, as the financial sector develops following domestic financial liberalization and as current international transactions are liberalized, capital controls become more difficult to enforce. Argentina, Israel, Mexico, and Uganda provide examples of countries that have moved toward liberal systems for capital flows rather than trying to reinforce controls as loopholes are progressively exploited.

Recourse to New Capital Controls

Notwithstanding the general trend toward liberalization, during 1993–97 there were 106 instances involving 29 countries where new capital controls were imposed or existing ones intensified. Over half the measures were implemented by middle-income countries (mainly by Brazil, Colombia, Malaysia, the Philippines, Thailand, and Turkey). Most restrictions were specific to banks (especially related to various forms of open-position limits and transactions with nonresidents) and credit controls (financial credits from nonresidents), and some were temporary. Of the above, 34 measures were introduced or tightened in 1997 by seven countries.

A range of different motivations and justifications have been ascribed to the use of capital controls, ranging from maintaining domestic monetary autonomy in an inflexible exchange rate regime, to protecting nascent financial sectors, to the need to cope with irrationally volatile international financial markets. Tightening measures relating to capital outflows have often been spurred by currency crises and associated "contagion" (or fear thereof), such as the events associated with the currency crises in the countries of the European Monetary System (EMS) (1992–93), Mexico (1994–95), and most recently Asia. The East Asian countries—especially the Philippines and, to a lesser extent, Thailand—accounted for about two-thirds of the new or tightened controls introduced in 1997. The measures chiefly related to forward or other derivative transactions and their financing and, in some cases, attempted to distinguish between nonresident and resident counterparties, or between speculative and nonspeculative capital transactions. In many cases, the new controls were quite short-lived—for example, in early 1998, Thailand removed most of the additional controls it had introduced several months earlier at the peak of its currency crisis. In Korea, not only was there an avoidance of new controls on outflows, but further liberalization of capital controls related to inflows was also an important part of the reform and stabilization package. (The use of controls in the Asian crisis is discussed further in Part II, Section VI.)

Policy autonomy has been another important motivation behind the imposition or maintenance of capital controls. There are a number of cases where controls have been reintroduced mainly because of surges in capital inflows rather than currency crises. For example, in recent years, several countries (including Brazil, Chile, Colombia, and Slovenia) have introduced or tightened reserve requirements and similar measures applied to various types of inflows, especially shorter-term inflows. Such measures have been motivated by concerns about the volatility of shorter-term inflows, and loss of monetary policy autonomy under relatively inflexible exchange rate regimes. In essence, capital controls are used in an attempt to reconcile the use of interest rates and the exchange rates to pursue, simultaneously, at least partially inconsistent internal and external balance objectives. The measures generally include compulsory, non–interest-

---

[9]On the effectiveness of controls on capital inflows, see, for example, Cardoso and Goldfajn (1997); Edwards (1998); Soto (1997). On the effectiveness of controls on capital outflows, see, for example, Johnston and Ryan (1994).

bearing, deposit requirements, set as a proportion of the affected foreign inflows. Such measures constitute an implicit tax that discriminates against foreign inflows, because the levels of the requirements are typically significantly higher than the level of reserve requirements against local funding obtained by resident banks, and are not new. For example, during the 1970s, the German authorities applied such measures. Between 1973 and 1974, Germany also applied a 60 percent reserve requirement on the growth of banks' foreign liabilities, and under the Bardepot Law imposed a 50 percent reserve requirement against foreign loans contracted by German companies. Together, these measures appeared to insulate the German domestic market from short-term capital inflows during 1973.

Capital Account Liberalization in the Asian Crisis Economies

Part II, Section VI examines the sequencing of the liberalization of controls on capital inflows in Indonesia, Korea, and Thailand over the period 1985–97 and the role that such sequencing may have played in the currency crises, given that large accumulations of short-term foreign liabilities played an important part in each crisis. Contrary to some perceptions, the approaches to capital account liberalization in these countries were markedly different: Indonesia liberalized outflows relatively early and liberalized inflows progressively, but reimposed controls on external borrowing by banks in the early 1990s; Korea followed a very gradual approach to capital account liberalization, with more emphasis on outflows at first, but beginning to address liberalization of inflows in steps from 1992–93; and Thailand attracted capital inflows quite aggressively, while liberalizing outflows more gradually.

Overall, there was no clear pattern of regulatory measures directly favoring shorter-term inflows over longer-term inflows, except in one aspect of the Korean regime. In 1994, Korea liberalized bank lending in foreign exchange while retaining restrictions on longer-term external borrowing, thus encouraging shorter-term borrowings. Perhaps more important, however, is that certain aspects of the reforms, and the broader policy frameworks in some countries, may have encouraged excessive reliance on shorter-term inflows in a more indirect fashion. Specifically, in Korea and Thailand in particular, there was a policy bias toward inflows intermediated by banks; for instance, the introduction of the Bangkok International Banking Facility (BIBF) in Thailand in 1992, and, in Korea, the limitation on direct borrowing by corporations, as well as the restrictions on access by nonresidents to the domestic bond and security markets. The emphasis on banking flows probably contributed to the short-term composition of inflows. Nevertheless,

in Indonesia, where foreign borrowing by banks was controlled, a large part of the inflows went directly to the corporate sector and was short term (commercial credits). Therefore, it may be reasonable to conclude that other micro- and macroeconomic incentives, including issues of moral hazard, were important in explaining the short-term composition of capital inflows.

Promoting Capital Account Liberalization

In recent years, staff have focused on ways of strengthening discussions with member countries on capital account convertibility. This section reviews some of the work that is under way, focusing on the information systems, technical assistance, regulatory frameworks and safeguards, financial sector surveillance, and collaboration with other agencies.

Information on Capital Controls

Work to improve the information in the *AREAER* database is continuing, by filling significant gaps in the data, eliminating remaining data inconsistencies across members and increasing the frequency of updates, and the accessibility of the information. Proposals are also being developed to make the database accessible on the Internet. Presently, the information does not cover in detail controls on foreign direct investment inflows.

The development of more comprehensive information on the controls maintained by members on payments and transfers for current international transactions and capital movements has allowed the staff to develop indices of the extensiveness of exchange and capital controls (see Part II, Section VI). While such indices have a number of potential shortcomings, they are useful as a way of summarizing the overall restrictiveness of exchange systems for analysis and research and for tracking the evolution of individual country's exchange system. More restrictive exchange and capital control systems, as measured by the indices, are found to be positively related to the size of the black, parallel, or free market premium, the volatility of exchange rates, and the inefficiency and low depth of financial systems. Lower levels of exchange and capital controls are found to be positively related with the level of economic development, and the volume of trade and capital flows, both in absolute terms and as a ratio to GDP.

Technical Assistance Advice

The IMF has traditionally provided technical assistance to liberalize exchange systems for current international transactions and to establish or further develop foreign exchange markets. An increasing

Table 7. Technical Assistance on Exchange Systems and Conditionality Under IMF-Supported Programs, 1994–97

	AFR	APD	EURI	EURII	MED	WHD
Number of countries	13	9	5	13	8	6
Instances of technical assistance						
Market development	10	7	4	13	5	3
Regulatory framework						
Current account transactions	9	7	4	13	5	2
Acceptance of Article VIII	6	5	4	8	3	1
Capital account transactions	4	4	2	4	2	1
Exchange regime	1	3	2	4	2	1
Central bank operations						
Central bank intervention	8	6	3	9	4	3
Coordination of policies	4	6	2	8	3	1
Reserve management	3	4	1	12	3	1
Conditionality under an IMF-supported program						
Countries with an IMF-supported program	6	2	2	9	4	2
Conditionality						
Current account related	1	—	1	5	4	—
Capital account related	2	1	—	3	1	1
Central bank operations related	—	2	—	—	–	—
Interbank market related	2	2	1	3	3	—
Exchange regime related	1	1	1	—	2	—

Source: Section VIII, Appendix.

Notes: AFR = African Department; APD = Asia and Pacific Department; EURI = European I Department; EURII = European II Department; MED = Middle East Department; and WHD = Western Hemisphere Department.

number of members are seeking assistance on the liberalization of their capital accounts. Among the 54 countries that received technical assistance on exchange systems during the period under review, most required assistance for exchange market development, a majority in the liberalization of current international transactions, and about one-fourth received assistance on capital account liberalization (see Table 7).

Technical assistance on exchange systems is integrated with policy discussions, including within the context of discussions and negotiations for an IMF program. For most of the 20 countries using IMF resources and receiving technical assistance on exchange system issues, programs agreed with the IMF included measures on the regulatory framework for foreign exchange transactions or foreign exchange market development, or both. Part II, Section VIII provides examples of technical assistance, general approaches adopted, and issues discussed on exchange systems. The discussion of capital account liberalization in Asia (above, and in Part II, Section VI) reconfirms and highlights the importance of very similar issues.

Integrating Advice on Capital Account Liberalization with Financial Sector Reform

The increased attention to capital account issues has involved an emphasis on an integrated approach to reform covering both external transactions and the development of domestic financial markets and institu-

tions. This integrated approach has reflected a number of considerations (see Johnston, Darbar, and Echeverria, 1997). In particular:

- the stage of development and the stability of domestic financial systems are critical in the approach to opening the capital account. Countries with developed financial markets and institutions have been better able to attract portfolio capital flows and to withstand the consequences of reversals in capital inflows than countries where such markets were just emerging;

- the opening of the capital account can have important implications for the development and stability of financial markets and institutions. In many cases, the implications are positive in that the liberalizations help develop deeper, more competitive, and more diversified financial markets. However, capital account liberalization can also increase financial sector risks if it accelerates the deregulation of the financial system without critical supporting reforms;

- the extent to which capital flows contribute to sustained improvements in economic performance depends on the stage of development and the efficiency of the domestic financial system. The central role of banking systems in allocating financial resources points to the importance of focusing attention on the incentives under which those institutions operate, including those associated with connected or politically motivated lending; developing a psychology attuned to the need for active management and hedging of currency and related risks; avoiding expectations of government support should problems arise; supervising banks effectively, including their liquidity management; and disposing of an efficient legal framework to enforce financial contracts, debt recovery, bankruptcies, and the like; and

- inconsistent monetary and exchange rate policies can create incentives for significant short-term capital flows, hence, increasing the vulnerability of the economy to reversals in capital inflows when policies or circumstances change. Moreover, high capital mobility alters the effectiveness of different monetary instruments in achieving the objectives of monetary policy. Instruments that impose a high cost or administrative constraint on the banks become less effective than indirect monetary instruments, which operate on the overall cost of money or credit in financial markets. The opening of the capital account, therefore, needs to be accompanied by the adoption of indirect methods of monetary control.

Monetary and exchange rate management and banking supervision have thus received particular attention in the context of technical assistance on the capital account. Countries are advised to develop the capacity of financial institutions to assess and manage risk (e.g., credit, liquidity, and foreign exchange risk associated with large capital inflows), and to strengthen their regulatory authorities and the capacity to provide effective supervision of their financial systems. Monetary authorities are advised to develop their capacity to implement monetary policy based on indirect instruments in order to be able to fully and durably liberalize their capital account.

Designing the Sequencing of Liberalization

As emphasized in earlier discussions, a key policy issue is how to maximize the benefits and minimize the risks of capital account liberalization. Issues of the pacing and sequencing are central to this objective. Beyond the general proposition of the need to follow an integrated and comprehensive approach to liberalization, designing the precise operational sequencing of the reforms to the capital account presents a difficult and complex challenge as it depends on the nature of the capital controls that are being liberalized, the objectives of the reforms, and the starting position of each member. Liberalizations of direct investment inflows have, for example, often gone hand in hand with reforms aimed at strengthening the real sector and export potential of the economy, including reforms to the trade and investment regimes, exchange rate adjustments to improve competitiveness, and liberalization of exchange controls on current international transactions. Liberalizations of portfolio capital flows have tended to be coordinated with domestic financial sec-

tor liberalization and reforms—liberalization of interest rates, development of indirect monetary control procedures, and strengthening banks and capital markets.

The precise approaches to sequencing liberalizations will depend on the balance of benefits, costs, and risks in any particular member, and will have to be developed based on research and experience. Such approaches would normally be guided, though, by the objectives of improving efficiency in the mobilization and allocation of financial resources, and promoting macroeconomic and financial sector stability. The structural benefits of liberalizations would be emphasized, including those that (1) help diversify financial systems and make them more efficient by introducing new technologies and instruments and by promoting competition for financial products; (2) improve financial discipline by facilitating market oversight through transparency and competition while avoiding moral hazard—for example, by providing a catalyst for introducing new accounting and disclosure requirements; (3) help revise out-of-date regulatory structures and weak or ineffective supervisory arrangements; (4) introduce new instruments for hedging and managing risks that provide scope for greater diversification of funding sources and asset distribution; and (5) favor the channels where regulatory systems are more developed and governance can be stronger.

Developing Regulatory Frameworks Consistent with an Open Capital Account

Comprehensive liberalization of capital transactions and transfers does not signify an abandonment of all rules and regulations connected to foreign exchange. Countries that have opened up their capital account have maintained a minimum set of rules, either in the form of the foreign exchange law (or its equivalent) or ensuring that the necessary legal framework is in other pieces of legislation. The important regulations that remain in force are connected to (1) reporting by market participants ensuring the timely and accurate compilation of balance of payments data; (2) prudential regulations related to nonresident and foreign exchange transactions and transfers; and (3) measures designed to prevent tax evasion and money laundering.

Attention is given to avoiding a less-than-level playing field that would favor short-term over long-term capital flows, recognizing, however, that the distinction between different types of flows is not clear-cut. The economic incentives for accumulating short-term liabilities are linked to the country risk, which generally induces international lenders to reduce the maturity of their exposure; to possible distortions in yield curves due to inefficient or underdeveloped domestic markets; to interest rate differentials that induce firms to take loans in foreign currency without paying attention to currency risk; and to the regulatory framework that might favor short-term over long-term flows. In the initial stage of liberalization, international investors may test the market by making primarily short-term investments, especially in countries without a record of sound macroeconomic management.

Thus, emphasis has been given to safeguards to help ensure that the shorter-term flows are not disruptive. In addition to avoiding the incentives for such inflows created by inconsistent monetary and exchange rate policies, the most important elements are an adequate system of prudential regulations for the banking system and other relevant financial institutions that encourages adequate attention to the scope and timing of access by banks to international markets and an effective management of open foreign exchange and short-term liquidity risks with a view to preventing excessive maturity mismatches.[10] As discussed above, a number of countries have also imposed discriminatory reserve requirements on short-term borrowing from abroad; however, if not applied comprehensively to all short-term sources of foreign capital inflows such measures may result in the channeling of the short-term flows through other instruments. For example, over time, Chile progressively extended the instruments covered by its reserve requirement to all short-term inflows. Also the effectiveness of the measures in Germany, noted above, appeared to depend on whether they were accompanied by limitations on foreign borrowing by German companies. Also the controls on bank borrowing in Indonesia may have contributed to the increase in direct corporate foreign borrowing.

---

[10]See the Basle Committee's 1992 "Framework for Measuring and Monitoring Liquidity." For instance, the measures taken by Korea in the context of the second quarterly review under the Stand-By Arrangement with the IMF required banks to: (1) introduce internal liquidity control systems based on a maturity ladder approach; and (2) agree with the supervisory body allowable maturity mismatches for sight to 7 days; 7 days to 1 month; 1 to 3 months; 3 to 6 months; 6 months to 1 year; and over 1 year. The supervisory body will monitor implementation of the banks internal liquidity controls on a monthly basis, and banks will publicly disclose statistics on foreign currency liquidity.

Financial Sector Surveillance

A further step has been taken to integrate assessments and advise on external liberalization and financial sector development in the context of discussions with country officials on financial sector surveillance in Article IV and Use of Fund Resources. Greater attention is given to the information to be collected and assessed on the financial system in the context of Article IV surveillance, consistent with the increased attention to the development of sound financial markets and institutions, the move to capital account convertibility, and the management of short-term capital flows. Such surveillance focuses, inter alia, on the risks to domestic financial institutions and corporations when operating in sophisticated international markets, and on the supervision and management of the risks to the financial systems; identifies incentives in the regulatory framework that could induce financial institutions and corporations to resort to excessive short-term borrowing; and assesses the vulnerability of the financial system to a decrease or reversal of capital flows.

Coordination with Other Agencies

Staff have also strengthened contacts and the exchange of information with other relevant organizations on issues related to financial systems and capital account liberalization, inter alia, the OECD and the World Bank, including the Multilateral Investment Guarantee Agency (MIGA). Staff have also been involved in the discussions of the safeguard provisions in the proposed Multilateral Agreement on Investment (MAI). In addition, advice on the use of prudential measures in the context of the move to capital account convertibility is guided by the prudential principles, standards, and best practices recommended by international organizations, including the Basle Committee on Banking Supervision, and the International Organization of Securities Commissions (IOSCO).[11]

---

[11]See Basle Committee on Banking Supervision (1997).

IV

Developments in Exchange Rate Arrangements and Markets

According to the IMF's official classification of exchange arrangements, there has been a gradual move away from pegged regimes into more flexible arrangements. This classification scheme has, however, a number of shortcomings, and, in particular when members' de facto exchange arrangements are taken into account, the trend to more flexible arrangements becomes much less marked. In fact, accounting for members' de facto arrangements suggests that exchange rate targeting has remained the predominant exchange rate arrangement, and thus, the existing official classification scheme can be misleading in this regard. This section first discusses the trend in exchange rate regimes under the official classification scheme; second, it discusses the shortcomings of this scheme and proposes an alternative classification scheme; third, it reviews some of the factors underlying the evolution in exchange regimes; and finally, it reviews developments and features of foreign exchange markets and international payments instruments.

Characteristics of Members' Exchange Rate Regimes According to the IMF Classification Scheme

The main characteristics of the official classification scheme, and the trend in arrangements classified under this scheme, are discussed in Box 1 and provided in Table 8. The percentage of members maintaining pegged arrangements declined from about 77 percent in 1975 and to 36 percent in 1997, while the percentage of countries with free floating exchange rate regimes increased from 12 percent in 1975, to 25 percent in 1997 (Figure 5). There has also been an increase in the recourse to intermediate arrangements, such as limited flexibility (mainly among industrial countries) and managed floating (mainly among developing countries).

In the industrial countries, over one half of the members, including countries participating in the exchange rate mechanism (ERM) of the European Monetary System (EMS), maintained pegged exchange rates until the early 1990s. The exchange rate crisis of 1992–93 within the ERM, however, brought greater flexibility to exchange rate regimes of several European countries as the ERM fluctuation bands were widened for most ERM members, and several countries suspended their formal pegs during the currency turmoil. Italy and the United Kingdom suspended their ERM membership, and Finland, Norway, and Sweden abandoned their link to the European currency unit (ECU) in Fall 1992.[12]

A number of countries, however, recently joined the ERM in a step toward joining the European Economic and Monetary Union (EMU). Finland and Italy (re)joined the ERM in 1996, and Greece, which maintained a de facto crawling peg mechanism under its formally announced managed floating regime, joined the ERM in 1998.

The gradual shift from fixed exchange rate systems to more flexible arrangements has been more clearly demonstrated in the developing countries. In 1975, 87 percent had some type of pegged exchange rate. By 1997, the percentage pegging their currencies had fallen to some 40 percent. A number of developing countries continued to pursue fixed rates in the context of monetary unions (e.g., the CFA franc and several Caribbean countries), and some reverted back to pegged systems after periods of applying more flexible arrangements (e.g., Angola, Argentina, Bulgaria, Guinea-Bissau, and Venezuela). Among the emerging market economies, the ratio of those members that maintained pegged exchange rates fell from around 40 percent in the late 1970s to less than 10 percent in 1997, a much smaller percentage than developing countries as a whole. Greater flexibility has in general taken the form of a managed float rather than an independent float.

In 1992, when most transition economies joined the IMF, about 41 percent adopted pegged exchange rates vis-à-vis a single currency, and an equal number adopted freely floating rates. A number of these countries were using the Russian ruble as legal tender at the

---

[12]Under the existing classification scheme, members of the ERM have been classified as maintaining regimes of limited flexibility within cooperative arrangements since 1979, although the ERM has the features of a formal pegged exchange rate system that involves pegging the member currencies vis-à-vis the ECU within a given fluctuation margin. Widening of the ERM bands from ±2.25 percent to ±15 percent in August 1994 did not affect the classification of the member countries' arrangements, although it implied a de facto move toward greater flexibility.

Box 1. Exchange Rate Classifications

Following the collapse of the par value system and introduction of generalized floating of the major currencies in 1973, members' obligations regarding their exchange rate policies changed significantly from those embodied under the Bretton Woods system. Under the Second Amendment of the IMF's Articles of Agreement, members were formally given the freedom to choose their own form of exchange rate arrangements, subject only to minor limitations (namely, a peg in terms of gold and pursuit of multiple exchange rates), reflecting a recognition that the precise nature of such arrangements was of less importance than the manner in which a member conducts its policies under the exchange arrangements of its choice. Members agreed to comply with certain broad obligations, including to assure that their exchange rates and macroeconomic policies foster orderly balance of payments adjustment. The IMF would exercise firm surveillance over the exchange rate policies of members, and each member would be required to provide the IMF with the information necessary for such surveillance. Figure 5 shows the current status of members' exchange rate arrangements.

Members are obliged to notify the IMF of the exchange arrangements of their choice, within 30 days of becoming a member and promptly thereafter of any changes in their arrangements. Based on these notifications, the IMF summarizes members' arrangements by an exchange rate classification scheme that was first introduced in mid-1975 as part of its oversight function of the evolution of the international monetary system. This classification system grouped members' exchange rate arrangements according to the degree of flexibility with which the arrangements have been implemented, and has been broadly unchanged for over 14 years.[1]

The classification scheme distinguishes between three main groups: pegged exchange rate arrangements, where the exchange rate is fixed vis-à-vis a single currency or a currency composite; limited flexibility, where the exchange rate is allowed to move within bands vis-à-vis a single currency or within a cooperative arrangement; and more flexible arrangements, in which the exchange rate is managed or allowed to float freely. The distinction between managed and independently floating arrangements aims to reflect the policy stance for full or limited market determination of the exchange rate. Under independently floating regimes, supply and demand is, in principle, in continuous equality, with intervention limited to smoothing excessive short-run fluctuations in the exchange rate without establishing a particular level for it. In countries with managed floating systems, the foreign exchange market does not necessarily clear without intervention by the central bank.

Fixed Rate Arrangements

Peg: Single Currency. The country pegs to a major currency—usually the U.S. dollar or the French franc—with infrequent adjustment of the parity.

Peg: Currency Composite. A weighted composite is formed from the currencies of major trading or financial partners. Currency weights are generally country-specific and reflect the geographical distribution of trade, services, or capital flows. They can also be standardized, such as those of the SDR and the ECU.

Flexible Rate Arrangements

Flexibility Limited vis-à-vis a Single Currency. The value of the currency is maintained within certain margins of fluctuation around the de facto peg, corresponding empirically to volatility within the regime of wider margins that preceded the Second Amendment.

Flexibility Limited: Cooperative Arrangements. This regime refers to countries in the exchange rate mechanism (ERM) of the European Monetary System (EMS) and is a conceptual cross between a peg of each EMS currency to others in the system (currently within wide margins), and a float of all EMS currencies jointly vis-à-vis non-EMS currencies.

More Flexible: Adjusted According to a Set of Indicators. The currency is adjusted more or less automatically in response to changes in selected quantitative indicators. A common indicator is the real effective exchange rate that reflects inflation-adjusted changes in the currency vis-à-vis major trading partners; another is a fixed, preannounced change. This category was merged with the More Flexible: Managed Float category below since 1997.

More Flexible: Managed Float. The central bank quotes and supports the rate but varies it frequently. Indicators for adjusting the rate are broadly judgmental, including, for example, the balance of payments position, international reserves, or parallel market developments, and adjustments may not be automatic.

More Flexible: Independent Float. Rates are market-determined, with any intervention aimed at the moderating rate of change, rather than at establishing a level for the rate.

---

[1]The scheme was revised slightly after the Second Amendment of the Articles and in 1982.

time of accession to membership in the IMF. Most transition economies that joined in 1993, however, adopted more flexible regimes. By the end of 1997, 22 out of the 26 transition economies were pursuing more flexible arrangements, although more than half of this group manage their exchange rates, rather than letting them float freely. A few transition economies (e.g., Latvia and Lithuania) that started with free floating exchange rates moved to pegged regimes, and two countries, Argentina and Bulgaria, recently reverted back to a pegged exchange rate mechanism in the context of a currency board (Part III, Table A7).

Table 8. Exchange Rate Arrangements as of December 31, 1997[1]

| Pegged | | | | | Flexibility Limited vis-à-vis a Single Currency or Group of Currencies | | More Flexible | |
| Single currency | | | Currency composites | | | | | |
U.S. dollar	French franc	Other	SDR	Other	Single currency[2]	Cooperative arrangements[3]	Other managed floating	Independently floating
Angola	Benin	Bhutan (Indian rupee)	Jordan	Bangladesh	Bahrain[6]	Austria	Algeria	Afghanistan, Islamic State of[5]
Antigua and Barbuda	Burkina Faso	Bosnia and Herzegovina (deutsche mark)	Latvia	Botswana[5]	Qatar[6]	Belgium	Belarus	Albania
Argentina*	Cameroon	Bulgaria* (deutsche mark)	Libya[4,5]	Burundi	Saudi Arabia[6]	Denmark	Bolivia	Armenia
Bahamas, The[5]	Central African Rep.	Brunei Darussalam (Singapore dollar)	Myanmar[5]	Cape Verde	United Arab Emirates[6]	Finland	Brazil[3,8]	Australia
Barbados	Chad	Estonia* (deutsche mark)		Cyprus[7]		France	Cambodia[5]	Azerbaijan
Belize	Comoros	Kiribati [2] (Australian dollar)		Fiji		Germany	Chile[5,9]	Canada
Djibouti*	Congo	Lesotho (South African rand)		Iceland[10]		Ireland	China	Congo, Democratic Republic of the[5]
Dominica	Côte d'Ivoire	Namibia (South African rand)		Kuwait		Italy	Colombia[11]	Eritrea
Grenada	Equatorial Guinea	Nepal (Indian rupee)		Malta		Luxembourg	Costa Rica	Gambia, The
Iraq[5]	Gabon	San Marino[12] (Italian lira)		Morocco		Netherlands	Croatia	Ghana
Lithuania*	Guinea-Bissau	Swaziland (South African rand)		Samoa		Portugal	Czech Republic	Guatemala
Marshall Islands[12]	Mali			Seychelles		Spain	Dominican Rep.[5]	Guinea
Micronesia, Federated States of[12]	Niger			Slovak Rep.[15]			Ecuador[13,5]	Guyana
Nigeria[5]	Senegal			Tonga			Egypt[5]	Haiti
Oman	Togo			Vanuatu			El Salvador	India
Palau[12]							Ethiopia	Indonesia
Panama[12]							Georgia	Jamaica
St. Kitts and Nevis							Greece	Japan
St. Lucia							Honduras[15,14]	Korea
St. Vincent and the Grenadines							Hungary[16]	Lebanon
Syrian Arab Rep.[5]							Iran, Islamic Rep. of[5]	Liberia
							Israel[17]	Madagascar
							Kazakhstan	Mexico
							Kenya	Moldova
							Kyrgyz Republic	Mongolia
							Lao P.D.R.	Mozambique
							Macedonia, former Yugoslav Republic of	New Zealand
							Malawi	Papua New Guinea
							Malaysia	Paraguay
							Maldives	Peru
							Mauritania	Philippines
							Mauritius	Rwanda
							Nicaragua	São Tomé and Príncipe[5]
							Norway	Sierra Leone
							Pakistan[5]	Somalia
							Poland[18]	South Africa
							Romania	Sweden
							Russia[19]	Switzerland
							Singapore	Tanzania
							Slovenia	Trinidad and Tobago
							Solomon Islands	Uganda
							Sri Lanka	United Kingdom
							Sudan[5]	United States
							Suriname	

25

Table 8 (concluded)

| Pegged | | | | | Flexibility Limited vis-à-vis a Single Currency or Group of Currencies | | More Flexible | |
| Single currency | | | Currency composites | | | | | |
U.S. dollar	French franc	Other	SDR	Other	Single currency[2]	Cooperative arrangements[3]	Other managed floating	Independently floating
							Tajikistan[5]	Yemen, Republic of
							Thailand	Zambia
							Tunisia	Zimbabwe
							Turkey	
							Turkmenistan[5]	
							Ukraine[20]	
							Uruguay	
							Uzbekistan[5]	
							Venezuela[21]	
							Vietnam[22]	

Note: An asterisk, *, indicates countries with currency board arrangements.

[1]The classification of members' exchange rate arrangements in this table reflects the official declaration of country authorities as well as staff views and may not reflect the actual or de facto policies they may follow.

[2]In all countries listed in this column, the U.S. dollar was the currency against which exchange rates showed limited flexibility.

[3]This category consists of countries participating in the exchange rate mechanism (ERM) of the European Monetary System (EMS). In each case, the exchange rate is maintained within a margin of ±15 percent around the bilateral central rates against other participating currencies, with the exception of the bilateral rate between Germany and the Netherlands, which is maintained within a margin of ±2.25 percent.

[4]The exchange rate is maintained within margins of ±47 percent.

[5]Member maintained exchange arrangement involving more than one market. The arrangement shown is that maintained in the major market.

[6]Exchange rates are determined on the basis of a fixed relationship to the SDR, within margins of up to ±7.25 percent. However, because of the maintenance of a relatively stable relationship with the U.S. dollar, these margins are not always observed.

[7]The exchange rate, which is pegged to the ECU, is maintained within margins of ±2.25 percent.

[8]The exchange rate is maintained within a band of R$1.05–1.14 per U.S. dollar.

[9]The exchange rate is maintained within a crawling band of ±12.5 percent on either side of a weighted composite of the currencies of the main trading areas. The exchange arrangement involves more than one market.

[10]The exchange rate is maintained within margins of ±6 percent.

[11]The exchange rate is maintained within a crawling band of ±7 percent.

[12]Country uses peg currency as legal tender.

[13]The exchange rate is maintained within a crawling band of ±10 percent.

[14]The exchange rate is maintained within margins of ±5 percent.

[15]The exchange rate is maintained within margins of ±7 percent with regard to the currency basket.

[16]The exchange rate is maintained within a crawling band of ±2.25 percent with regard to the currency basket.

[17]The exchange rate is maintained within an asymetric crawling band of width of 29 percent.

[18]The exchange rate is maintained within a crawling band of ±7 percent against a basket of currencies.

[19]The exchange rate is maintained within margins of ±5 percent.

[20]The exchange rate is maintained within a band of HRV 1.70–1.90 per U.S. dollar.

[21]The exchange rate is maintained within a crawling band of ±7.5 percent.

[22]The exchange rate is maintained within margins of ±10 percent.

Figure 5. Exchange Rate Arrangements of Member Countries
(In percent of total number of countries)

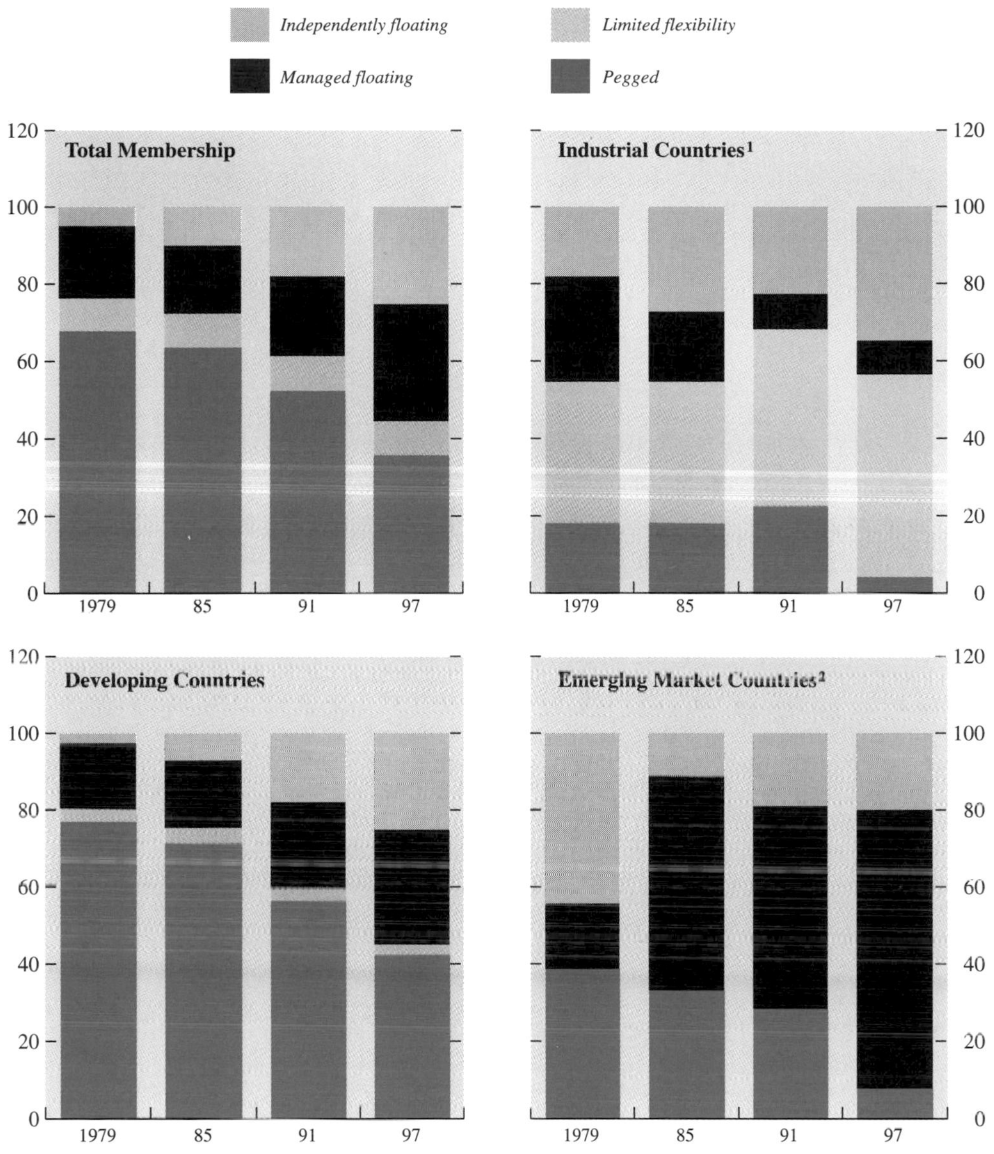

Sources: IMF, *Annual Report on Exchange Arrangements and Exchange Restrictions,* various issues.

[1]For continuity, the industrial and developing country classifications do not reflect the new *World Economic Outlook* reclassification of the three economies previously classified as developing countries. Thus, Israel, Korea, and Singapore are still included in the developing country group.

[2]Emerging market countries include (1) Asia Pacific: Indonesia, Korea, Malaysia, Philippines, Thailand, Singapore, and China; (2) South America: Argentina, Brazil, Chile, Colombia, Mexico, and Venezuela; (3) Eastern and Central Europe: Czech Republic, Slovak Republic, Poland, Slovenia, Hungary, and Russia; and (4) Others: India, Sri Lanka, Pakistan, Turkey, Israel and South Africa. From the group of Eastern and Central Europe, in 1979 only Slovenia is included, in 1985 Slovenia and Hungary are included, in 1991 Poland, Slovenia, Hungary, Czech Republic, and Slovak Republic are included. In 1997, all countries classified under Eastern and Central Europe are included.

Shortcomings of the Existing Classification Scheme and Proposed Modification

The existing exchange rate classification scheme has a number of shortcomings. As a result, a new exchange rate classification scheme has been developed.

Existing Classification Scheme

The existing exchange rate classification scheme has a number of well-recognized shortcomings.[13] First, there is considerable ambiguity as to what the scheme is intended to measure. There is a wide spectrum of exchange rate regimes beyond the traditional "fixed versus flexible" exchange rate dichotomy used in the official classification scheme with each regime affording a varying degree of monetary policy independence, which is not always apparent from the existing exchange rate classification. This is best illustrated by the group of countries that are classified as following managed floating regimes but use a range of different approaches to limit the flexibility of the exchange rate and to assign varying roles to the exchange rate as a nominal anchor. Several countries, for example, informally peg their currencies rather than using a single currency or a currency basket (e.g., Maldives and the former Yugoslav Republic of Macedonia). In a few others (e.g., Brazil and Ukraine), the exchange rate is pegged within a horizontal band. In some others, the currency is allowed to depreciate periodically at a rate that is preannounced or adjusted according to a set of indicators, with (e.g., as in Israel and Poland) or without bands around the central parity (e.g., in Costa Rica and Nicaragua). In these groups of countries, the de facto pegged exchange rate arrangement imposes similar constraints on monetary policy flexibility as in those with formal pegged arrangements though the restrictiveness of such constraints would clearly depend on the degree of flexibility of the pegged arrangement. The remaining countries within the managed floating group influence the movements of the exchange rate through active intervention without specifying a preannounced path for it and thus without constraining their monetary policies to that end.

The difficulties with the present classification scheme are also illustrated by the group of countries that are classified as maintaining pegged exchange rates. In countries that operate currency board arrangements (CBAs) (e.g., as in Argentina, Estonia, and Djibouti), in which the currency of another country circulates as legal tender (e.g., the Australian dollar in Kiribati) or maintain a currency union under which a common currency circulates at par among the members (e.g., the CFA franc zone), there is little or no scope for discretionary monetary policies. However, in countries that peg their currencies, including those pegging to a currency composite (e.g., Bangladesh, Fiji, and Malta), or that maintain pegged systems that allow the exchange rate to fluctuate within bands (e.g., Iceland, and the Slovak Republic), there is some limited degree of monetary policy discretion, with the degree of discretion depending on the band width.

The second, and perhaps more important, shortcoming of the present classification scheme is that there are sometimes important differences between the official classification, based on members' formally announced regimes, and the actual, de facto, exchange rate arrangements followed by members; such differences may reflect political considerations of the authorities, as well as policy dilemmas arising from trade-offs between various economic objectives. For example, some countries that are classified with pegged exchange rates have engineered frequent changes in the parity of their exchange rates (e.g., as in Bangladesh and Solomon Islands), making the arrangement less distinguishable from a more flexible regime. Other countries that are classified with managed or independently floating exchange rate arrangements have, de facto, followed fixed exchange rate arrangements (e.g., Georgia, Lebanon, and the Philippines until mid-1997). Some countries have also announced pegs to a currency basket but followed de facto pegs to a single currency (e.g., Thailand's peg to the U.S. dollar until July 1997 and Jordan, which has formally announced its peg to the SDR, but follows a de facto peg to the U.S. dollar). This divergence between members' formally announced and de facto regimes reduces the transparency of members' policy actions and the role of their exchange rate regimes in the overall policy framework, thus making effective surveillance over the policies of member countries more difficult.

In the period 1994–97, 33 members' exchange arrangements were reclassified from less flexible to more flexible arrangements, and 35 from more flexible arrangements to less flexible ones (see Part III, Tables A8 and A9 for further details on these changes). A closer look at the nature of these shifts indicates that some of the reclassifications from less flexible to more flexible involve the continued maintenance of exchange rate targeting of some form (e.g., in Venezuela and Hungary, the move from pegged exchange rates to greater flexibility took the form of a forward-looking crawling band system, thus maintaining the essence of the pegged regimes). In all, many of

---

[13]The last major review of the classification scheme was undertaken in 1982. The main changes involved introducing new categories for the nonpegged regimes to distinguish between managed floats and independent floats. The variability of exchange rates vis-à-vis a number of putative pegs was also reviewed, to identify "backward looking de facto pegs." This methodology was subsequently applied on a few occasions to help identify the de facto nature of regimes.

Table 9. Evolution of Pegged Exchange Rate Regimes in Official Versus De Facto Classification

	1991		1997	
	Number	Percent	Number	Percent
Pegged exchange rates (official classification)	81	52	65	36
Pegged exchange rates, including de facto fixed pegs and formal and informal bands[1]	102	66	96	53
Pegged exchange rates, including de facto fixed pegs, formal and informal bands, crawling pegs, and crawling bands[1]	118	76	114	63

Source: Information provided by the national authorities.

[1]Includes the countries with limited flexibility vis-à-vis a single currency and within a cooperative arrangement (ERM countries), where the exchange rate is allowed to fluctuate within established margins.

the exchange regime reclassifications in 1994–97 involved a move to intermediate exchange rate regimes from either pegged regimes or free floating systems, with about 50 percent of these intermediate regimes conveying the features of a pegged exchange rate system (e.g., El Salvador and the former Yugoslav Republic of Macedonia informally peg their currencies; Brazil, Croatia, Sudan, and Ukraine peg their currencies within formal or informal bands; Costa Rica maintains a crawling peg; and Honduras and the Russian Federation operate crawling band regimes). Among the 14 transition economies that manage their exchange rates, 9 do so in the context of regimes that share the features of a pegged exchange rate regime. The former Yugoslav Republic of Macedonia, for example, maintains an informal peg against the deutsche mark; Belarus (the latter part of 1997), Croatia, and Ukraine operate within formal or informal target bands; and Hungary, Poland, and Russia (between mid-1996 and the end of 1997) pursue crawling band regimes where the exchange rate is allowed to depreciate at a preannounced or forward looking rate. De facto arrangements indicate that a much larger percentage of the membership follows different forms of exchange rate targeting than is suggested by the official classification of members that peg their exchange rate. It also shows that exchange rate targeting has remained the predominant monetary arrangement followed by almost two-thirds of the membership (see Table 9, columns 3 and 4).

Expanded Information on Exchange Arrangements

In an attempt to overcome some of the shortcomings of the existing classification scheme, supplementary information on members' exchange rate arrangements has been developed:

- Additional information was provided on the nature of the exchange rate arrangements maintained by members that were classified as following pegged and managed floating arrangements under the present scheme, and on the choice of a nominal anchor in countries following floating exchange rates (Figure 6).
- Supplementary information compared members' formally announced exchange rate arrangements, as recorded in the current classification system, with their de facto arrangements, with the latter ranked to indicate the general role of the exchange rate as an anchor of monetary policy (Figure 7).
- An additional dimension was introduced to indicate members' choices of alternative nominal anchors in conducting monetary policy including the exchange rate anchor, targeting of monetary aggregates, and direct targeting of inflation (Figures 6 and 7). This additional information indicates that as members move toward greater exchange rate flexibility, they adopt additional or alternative anchors to ensure price stability. In some cases, countries maintain monetary targets along with exchange rate anchors (e.g., Greece, Poland, Sri Lanka, and so forth). A number of other countries (e.g., Australia, Canada, New Zealand, Sweden, and the United Kingdom) have chosen a direct targeting of inflation as the anchor of monetary policy, while some countries (e.g., Colombia, Finland, Israel, and Spain) combined inflation targets with exchange rate anchors, in some cases (e.g., Colombia and Israel) to reinforce price stability. It should be acknowledged, however, that it would not be possible, for practical reasons, to infer from Figure 7 which nominal anchor plays the principal role in conducting

Figure 6. Expanded IMF Classification of Exchange Rate Arrangements as of December 31, 1997[1]

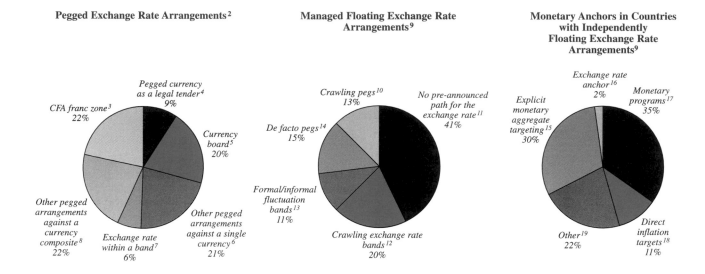

Source: IMF, Quarterly and Semiannual Reports on Exchange Rate Arrangements, various issues.

[1]Member countries of the ERM that maintain an exchange rate regime of limited flexibility within a cooperative arrangement are not reported in this figure.

[2]The following countries also have an IMF-supported program: Argentina, Bangladesh, Benin, Bulgaria, Burkina Faso, Cameroon, Chad, Republic of Congo, Côte d'Ivoire, Djibouti, Estonia, Gabon, Guinea Bissau, Jordan, Latvia, Lithuania, Mali, Niger, Senegal, and Togo.

[3]This group includes Benin, Burkina Faso, Cameroon, Central African Republic, Chad, Republic of Congo, Côte d'Ivoire, Equatorial Guinea, Gabon, Guinea Bissau, Mali, Niger, Senegal, and Togo.

[4]This group includes Kiribati, Marshall Islands, Micronesia, Republic of Palau, Panama, and San Marino.

[5]This group includes Antigua and Barbuda, Argentina, Bosnia and Herzegovina, Brunei Darussalem, Bulgaria, Djibouti, Dominica, Estonia, Grenada, Lithuania, St. Kitts and Nevis, St. Lucia, and St. Vincent and Grenadines.

[6]This group includes Angola, Bahamas, Barbados, Belize, Bhutan, Comoros, Iraq, Jordan, Lesotho, Namibia, Nepal, Oman, Syrian Arab Republic, and Swaziland.

[7]This group includes Cyprus (+/-2.25%), Iceland (+/-6%), Libyan Arab Jamahiriya (+/-47%), and Slovak Republic (+/-7%).

[8]This group includes Bangladesh, Botswana, Burundi, Cape Verde, Fiji, Kuwait, Latvia, Malta, Morocco, Myanmar, Samoa, Seychelles, Tonga, and Vanuatu.

[9]The following countries also have an IMF-supported program: Algeria, Bolivia, Croatia, Egypt, El Salvador, Ethiopia, Georgia, Hungary, Kazakhstan, Kenya, Kyrgyz Republic, Federal Yugoslav Republic of Macedonia, Mauritania, Pakistan, Romania, Russia, Thailand, Ukraine, and Uruguay.

[10]This group includes Bolivia, Costa Rica, Greece, Nicaragua, Solomon Islands, Tunisia, and Turkey.

[11]This group includes Algeria, Belarus, Cambodia, Czech Republic, Dominican Republic, Ethiopia, Kazakhstan, Kenya, Kyrgyz Republic, Lao Peoples Democratic Republic, Malawi, Malaysia, Mauritania, Mauritius, Nigeria, Norway, Romania, Singapore, Slovenia, Suriname, Tajikistan, Thailand, and Uzbekistan.

[12]This group includes the following: Chile (backward-looking crawl); Colombia, Honduras, Israel, Poland, Sri Lanka, Venezuela (forward-looking crawl); and Ecuador, Hungary, Russia, Uruguay (preannounced rate of crawl). Sri Lanka changed classifications to reflect the current information.

[13]This group includes Brazil (R$0.97–R$1.06/US$1), China (+/-0.3%), Croatia (HRK3.5–3.8/deutsche mark), Sudan (+/-2%), Ukraine (HRV 1.7–1.9/US$1), and Vietnam (+/-10%).

[14]This group includes Egypt, El Salvador, Georgia, Islamic Republic of Iran, Federal Republic of Macedonia, Maldives, Pakistan, and Turkmenistan.

[15]This group includes The Gambia, Ghana, Guinea, India, Jamaica, Korea, Mongolia, Philippines, São Tomé and Príncipe, Sierra Leone, South Africa, Switzerland, and Zimbabwe. Ghana, Guyana, Philippines, São Tomé and Príncipe, and Sierra Leone also have and IMF-supported or other monetary programs.

[16]This group includes Lebanon.

[17]This group includes Armenia, Azerbaijan, Haiti, Indonesia, Madagascar, Moldova, Mozambique, Peru, Tanzania, Uganda, and Zambia, which all have IMF-supported programs. This group also includes Albania, Mexico, Rwanda, Trinidad and Tobago, and Yemen, which have other monetary programs.

[18]This group includes Australia, Canada, New Zealand, Sweden, and the United Kingdom.

[19]This group includes Democratic Republic of Congo, Eritrea, Guatemala, Japan, Papua New Guinea, Paraguay, and the United States (which do not have explicit nominal anchor) and Afghanistan, Liberia, and Somalia (for which there is no recent information).

Figure 7. Exchange Rate Arrangements: Comparison of IMF Classification, De Facto Arrangements, and Choices of Monetary Anchors, as of December 31, 1997[1]

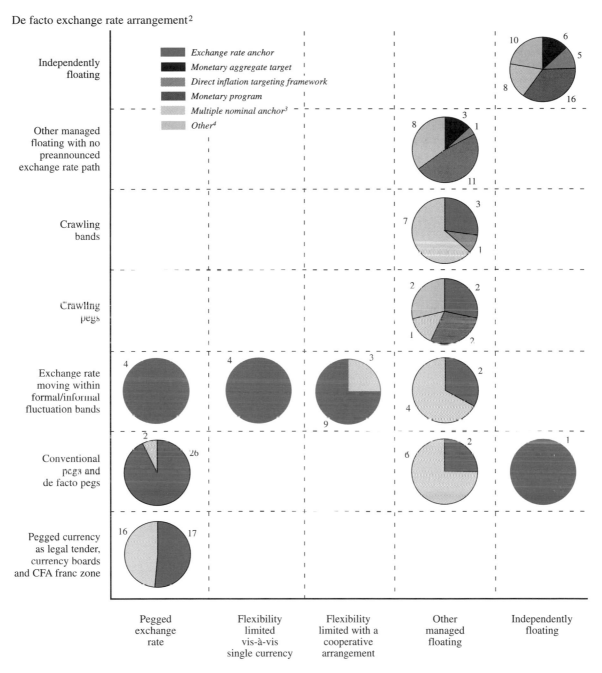

Formal exchange rate arrangement classification

[1]The number next to each pie slice indicates the number of countries following the classification outlined in the bottom axis.

[2]This exchange rate arrangement indicates the actual policy followed by the member country, as opposed to the formally announced exchange rate arrangement.

[3]This category indicates that the country adopts more than one nominal anchor (inflation targeting, exchange rate anchor, explicit monetary targets, or monetary targets of an IMF-supported program or other monetary program) in conducting monetary policy.

[4]This category indicates that there is no explicitly stated nominal anchor but the country monitors a multiple set of indicators in conducting monetary policy, or that no recent, relevant information is available for the country.

monetary policy. In addition, a number of countries adopt IMF-supported or other monetary programs, which implicitly impose limits on their credit aggregates such as net domestic assets or domestic credit (e.g., Peru and Romania). It should be recognized, however, that such credit aggregates are not effective nominal anchors, and countries typically missed targets for both money and inflation due to unexpectedly large foreign exchange inflows; thus many countries with independently floating exchange rates do not have an effective anchor.

This additional information serves to bring out the similarities between exchange rate arrangements and use of nominal anchors by members whose exchange rate arrangements are classified under different regimes according to the official classification system. For example, the arrangements in which the exchange rate fluctuates within bands can be found under the formal peg arrangements, as well as in limited flexibility and managed floating systems. Of the group of countries that are officially classified as maintaining more flexible arrangements, 9 have de facto fixed pegs, 6 limit the flexibility of their exchange rates within some formally announced or informal fluctuation bands, 7 allow their currencies to depreciate at a preannounced rate, and 11 do the same within bands crawling at a preannounced rate.

This additional information also indicates that within the group of exchange rate arrangements classified as pegged, there has been a marked shift away from conventional single currency or basket pegs toward more rigid forms of pegged exchange rate regimes (such as CBAs, currency unions, and regimes in which the pegged currency is the legal tender) (Figure 8). Moreover, within the more flexibly managed floating systems, there has been a marked shift toward arrangements where the authorities manage their exchange rates without establishing a preannounced path. These trends suggest that members have been moving toward more extreme regimes and may support the view that, as capital flows increase, the more extreme regimes become more viable: namely, floating regimes, where the exchange rate moves regularly in response to market forces, and truly fixed exchange rates with the strongest commitment to the exchange regime, whose sustainability depends on the implementation of a consistent set of economic policies (see Fischer, 1996, and Eichengreen and others, 1998).

Possible Revised Classification Scheme

Not characterizing members' exchange rate arrangements accurately may cloud the policy implications derived from the research and policy papers that base their analysis on the IMF's classification scheme. Moreover, classifying members' exchange

rate arrangements based on their de facto rather than their formally announced policies could bring greater transparency to members' policy actions and thus contribute to improve surveillance over the exchange rate policies of members. Bringing together information on both exchange rate arrangements and nominal anchors of monetary policy can also help make potential sources of inconsistency in the monetary-exchange rate policy mix more transparent and illustrate that different forms of exchange rate regimes can be consistent with similar monetary frameworks.

Accordingly, Table 10 and Box 2 present a revised classification scheme that addresses some key shortcomings of the existing system. Members' exchange rate regimes could be based on their de facto regimes. In addition, the new classification would present members' exchange rate regimes against alternative nominal targeting frameworks, with the intention of using both criteria as a way of providing greater transparency in the classification scheme. The scheme would continue to rank exchange rate regimes on the basis of the degree of flexibility of the exchange rate arrangement. However, it would distinguish between the more rigid forms of pegged regimes (such as CBAs);[14] other (conventional) fixed peg arrangements against a single currency or a currency basket; exchange rate bands around a fixed peg; crawling peg arrangements; and exchange rate bands around crawling pegs. The degree of flexibility of the band arrangements would depend on the width of the bands chosen. It would also introduce a new category to distinguish the exchange arrangements of those countries that have no separate legal tender. Adopting the currency of another country as legal tender or joining a monetary union in which the same legal tender is shared by the members of the union are forms of ultimate sacrifices for surrendering monetary control, where no leeway is left for national monetary authorities to conduct monetary policies. Traditionally, the classification scheme has treated such arrangements as pegged regimes. It should also be noted that some countries with pegged exchange regimes may have a bimonetary legal tender. This characteristic has been proven to enhance stability (e.g., in Argentina) by facilitating orderly redenomination of financial assets in domestic financial markets during heightened uncertainty.

In addition to their exchange rate regimes, members would also be classified by their choices of alternative nominal anchors in conducting monetary policy. Countries that maintain multiple anchors of monetary policy appear in more than one column in Table 10. Replacement of the national currencies of countries participating in EMU with a common cur-

---

[14]Countries may still exercise some degree of flexibility under such arrangements, however, depending on how strict the rules of the boards are established (see Baliño, and others, 1997).

Figure 8. Evolution of Exchange Rate Regimes—Expanded Classification

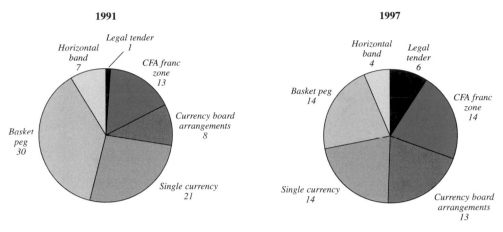

Pegged Exchange Rate Regimes

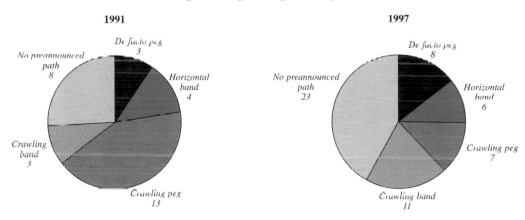

Managed Floating Exchange Rate Regimes

Source: IMF, *Annual Report on Exchange Rate Arrangements and Exchange Restrictions,* various issues.

rency, the euro, will raise an issue for the classification scheme.

The exchange rates of the national currencies were irrevocably locked on January 1, 1999. National currencies had continued to circulate as legal tender in their country of issue since January 1, 1999. Since that time, they have acted, however, no longer as separate currencies but as subdivisions of the euro. Euro notes and coins will be introduced on January 1, 2002. National currencies will be withdrawn and after July 1, 2002 will cease to be legal tender. The question will arise how to classify the exchange arrangements of the individual countries of EMU. It would seem reasonable to classify the EMU members jointly under the new category for the countries that have no separate legal tender with the appropriate nominal anchor (e.g.,

direct inflation targeting). The proposed new classification became effective on January 1, 1999.

The new classification of members' exchange rate arrangements in Table 10 shows that contrary to the trends that emerge from the existing classification scheme, exchange rate arrangements, in which the exchange rate plays the role of the nominal anchor of monetary policy, are still the dominant type of monetary arrangements. It is also interesting to note that a significant part of the IMF membership (about 56 percent) that maintains some sort of pegged arrangements seems to continue to adopt conventional peg arrangements, with or without bands.

The adoption of the new classification system would involve a departure from the long-standing practice of classification by members' formally an-

Table 10. New IMF Exchange Rate Classification as of December 31, 1997[1]

Exchange Rate Regime (number of countries)	Monetary Policy Framework				
	Exchange rate anchor	Monetary aggregate target	Inflation targeting framework	IMF supported or other monetary program	Other
Exchange arrangements with no separate legal tender (26)	*Another currency as legal tender:* Kiribati, Marshall Islands, Micronesia, Palau, Panama, San Marino — *ECCM[2]:* Antigua and Barbuda, Dominica, Grenada, St. Kitts and Nevis, St. Lucia, St. Vincent and the Grenadines — *CFA franc zone — WAEMU:* Benin*, Burkina Faso*, Côte d'Ivoire*, Guinea-Bissau, Mali*, Niger*, Senegal*, Togo — *CAEMC:* Cameroon*, Central African Rep.*, Chad*, Congo, Rep. of*, Equatorial Guinea, Gabon			Benin*, Burkina Faso*, Cameroon*, Chad*, Congo, Rep. of*, Côte d'Ivoire*, Gabon*, Guinea-Bissau*, Mali*, Niger*, Senegal*, Togo*	
Currency board arrangements (6)	*Another currency as legal tender:* Argentina*, Brunei — Estonia, Lithuania			Djibouti, Estonia*	Argentina*, Bulgaria
Other conventional fixed peg arrangements (including de facto peg arrangements under managed floating) (38)	*Against a single currency (22):* Angola, Bahamas, The, Barbados, Belize, Bahrain, Bhutan, Comoros[3], Egypt*[4], Georgia*[4], Iran, Islamic Rep. of[4], Iraq, Jordan*[4], Lebanon[4], Lesotho, Macedonia, FYR*[4], Maldives*[4], Namibia, Nepal, Nigeria, Oman, Syrian Arab Republic, Swaziland — *Against a composite (15):* Botswana, Burundi, Cape Verde, Fiji, Kuwait, Latvia*, Malta, Morocco, Myanmar, Pakistan*[4], Samoa, Seychilles, Tonga, Vanuatu, Turkmenistan[4], Vanuatu			Bangladesh, Egypt[5], El Salvador*[4], Georgia*[4], Jordan*, Latvia*, Macedonia, FYR*[4], Maldives*[4], Pakistan*[4]	
Pegged exchange rates within horizontal bands (26)	*Within a cooperative arrangement (12):* Austria, Belgium, Denmark, Finland*, France, Germany*, Ireland, Italy, Luxembourg, Netherlands, Portugal, Spain* — *Other band arrangements (6):* Bahrain, Brazil[4], China*[4], Croatia*[4], Cyprus, Iceland, Libya, Qatar, Saudi Arabia, Slovak Republic, Sudan[4], Ukraine*[4], United Arab Emirates, Vietnam*	China*[4], Germany*	Finland*, Spain*	Croatia*[4], Ukraine*[4,6], Vietnam*[4]	

Table 10 (*concluded*)

Exchange Rate Regime (number of countries)	Monetary Policy Framework					
	Exchange rate anchor		Monetary aggregate target	Inflation targeting framework	IMF supported or other monetary program	Other
Crawling pegs (7)[4]	*Within a cooperative arrangement (12)* Costa Rica	*Other band arrangements (14)* Greece* Nicaragua	Greece*		Bolivia Tunisia	Turkey[5] Solomon Islands[5]
Exchange rates within crawling bands (11)[4]	Colombia* Ecuador Honduras Hungary*	Israel* Poland* Russia* Sri Lanka* Uruguay* Venezuela	Poland* Sri Lanka*	Chile Colombia* Israel[4]	Hungary* Russia* Uruguay*	
Managed floating with no preannounced path for exchange rate (23)			Czech Rep. Lao PDR Slovenia Jamaica[4] Mauritius[4]	Singapore	Algeria Ethiopia Kazakhstan Kenya Kyrgyz Rep. Malawi Mauritania Romania Tajikistan Thailand	Belarus[5] Cambodia[5] Dominican Rep.[5] Malaysia[5] Norway[5] Suriname[5] Uzbekistan[5]
Independently floating (44)			Ghana Guinea* Guyana* India Korea* Mongolia* Peru* Philippines* São Tomé and Príncipe* Sierra Leone* South Africa Switzerland Zimbabwe	Australia Canada New Zealand Sweden United Kingdom	Albania Armenia Azerbaijan Guinea* Guyana* Haiti Indonesia Korea* Madagascar Mexico Moldova Mongolia* Mozambique Peru* Philippines* Rwanda São Tomé and Príncipe* Sierra Leone* Tanzania Trinidad and Tobago Uganda Yemen Zambia	Afghanistan, Islamic State of[6] Congo, Dem. Rep. of the[5] Eritrea[5] Gambia, The[6] Guatemala[5] Japan[5] Liberia Paraguay[5] Papua New Guinea Somalia[6] United States[5]

Sources: Information provided by country authorities.

[1]A country with an asterisk, *, indicates that the country adopts more than one nominal target in conducting monetary policy.

[2]These countries also have a currency board arrangement within the common market.

[3]Comoros has the same arrangement with the French treasury as do the CFA franc zone countries.

[4]The indicated country has a de facto arrangement under a formally announced policy of managed or independent floating. In the case of Jordan, it indicates that the country has a de jure peg to the SDR but a de facto peg to the U.S. dollar. In the case of Mauritius, the authorities have a de jure policy of managed floating, but a de facto policy of independent floating, with only infrequent intervention by the central bank.

[5]The country has no explicitly stated nominal anchor but rather monitors various indicators in conducting monetary policy.

[6]There is no relevant information available for the country.

35

Box 2. New IMF Exchange Rate Classification System

The IMF's new classification system is based on the members' actual, de facto, regimes that may differ from their officially announced arrangements. The system ranks exchange rate regimes on the basis of the degree of flexibility of the arrangement. It distinguishes between the more rigid forms of pegged regimes (such as currency board arrangements); other conventional fixed peg regimes against a single currency or a basket of currencies; exchange rate bands around a fixed peg; crawling peg arrangements; and exchange rate bands around crawling pegs, in order to help assess the implications of the choice of exchange rate regime for the degree of independence of monetary policy. This includes a category to distinguish the exchange arrangements of those countries that have no separate legal tender. The new system presents members' exchange rate regimes against alternative monetary policy frameworks with the intention of using both criteria (i.e., policy frameworks and current regime) as a way of providing greater transparency in the classification scheme and to illustrate that different forms of exchange rate regimes could be consistent with similar monetary frameworks. The following explains the categories.

Exchange Rate Regime

Exchange Arrangements With No Separate Legal Tender

The currency of another country circulates as the sole legal tender or the member belongs to a monetary or currency union in which the same legal tender is shared by the members of the union. Adopting such regimes is a form of ultimate sacrifice for surrendering monetary control where no scope is left for national monetary authorities to conduct independent monetary policy.

Currency Board Arrangements

A monetary regime based on an implicit legislative commitment to exchange domestic currency for a specified foreign currency at a fixed exchange rate, combined with restrictions on the issuing authority to ensure the fulfillment of its legal obligation. This implies that domestic currency be issued only against foreign exchange and that new issues are fully backed by foreign assets, eliminating traditional central bank functions such as monetary control and the lender of last resort and leaving little scope for discretionary monetary policy; some flexibility may still be afforded depending on how strict the rules of the boards are established.

Other Conventional Fixed Peg Arrangements

The country pegs its currency (formally or de facto) at a fixed rate to a major currency or a basket of currencies, where a weighted composite is formed from the currencies of major trading or financial partners and currency weights reflect the geographical distribution of trade, services, or capital flows. In a conventional fixed pegged arrangement the exchange rate fluctuates within a narrow margin of at most ±1 percent around a central rate. The currency composites can also be standardized, such as those of the SDR (special drawing right). The monetary authority stands ready to maintain the fixed parity through intervention, limiting the degree of monetary policy discretion; the degree of flexibility of monetary policy, however, is greater relative to currency board arrangements (CBAs) or currency unions, in that traditional central banking functions are, although limited, still possible, and the monetary authority can adjust the level of the exchange rate, although infrequently.

Pegged Exchange Rates Within Bands

The value of the currency is maintained within margins of fluctuation around a formal or de facto fixed peg that are wider than ±1 percent around a central rate. It also includes the arrangements of the countries in the exchange rate mechanism (ERM) of the European Monetary System (EMS) (replaced with ERM-II on January 1, 1999). There is some limited degree of monetary policy discretion, with the degree of discretion depending on the band width.

Crawling Pegs

The currency is adjusted periodically in small amounts at a fixed, preannounced rate or in response to changes in selective quantitative indicators (past inflation differentials vis-à-vis major trading partners, differentials between the target inflation and expected inflation in major trading partners, and so forth). The rate of crawl can be set to generate inflation adjusted changes in the currency's value ("backward looking"), or at a preannounced fixed rate below the projected inflation differentials ("forward looking"). Maintaining a credible crawling peg imposes constraints on monetary policy in a similar manner as a fixed peg system.

---

nounced regimes. The revised scheme requires an interpretation by IMF staff of the actual exchange rate arrangements and the monetary anchors that are pursued by members. Such an understanding of members' exchange arrangements is already a central part of the IMF's surveillance over the exchange rate policies of its members in the context of Article IV consultations. The adoption of a new classification scheme would make the assessment a more formal requirement and have the advantage of making more transparent the role of members' exchange rate arrangements as part of their overall macroeconomic and monetary policies.

As a practical matter, it could be envisaged that the Article IV consultations would be a first step in discussing with the authorities, in cases where there are

Exchange Rates Within Crawling Bands

The currency is maintained within certain fluctuation margins around a central rate that is adjusted periodically at a fixed preannounced rate or in response to changes in selective quantitative indicators. The degree of flexibility of the exchange rate is a function of the width of the band, with bands chosen to be either symmetric around a crawling central parity or to widen gradually with an asymmetric choice of the crawl of upper and lower bands (in the latter case, there is no preannouncement of a central rate). The commitment to maintain the exchange rate within the band continues to impose constraints on monetary policy, with the degree of policy independence being a function of the band width.

Managed Floating With No Preannounced Path For the Exchange Rate

The monetary authority influences the movements of the exchange rate through active intervention in the foreign exchange market without specifying, or precommitting to, a preannounced path for the exchange rate. Indicators for managing the rate are broadly judgmental, including, for example, the balance of payments position, international reserves, parallel market developments, and the adjustments may not be automatic.

Independent Floating

The exchange rate is market determined, with any foreign exchange intervention aimed at moderating the rate of change and preventing undue fluctuations in the exchange rate, rather than at establishing a level for it. In these regimes, monetary policy is in principle independent of exchange rate policy.

Monetary Policy Framework

Members' exchange rate regimes are presented against alternative monetary policy frameworks to present the role of the exchange rate in broad economic policy and help identify potential sources of inconsistency in the monetary and exchange rate policy mix.

Exchange Rate Anchor

The monetary authority stands ready to buy and sell foreign exchange at given quoted rates to maintain the exchange rate at its preannounced level or range (the exchange rate serves as the nominal anchor or intermediate target of monetary policy). These regimes cover exchange rate regimes with no separate legal tender, CBAs, fixed pegs with and without bands, and crawling pegs with and without bands, where the rate of crawl is forward looking.

Monetary Aggregate Anchor

The monetary authority uses its instruments to achieve a target growth rate for a monetary aggregate (reserve money, M1, M2, and so forth) and the targeted aggregate becomes the nominal anchor or intermediate target of monetary policy.

Inflation-Targeting Framework

A framework that targets inflation involves the public announcement of medium-term numerical targets for inflation with an institutional commitment by the monetary authority to achieve these targets. Additional key features include increased communication with the public and the markets about the plans and objectives of monetary policymakers and increased accountability of the central bank for obtaining its inflation objectives. Monetary policy decisions are guided by the deviation of forecasts of future inflation from the announced inflation target, with the inflation forecast acting (implicitly or explicitly) as the intermediate target of monetary policy.

IMF-Supported or Other Monetary Program

An IMF-supported or other monetary program involves implementation of monetary and exchange rate policy within the confines of a framework that establishes floors for international reserves and ceilings for net domestic assets of the central bank. As the ceiling on net domestic assets limits increases in reserve money through central bank operations, indicative targets for reserve money may be appended to this system.

Other

The country has no explicitly stated nominal anchor but rather monitors various indicators in conducting monetary policy, or there is no relevant information available for the country.

significant divergences between de facto and formally announced regimes and the merits of reporting more realistic descriptions of exchange rate regimes. This should also help minimize the potential risks of misinterpretation by IMF staff of the true nature of the members' arrangements, as well as any potential disagreements with the authorities regarding the description of the nature of their arrangements. Exchange regimes for a particular currency can vary between Article IV consultations; thus, keeping the classification scheme current would require more frequent monitoring of monetary frameworks and exchange of information with the authorities. Both schemes would be maintained during a transition period over which the de facto and formally announced regimes are expected to conform with each other.

Factors Underlying the Evolution of Exchange Rate Regimes

Although less pronounced than suggested by the IMF classification scheme, there has been, in recent years, a shift away from pegged regimes to more flexible ones. This reflected a variety of factors including the changing economic conditions and policy objectives of countries over time, the liberalization and globalization of financial markets, and the accompanying increase in capital mobility.

Tensions Between Economic Objectives

The emergence of tensions between the objectives of lower inflation and external competitiveness over short time frames has been one significant factor in countries' adopting more flexible exchange rate arrangements. During the initial phase of stabilization, many countries adopted pegged exchange rate regimes to help stabilize inflationary expectations and increase economic policy credibility. The advantages of fixed exchange rates have been particularly relevant for countries that suffered from hyperinflation and those in the process of transition to a market-based economy. The disadvantage is that fixed exchange rates have also been associated with sizable appreciations in real exchange rates reflecting the period needed to reduce inflation rates to the levels of major trading partners. In some cases, real exchange rate appreciations reflected the choice of an exchange rate peg that did not reflect the pattern of international trade, such as in some Asian economies. Real appreciations have in turn been associated with a deterioration of competitiveness and external imbalances, particularly when exchange rate policy was not adequately supported by consistent structural policies to improve competitiveness, or where the real exchange rate was not significantly undervalued initially. In such circumstances, a number of countries have abandoned pegged exchange rate arrangements. In some, the pegged exchange rates were abandoned as a result of speculative attacks. Factors that contributed to such crises included contagion effects, inconsistencies of fiscal policies with the pegged exchange rate, as well as severe problems in the financial system, high public or private indebtedness, and economic slowdown, which made it costly for the authorities to maintain and defend fixed parities (e.g., Finland, Italy, the United Kingdom, and Sweden in 1992; Mexico in 1994; and the Czech Republic, Indonesia, Korea, the Philippines, and Thailand in 1997). In several other countries, the move to greater exchange rate flexibility has been the result of a deliberate policy choice. Some countries adopted a progressive, step-wise approach toward more flexible exchange rates, and others a pragmatic approach.

A number of members have sought to address the tensions between inflation and external objectives by adopting crawling band arrangements. Chile, Israel, and Poland, for example, started their stabilization efforts with fixed exchange rates but moved to crawling pegs or horizontal bands, and eventually to crawling bands in an attempt to allow for greater exchange rate flexibility that, nevertheless, continued to maintain the anchor role of the exchange rate. Such arrangements retain an anchor role for the exchange rate by committing to a preannounced schedule of mini-devaluations, while, at the same time, avoiding serious real exchange rate misalignment that would hurt competitiveness.[15] The choice of the rate of crawl of the band in general reflected differing policy priorities assigned to price stability and competitiveness objectives: in most cases, the rate of crawl was set in a "forward-looking" manner where the authorities assigned a greater weight to disinflation; in a few cases, the rate of crawl was determined in a "backward-looking" manner where competitiveness was given a higher priority (see Part III, Table A10). As indicated in Figure 8, the number of members adopting crawling band arrangements increased significantly in recent years (from about 10 percent of the managed floating arrangements in 1991 to about 22 percent in 1997), reflecting the advantages of such arrangements to minimize the trade-off between inflation and competitiveness objectives, as well as to provide greater monetary policy autonomy in the face of increasing capital mobility (see below).

Moves Toward Currency Convertibility

Moves toward greater currency convertibility have been associated with the adoption of more flexible, market-based exchange rates. First, as countries eliminated exchange restrictions on payments and transfers for current international transactions and liberalized capital movements, conditions were created for the development of domestic foreign exchange markets where exchange rates could be determined in a more flexible manner in response to supply and demand conditions. There is a positive correlation (0.87) between the share of members with Article VIII status and with flexible exchange rate regimes (managed or free floating regimes). The percentage of countries with Article VIII status increased from about 35 percent in 1978 to 78 percent in 1997, while the share of members with flexible exchange rates more than doubled within the same period.

Second, the elimination of exchange restrictions and in particular multiple exchange rates in itself often involved the adoption of market-determined exchange rates. Recent trends in multiple exchange rate

---

[15]See Williamson (1996).

38

practices are discussed in more detail below. Of a total of 39 countries that moved to greater exchange rate flexibility during 1991–94, 14 adopted floating rates upon unification of exchange rates and 9 introduced interbank foreign exchange markets or auctions and shifted transactions to the free market.[16] In 1994–97, the elimination of multiple exchange rates was also associated with the move to floating exchange rates in the case of Angola, Azerbaijan, Lao People's Democratic Republic, Venezuela, Yemen, and Zimbabwe, and with the introduction of interbank foreign exchange markets (e.g., Guinea, Madagascar, Mauritius, and Papua New Guinea). Of the 43 countries that maintained multiple exchange rate systems at the end of 1997, about 56 percent pursued less flexible exchange rate regimes (Table 11).[17] The exchange rate classification scheme classifies members' arrangements based on the dominant foreign exchange market, and thus, multiple exchange rate systems are also found in some countries with floating exchange rate systems.

Third, many countries support their pegged exchange rates through administered constraints on the sale of export proceeds and have abandoned pegged exchange rates as they eliminate such constraints. Some two-thirds of countries that still require export receipts to be repatriated and surrendered to the central bank or the banking system maintain, formally or informally, pegged exchange rate regimes.

The relationship between the choice of the exchange rate system and the degree of restrictiveness of the exchange regime, for a sample of 41 countries for which the degree of restrictiveness of the current account, capital account, and the overall exchange regime has been calculated in terms of an index, is examined in Part III, Table A11. The countries identified as having more restricted exchange regimes seem to pursue more flexible exchange rate systems according to the official exchange rate classification. However, taking into consideration the members' de facto policies shows that more than 75 percent of the countries with more restricted exchange regimes have some kind of a pegged exchange rate arrangement. Among those countries with less-than-average restrictiveness, no clear pattern is identified. This is consistent with the fact that the introduction of convertibility did not involve floating exchange rates in a number of cases where monetary policy was clearly subordinated to maintaining the exchange rate objective.

Responses to Increased Capital Flows

The increase in capital flows places a premium on countries following consistent monetary and exchange rate policies. Thus, countries attempting to maintain a fixed or a crawling peg have a limited capacity to set their domestic interest rate independent of the foreign interest rate without risking significant capital flows.

In general, the first policy reaction to strong capital inflows with a pegged exchange rate has been to conduct sterilized intervention to limit the impact of such flows on monetary aggregates. However, such intervention involves quasi-fiscal costs and is generally of limited effectiveness since it serves to keep interest rates high, attracting further capital inflows. A variety of other instruments and policies have, therefore, been brought into play in responding to capital inflows. These included a tightening of fiscal policy, imposition of controls on capital inflows, relaxation of controls on outflows, and a tightening of financial and prudential regulations, or a combination of a number of different measures.[18]

As an alternative response to increased capital inflows, and in many cases as a supplementary measure, a number of countries have moved toward more flexible exchange rate arrangements, inter alia, to insulate the domestic money base from the expansionary effects of capital inflows and to increase perceived exchange risk that may help deter speculative and potentially destabilizing short-term inflows. Several countries allowed their exchange rate to adjust through an appreciation of the exchange rate in a floating system; a revaluation of the pegged exchange rate; and an introduction of greater flexibility within their pegged or managed exchange rate systems (see Table 12). The latter has taken many different forms, including the introduction of fluctuation bands around a central parity, a move from horizontal band systems to crawling bands, successive adjustments in the band width, or the abandonment of the pegged systems altogether and moving to managed or floating exchange rates.

In some countries, the prolonged maintenance of pegged exchange rates may have been seen as implicit exchange rate guarantees and encouraged external borrowing. This, in turn, led to excessive exposure to foreign exchange risk in the financial and corporate sectors and increased vulnerability to a sudden change in market sentiment. In several Southeast Asian countries (Indonesia, Korea, the Philippines, and Thailand), as well as Mexico in 1994, floating the exchange rate was the main response when countries faced a subsequent significant outflow of capital and a weak international reserve position, and when increases in domestic interest rates proved insufficient

---

[16]See IMF (1995a).

[17]If the IMF classification system were to be used, which would include the countries with informal pegs among the flexible exchange rate group, one could reach the conclusion that countries with dual exchange rate systems tend to pursue more flexible exchange rates.

[18]See IMF (1995b).

Table 11. Exchange Rate Regime and Various Aspects of Exchange Systems, End of 1997

(Number of countries)

Exchange Rate Regime	Surrender Requirements	Repatriation Requirements	Multiple Exchange Rate Systems			Memo Item: Total Members
			With MCPs	Without MCPs	Total	
Pegged exchange rate	40	47	5	5	10	66
Limited flexibility	1	1	0	0	0	16
Managed float (with preannounced exchange rate path)	16	18	8	6	14	29
Managed float (with no preannounced exchange rate path)	14	18	9	1	10	21
Independent float	15	28	8	1	9	49
Total	85	112	30	13	43	181
(In percent of total members within each exchange arrangement)						
Pegged exchange rate	60.6	71.2	7.6	7.7	15.2	100.0
Limited flexibility	6.2	6.2	0.0	0.0	0.0	100.0
Managed float (with preannounced exchange rate path)	55.2	62.1	27.6	21.4	48.3	100.0
Managed float (with no preannounced exchange rate path)	66.7	85.7	42.9	5.3	47.6	100.0
Independent float	30.6	57.1	16.3	1.9	18.4	100.0
Total	47.0	61.9	16.6	23.8	23.8	100.0

Source: IMF, *Annual Report on Exchange Arrangements and Exchange Restrictions* (1997).

to encourage a reversal of the capital outflows. Among other factors that contributed to the crises in these countries are a buildup of overheating pressures; lack of enforcement of prudential rules and inadequate supervision of financial systems, together with direct-lending practices by the government; problems in disclosure and transparency of data and information and in governance; and movements in international competitiveness due to wide fluctuations in exchange rates.

Developments in Foreign Exchange Markets

At a global level, exchange rate arrangements have generally become more market-based, with greater reliance on interbank exchange markets as the core of wider currency markets in developing and emerging market economies. At the same time, in the most developed markets, traditional interbank foreign exchange trading appears to be declining somewhat in relative importance.

Foreign Exchange Markets in Industrial Countries

In the major industrial countries, the importance of traditional interbank operations in spot and forward foreign exchange markets appears to have been declining in importance relative to other forms of foreign exchange trading, especially trading in deriva-

tives. As discussed in Part II, Section IX, Bank for International Settlements (BIS) data on total foreign exchange trading for 1995 show continued growth of around 30 percent between the triennial surveys, with total surveyed trading averaging $1.26 trillion daily. Traditional spot, forward, and swap transactions still account for the majority of this by far, but trading in currency futures and options is growing rapidly, and accounted for around 6 percent of daily turnover in 1995. A similar pattern is reflected in bank income trends: foreign exchange dealing as a profit center for major international banks is reported to be declining, with greater emphasis being placed on client business, especially in relatively complex derivative products. Other factors contributing to the trend include the growing power of nonbank financial institutions and other end users that, inter alia, has made it somewhat more difficult for traditional dealers to read short-term market developments (their traditional speciality); intense competition from electronic deal-matching systems; and to some extent also the convergence toward EMU. More generally, greater exchange rate confidence and lower volatility reduce the demand for speculative position taking and, to that extent, the return to market making. With reduced volatility of the exchange rate, the number of institutions actively making markets often tends to decline.

At the same time, a trend toward growing concentration in the major foreign exchange markets continues. In addition to factors such as those mentioned

Table 12. Exchange Rate Regime Response to Capital Inflows

Country	Exchange Regime at Start of Inflows (De Facto Regime)	Exchange Regime Response
Brazil	Independent float	Allowed the exchange rate to appreciate within a flexible regime. Switched to managed float in 1994 and widened the de facto band in 1995–97.
Chile	Managed float (crawling band)	Widened the band width five times in 1988–97 from ±3 percent to ±12.5 percent in 1997. Revalued the central rate several times in 1992–96.
Colombia	Managed float (crawling band)	Allowed the exchange rate to move within the de facto ±7 percent crawling band. Revalued the band twice in January and December 1994.
Czech Rep.	Basket peg	Widened the trading band from ±0.5 percent to ±7.5 percent in February 1996. Abandoned the horizontal band in May 1997 and moved to managed float with no preannounced path.
Hungary	Basket peg	Switched to managed float in 1995. Reduced the rate of crawl twice in 1997.
Indonesia	Managed float (crawling peg)	Introduced a crawling band in 1994. Widened the band width seven times in 1994–97. Switched to free float in August 1997 under market pressure.
Israel	Managed float (horizontal band)	Switched to crawling band in January 1992. Widened the band three times in 1993–97 from ±5 percent to +7 percent then to ±15 percent, finally widened only the upper band keeping the lower band unchanged.
Korea	Managed float	Introduced a horizontal band, widened the band width in steps in 1992–95.
Malaysia	Basket peg with band	Moved to managed float with no preannounced path for the exchange rate and allowed for greater degree of flexibility.
Mexico	Managed float (crawling peg)	Moved to a gradually widening crawling band in November 1991, but in practice heavy intramarginal intervention was used to keep the rate within a tight inner band.
Peru	Independent float	Exchange rate was allowed to adjust within a flexible regime.
Philippines	Independent float	Exchange rate was initially allowed to adjust within a flexible regime. Starting from 1995 a de facto peg was adopted.
Poland	Managed float (crawling peg)	Switched to crawling band in 1995, but in practice kept a narrower inner band. Revalued in 1996 and reduced the crawl rate in five steps in 1991–96 to curb appreciation.
Russia	Managed float (de facto horizontal band)	Switched to crawling band in 1996. Adjusted the band width on a number of occasions.
South Africa	Independent float	Exchange rate was allowed to adjust within a flexible regime.
Slovak Rep.	Basket peg	Widened the trading band in two steps from ±1.5 percent to ±7 percent in 1996–97.
Turkey	Managed float (crawling peg)	Devalued the lira in 1994 and allowed for more flexibility within a flexible regime.
Venezuela	Independent float	Exchange rate was allowed to adjust within a flexible regime in response to market forces in early 1990s. Subsequently moved to managed float, and then to single currency peg, and back to managed float with a crawling band in 1996.

above that are more specific to foreign exchange markets, this trend is in part symptomatic of broader developments in financial markets. It reflects the same sorts of intense competitive pressures in the financial sector that are encouraging rationalizations and mergers and acquisitions, as previously distinct (if not protected) market segments are breaking down internationally, and as the differences between commercial banks and other financial institutions also continue to erode significantly. While regulatory changes act as a spur to some of these trends, the regulatory changes are themselves in part a response to underlying market trends—including those associated with globalization, innovation, and rapid technological progress—that would simply make their presence felt in other ways in the absence of regulatory changes. A case in point is the trend toward rationalization in the United States, as previously separate regional banking markets integrate further, and as the barriers between investment and commercial banking erode, notwithstanding the failure to date of attempts to repeal the Glass-Steagall Act itself. Similar market pressures have their reflection at the supervisory level, where some countries have moved to more closely integrate domestic supervision and regulation of a range of different financial market sectors, and where coordination has been growing between international supervisory bodies for banking, insurance, and securities markets. At an organizational level, there is some trend also toward closer global integration of major financial institutions' activities internationally, including in some cases a global centralization of institutional risk management functions.[19]

The review of exchange market behavior in Part II, Section IX concludes that the key issue for public policy is to improve the environment in which markets work, rather than to intervene directly in market behavior. In particular, while there are aspects of shorter-term dealer behavior that are not immediately driven by an analysis of economic "fundamentals," the review notes that this does not mean that such behavior is unconstrained by those fundamentals. Indeed, one would expect the payoff to good economic analysis to be largest precisely when the fundamentals are changing significantly. In general, then, extrapolating from short-term dealer behavior may give a misleading impression of (the lack of) "rationality" or "efficiency" in the foreign exchange market. At the level of the dealers specifically, direct interventions in dealer activity that restrict their ability to earn dealing profits will likely have the negative consequences of either reducing the amount of market-making activity (a form of public good) below what is appropriate given the general market environment or result in a relocation of dealing activity to a different jurisdiction to avoid the effect of the regulatory intervention. More often that not, it is not particularly difficult technically to trade a currency in offshore markets, even if indirectly through various sorts of synthetic instruments.[20]

Foreign Exchange Markets in Developing Countries

The market structures for foreign exchange trading in developing countries have been organized as both interbank markets (as observed in developed and more advanced developing countries) and auction-type arrangements. The choice between market structures in general depends on a range of factors, including the initial institutional and regulatory circumstances.

Auction-type arrangements still exist in a significant number of IMF member countries (Angola, Azerbaijan, Belarus, Bolivia, Congo, Ethiopia, Georgia, Honduras, Kazakhstan, the Kyrgyz Republic, Moldova, Papua New Guinea, Russia, the Slovak Republic, Tajikistan, Turkmenistan, Ukraine, Uzbekistan, Vietnam, and Zambia). Auctions continue to be

the dominant market structure in several of these countries while in others the role of the auction market (mostly in the form of fixing sessions) has been significantly reduced concurrent with the development of interbank markets (Part III, Table A12). In the early stages of market development, when the volume of foreign exchange trading is limited, voluntary auction-type arrangements, such as an interbank auction or fixing arrangements, have offered a useful transitional arrangement toward an interbank exchange market.

Several countries introduced interbank foreign exchange markets only recently (e.g., Azerbaijan, Guinea, Iceland, Madagascar, Mauritius, Morocco, Mozambique, Nigeria, Tunisia, and Vietnam), and in several countries, interbank markets have developed significantly in depth and sophistication with transactions taking place through electronic and computer systems (e.g., Armenia, Bulgaria, China, Chile, Colombia, Costa Rica, Egypt, Estonia, Mexico, Moldova, the Philippines, Poland, Romania, Russia, and the Slovak Republic). While there are significant benefits from continuous interbank market structures because of the relative liquidity and efficiency of such arrangements, the development of such markets can be impeded by various factors. These include the instability and low volume of foreign exchange flows; insolvency problems with commercial banks; lack of trust between market dealers; inefficiencies in banking, payments, and communication systems; and the presence of official regulations and practices and exchange controls. As Part II, Section IX notes, broader international trends have combined in recent years to heighten the interest of international banks in the foreign exchange markets of at least some developing and transitional economies. This interest can provide a significant fillip for the further development of those markets but is in turn predicated on some minimum requirements in terms of size, structure, and efficiency.

Active foreign exchange bureau markets where cash and retail transactions take place continue to exist in many developing countries. In some countries, the importance of exchange bureau markets reflects continued restrictions on interbank market trading and limitations on access to foreign exchange in the official markets. In addition, parallel markets for foreign exchange continue to exist in a number of countries where access to foreign exchange has been restricted. The existence of officially sanctioned parallel markets (e.g., the curb market in Pakistan) can also provide a significant degree of capital account convertibility.

As part of its technical assistance work on exchange systems, the IMF has assisted member countries in developing an efficient interbank foreign exchange market. In creating such a market, the staff emphasized, inter alia, the need to eliminate barriers arising from official regulations and practices, and exchange controls, that might hinder foreign exchange dealings; the

---

[19]For further discussion on issues related to those mentioned in the last two paragraphs, see IMF (1997b).

[20]A recent hedge fund study reached similar conclusions about the need for caution in considering direct intervention in the market activities of institutional investors and collective investment schemes. See Eichengreen, Masson, and others (1998).

establishment of codes of conduct for dealings among market participants and the imposition of information technology to facilitate interbank dealings; the strengthening of payments and clearing arrangements; and the introduction of prudential guidelines and reporting requirements for authorized dealers. Some of the aspects involved in the development of interbank markets are discussed in Part II, Section VIII.

Forward Exchange Markets

As regards forward exchange markets, most industrial countries have eliminated restrictions on access to forward markets and limits on forward exchange transactions. Except for Greece, where the central bank provides forward cover to credit institutions, all industrial countries now have market-determined forward markets. Significant progress has also been made in a number of developing countries in terms of forward market development, with many countries allowing the banking system to provide forward cover for foreign exchange risk (see Part III, Table A12). About half of the developing countries allow forward cover in financial transactions, although official approval for the provision of cover or for conducting transactions in the forward market is still necessary in some cases.

About 70 IMF developing member countries have no formalized markets for forward transactions, and in the remaining developing countries the forward markets are either not very active (e.g., Algeria, Belarus, Jamaica, Lesotho, Madagascar, and Slovenia) or are subject to certain restrictions and limitations, particularly on the type of transactions for which forward operations and cover are permitted. Table 13 presents summary information on the features of the forward markets as well as their relationship with the exchange rate regimes in these countries. As the table indicates, there appears to be a close relationship between the lack of development of forward markets and maintenance of pegged exchange rates: almost all the countries that require prior approval for forward foreign exchange transactions or allow forward cover only for trade transactions and prohibit those for financial transactions have pegged exchange rates; and more than 11 of the 19 countries in which forward cover is provided by the monetary authority maintain formal or informal pegs. This tendency reflects both the fact that the spot markets are not sufficiently developed to support an efficient and smooth functioning forward market and restrictions on forward markets, which are more often associated with pegged exchange arrangements.

As discussed more fully in Part II, Section IX, central bank activity in non–spot markets, including through currency futures or derivatives markets, as well as forward contracts, per se, can sometimes be quite problematic. This discussion does not relate to the use of such transactions for foreign reserves management, as distinct from exchange rate intervention. Nor does it relate to forward foreign exchange transactions where these are part of a foreign currency swap (where the two sides of the swap transaction largely eliminate the direct exchange rate effect, but affect domestic bank liquidity). Foreign currency swaps have been used as an important monetary management instrument in a number of countries, Switzerland being perhaps the best known case. The problems with some forms of forward or derivative foreign exchange intervention are that there can be a strong temptation for overuse, as the non–spot interventions economize on the immediate use of official foreign reserves and are frequently less transparent than spot operations. They can disguise significant foreign exchange losses, as has been amply demonstrated by the experiences of Thailand and Korea during the buildup to their currency crises in 1997. In addition, the Brazilian authorities used currency intervention in futures markets as part of their defense of the real during 1997–98.

Multiple Exchange Rate Systems

Some 43 IMF members maintained multiple exchange rate systems at the end of 1997. In 30, the multiple exchange rates gave rise to a multiple currency practice subject to the IMF's jurisdiction. (See Part III, Table A13 for a more detailed description of these regimes and Box 3 for a discussion of such practices and the IMF's jurisdiction). Most multiple currency practices arose from the practice of applying different exchange rates to different transactions, from the existence of dual markets with spreads between official and market rates in excess of 2 percent, and from the imposition of various taxes or subsidies or provision of official exchange rate guarantees (see Table 14). In the remaining 13 countries, the multiple exchange rate systems did not give rise to multiple currency practices subject to the IMF's jurisdiction, as the spread between different effective rates remained within 2 percent or because the different exchange rates were applied to capital transactions (e.g., the Bahamas, Brazil, and Chile).

Since late 1994, 18 members eliminated multiple currency practices or unified their exchange rate systems or both (Azerbaijan, the Czech Republic, Ethiopia, Georgia, Lao People's Democratic Republic, Lesotho, Malta, Mauritania, Mauritius, Moldova, Namibia, Nicaragua, Poland, Slovak Republic, South Africa, Tajikistan, Ukraine, and Yemen). Some countries (e.g., Venezuela) unified their exchange rates after temporarily introducing multiple exchange rates or engaging in multiple currency practices during the same period. As already noted, a number of the unifications were associated with a move to floating exchange rate regimes (e.g., Azerbaijan, Lao People's

Table 13. Summary Features of Forward Exchange Markets in Selected Developing Countries, End of 1997

Country	Exchange Rate Regime	Forward Cover/Transactions		Official Forward Cover	Prior Approval for Forward Transactions
		Financial	Commercial		
Argentina	SCP	Yes	Yes	No	
Armenia	FF	Yes	Yes	Yes	
Bahamas, The	SCP	Yes	Yes	No	Yes
Bahrain	LF	Yes	Yes	No	
Barbados	SCP	Yes	Yes	No	
Bangladesh	BP	No	Yes	No	
Benin	SCP	No	Yes	No	Yes
Botswana	BP	No	Yes	Yes	
Burkina Faso	SCP	No	Yes	No	Yes
Burundi	BP	Yes	Yes	No	
Cameroon	SCP	...	...	No	Yes
Chad	SCP	No	Yes	No	Yes
Colombia	MF (CB)	Yes	Yes	No	
Comoros	SCP	No	Yes	No	Yes
Côte d'Ivoire	SCP	No	Yes	No	Yes
Croatia	MF (HB)	...	...	Yes	
Cyprus	BP (HB)	...	...	Yes	
Ecuador	MF (CB)	Yes	Yes	No	
Egypt	MF (DP)	Yes	Yes	No	
Fiji	BP	No	Yes	No	
Guyana	FF	...	...	Yes	
Hungary	MF (CB)	Yes	Yes	No	
India	FF	No	...	Yes	
Indonesia	FF	...	...	Yes	
Jordan	BP	No	Yes	Yes	
Kenya	MF	Yes	Yes	No	
Kuwait	BP	...	...	Yes	
Lebanon	FF (DP)	No	Yes	No	
Macedonia, FYR	MF (DP)	No	Yes	Yes	
Madagascar	FF	...	No		
Malaysia	MF	Yes	Yes	No	Yes[1]
Mali	SCP	No	Yes	No	Yes
Malta	BP	...	Yes		
Marshall Islands	SCP	Yes	Yes	No	
Mauritius	MF	Yes	Yes	No	
Mexico	FF	Yes	Yes	No	
Micronesia	SCP	Yes	Yes	No	
Morocco	BP	Yes	Yes	No	
Namibia	SCP	Yes	Yes	Yes	
Nepal	SCP	No	Yes	No	
Niger	SCP	No	Yes	No	Yes
Nigeria	SCP	Yes	Yes	No	
Oman	SCP	...	...	Yes	
Pakistan	MF (DP)	...	...	Yes	
Papua New Guinea	FF	No	Yes	No	
Paraguay	FF	No	Yes	No	
Peru	FF	Yes	Yes	No	
Philippines	FF	Yes	Yes	Yes	Yes
Qatar	LF	No	Yes	No	
Russia	MF (CB)	Yes	Yes	Yes	
Saudi Arabia	LF	Yes	Yes	No	
Senegal	SCP	No	Yes	No	Yes
Singapore	MF	Yes	Yes	No	
Solomon Islands	BP	Yes	Yes	No	
South Africa	FF	Yes	Yes	Yes	
Sri Lanka	MF	No	Yes	No	
Swaziland	SCP	Yes	Yes	No	
Tanzania	FF	No	Yes	No	
Thailand	MF	Yes	Yes	No	
Togo	SCP	No	Yes	No	Yes
Tonga	BP	Yes	Yes	No	Yes
Trinidad and Tobago	FF	Yes	Yes	No	
Tunisia	MF (CP)	No	Yes	Yes	
Turkey	MF (CP)	Yes	Yes	No	
United Arab Emirates	LF	No	Yes	Yes	
Uganda	FF	No	Yes	No	
Vanuatu	BP	Yes	Yes	No	
Zimbabwe	FF	No	Yes	No	

Notes: BP = basket peg, CB = crawling band; CP = crawling peg; DP = de facto peg; FF = free float; HB = horizontal band; LF = limited flexibility; MF = managed float; SCP = single currency peg.
[1]For financial transactions.

44

Box 3. Multiple Exchange Rate Systems

According to the IMF's policy on multiple currency practices (MCPs), "action by a member or its fiscal agencies that of itself gives rise to a spread of more than 2 percent between buying and selling rates for spot exchange transactions between the member's currency and any other member's currency would be considered a multiple currency practice" subject to IMF jurisdiction under Article VIII. The approval policies have been flexible and responsive to each country's circumstances. In approving MCPs, the IMF has taken into consideration whether they are intended to be temporary and introduced or maintained for balance of payments reasons, and whether they discriminate between IMF members. The approval is also contingent on the existence of a clear plan designed to bring about unification over a specific and appropriately brief period of time. The IMF's policy toward MCPs and country experiences with multiple exchange rates were last reviewed by the Executive Board in April 1984 and February 1985.

Multiple currency practices can take a number of forms:

1. *Different rates for different transactions.* A typical multiple currency practice may take the form of the setting by the central bank of different exchange rates applying to different categories of transactions (e.g., official, commercial, tourist transactions, and so forth), which result in spreads of more than 2 percent between these rates.

2. *Dual or multiple exchange markets.* A multiple currency practice would arise if the authorities were to establish separate exchange markets and the coexistence of these markets results in spreads of more than 2 percent between the rates in the different markets. A multiple currency practice would also arise if, having established an official market, the authorities were also to allow the existence of a free market without establishing any mechanism to ensure that spreads of more than 2 percent would not arise between the rates in these markets.

3. *Exchange taxes or subsidies.* A tax or subsidy payable on exchange transactions or the purchase or sale of a foreign currency may be part of the effective exchange rate on a foreign exchange transaction and thus give rise to a multiple currency practice.

4. *Exchange guarantees.* Exchange guarantees provided by a member or its fiscal agencies to cover exchange risks are viewed as a provision of subsidized exchange rate by the member. Under many of these systems, compensation for exchange losses is not a part of the nominal exchange rate applied to the purchase of foreign exchange by the beneficiary of the guarantee, but it is a part of the effective exchange rate because the benefit of the coverage flows directly from exchange losses and thus from the exchange transaction in which these losses are realized. A system for covering exchange risk managed by the official authority would not be a multiple currency practice if it is self financed (i.e., the premium paid by the beneficiaries are sufficient to cover the exchange risk).

5. *Broken cross rates.* Broken cross rates arise from an action by a member or its fiscal agencies that results in midpoint spot exchange rates of other members' currencies against its own currency in a relationship that differs by more than 1 percent from the midpoint spot exchange rates for these currencies in their principal markets.

Multiple exchange rate regimes have in general been used (1) for balance of payments purposes (e.g., to prevent large exchange rate depreciations from affecting the domestic price of essential commodities, or to prevent sudden one way pressures on the capital account from affecting trade relations and international reserves); (2) to raise tax revenue through the exchange system; (3) to promote or discourage certain types of transactions or sectors through what effectively amounts to a set of effective taxes and subsidies; and (4) as a temporary measure before liberalizing transactions.

Experience with multiple exchange rate systems has shown that such regimes have more drawbacks than advantages, namely that they can distort economic incentives and impose costs on the economy by misallocating resources for production and consumption. Moreover, the maintenance of such systems generally requires a complex and costly system of controls administered by using public sector resources, and when administrative and institutional systems are weak and scarce resources are employed toward sustaining such systems, foreign exchange pressures may reemerge, manifesting themselves either directly through reserve losses or indirectly through a growing informal sector.

Since the 1950s, there has been a trend away from multiple exchange rates, although progress has not been continuous. Significant progress was made by members in simplifying their exchange systems in the late 1950s and early 1960s, but thereafter progress was mixed, with an increased use of multiple exchange rates in the late 1960s and early 1970s, and again in the early 1980s in response to widespread balance of payments difficulties. The number of countries operating some form of multiple exchange rate regimes somewhat declined from 46 (30 percent of membership) in 1986 to 43 members in 1997 (about 24 percent).

Democratic Republic, Mauritania, Venezuela, and the Republic of Yemen).

Despite the general tendency toward unification of exchange systems, new multiple currency practices also emerged in a number of countries since 1994. Some of these countries include Cambodia, the Dominican Republic, Honduras, Mongolia, Nigeria, São Tomé and Príncipe, Sudan, Suriname, Uzbekistan, and Zimbabwe (introduced in early 1994 but abolished in July 1997). In some of these cases, multiple currency practices emerged as a result of a significant deviation between the exchange rates prevailing in different ex-

Table 14. Summary of the Nature of Members' Multiple Exchange Rate Regimes, End of 1997

Nature of the Multiple Exchange Rate (MER) Regime	Number of Countries Maintaining the System
Countries with MER that have jurisdictional implications (multiple currency practices)	30
Dual markets or different rates for different transactions	17
Exchange tax or subsidy	4
Exchange guarantee	4
At least two of the above	5
Countries with MER that do not have jurisdictional implications	13
Dual markets or different rates for different transactions	5
Exchange tax or subsidy	4
Exchange guarantee	0
At least two of the above	4
Total	43

Source: Table A13.

change markets, which were in turn the result of shortages of foreign exchange, downward pressure on domestic currencies for balance of payments reasons, or absence of a firm commitment to unified exchange rates. In Nigeria, where the official exchange rate is pegged, a dual exchange market was introduced to liberalize the foreign exchange market and enhance the role of market forces as part of an overall strategy for economic liberalization.

Payment Systems Issues

As foreign exchange markets have evolved, international payments have been characterized by a rapid growth in the volume of international transactions, as well as the application of new technologies. Electronically based technologies have become prevalent, reducing transactions costs and payment lags and improving the security and reliability of individual transactions. The number and volume of international payment transactions have increased pressures to upgrade payment systems and harmonize procedures for specific categories of payment transactions.

Central banks, and other supervisory agencies, have been focusing on means to improve risk management in international payment and settlement systems since the early 1980s.[21] There have been numerous studies of the risks associated with cross-border transactions, particularly by the Bank for International Settlements and its Committee on Payment and Settlement Systems (CPSS). In 1994, recognizing the importance of foreign exchange settlement risk, the CPSS formed a Steering Group on Settlement Risk in Foreign Exchange Transactions. The group suggested a strategy for controlling foreign exchange settlement risks that relies on collective as well as individual action by private banks. The collective initiatives taken by private banks (particularly the so-called "Group of 20 banks") are seeing the development of new settlement facilities known as continuous linked settlement (CLS). This involves the creation of a limited-purpose bank, the CLS bank, to offer users multicurrency accounts. Settlement risk will be eliminated by the CLS bank settling the different legs of foreign exchange transactions simultaneously. Two existing foreign exchange clearing houses operating multilateral netting services, the Exchange Clearing House (ECHO) and Multinet International Bank, merged with CLS Services, and the new entity will thus provide both continuous linked settlement services and netting services. The central banks of the Group of Ten countries have been actively cooperating with the private sector to facilitate these developments and are closely monitoring the impacts on risks in foreign exchange markets and whether there is need for any further action to mitigate these.

[21]A number of the IMF's *International Capital Markets* reports (especially the September 1996 report) have discussed such issues.

Part II

V

Phasing Exchange and Trade Liberalization

One of the purposes of the IMF is "to assist in the establishment of a multilateral system of payments in respect of current transactions between members and in the elimination of foreign exchange restrictions which hamper the growth of world trade" (Articles of Agreement, Article I (iv)). The IMF also seeks to assist members "to correct maladjustments in their balance of payments without resorting to measures destructive of national or international prosperity" (Articles of Agreement, Article I (v)). Exchange and trade restrictions are important factors inhibiting the growth of world trade and are destructive of national and international prosperity.

This section describes the main linkages between the liberalization of exchange controls (specifically, controls on current international payments and transfers) and trade barriers, and examines the phasing of exchange and trade reforms in five countries—China, India, Korea, Mexico, and Russia—to 1997. It focuses on phasing of exchange reform relative to trade reform rather than the optimal sequencing of exchange and trade reforms per se.[22] The case studies suggest that exchange liberalization tends to precede or accompany trade reforms and is often implemented at a relatively faster speed than trade liberalization. Exchange liberalization can provide an impetus to, and complement the reform of, the trade system, and can reinforce efficiency gains from, and the sustainability of, trade reform. Thus, coordination of exchange and trade reforms can help create a policy framework for an orderly development of a liberal external regime.

The liberalization of both controls on payments and transfers for current international transactions and controls on capital movements may be important for the phasing of trade liberalization. Liberalization of exchange controls for current international transactions has usually preceded the liberalization of controls on capital movements; this section focuses primarily on the historical relationship between such liberalization and trade reforms. The research in the appendix to the section shows, however, that in view

of the extent of liberalization of exchange controls on current international payments and transfers, controls on capital movements are *now* more significant nontariff barriers for trade to the developing countries than exchange controls on current international payments and transfers, and that the liberalization of capital controls could significantly increase trade.

Relationship Between Exchange and Trade Measures

Exchange controls affect foreign exchange transactions with nonresidents and encompass regulations pertaining to the acquisition, holding, or use of foreign exchange, or to the use of domestic or foreign currency in international payments or transfers.[23] Forms of exchange control are omnifarious, including foreign exchange budgets, advance import deposit schemes, currency repatriation and surrender requirements, limitations and prohibitions on payments and transfers, payments arrears, approval procedures, and multiple currency practices.[24]

Trade measures can be broadly categorized into tariff and nontariff barriers. The former include import tariffs and export taxes, and the latter encompass quotas, voluntary export restraints, and administrative barriers (such as licensing, government procurement, sanitary and phytosanitary standards; quality, safety, health, and environmental standards; trade-related intellectual property rights, local content requirements, and countervailing duties). Arguments for protection range from the promotion of domestic production and employment and the collection of tax revenue to the support of "infant" and increasing-returns-to-scale industries, the improvement of terms of trade, and national security. Trade policy, however, is typically not

---

Note: This section was prepared mainly by Natalia Tamirisa, an Economist in the IMF's Policy Development and Review Department.

[22]For the analysis of trade liberalization in the context of IMF programs, see IMF (1998).

[23]The IMF's jurisdiction under the Articles of Agreement extends to exchange control measures that restrict the making of payments and transfers for current international transactions or that give rise to discriminatory currency arrangements or multiple currency practices. To analyze the phasing of exchange and trade liberalization, this section focuses on exchange controls in general rather than exchange restrictions subject to IMF jurisdiction.

[24]For more details on various types of exchange control, see IMF (1997a).

the first-best instrument to achieve the above objectives. Although theoretical cases exist under which trade protection could improve welfare, governments are unlikely to have sufficient information to design such welfare-enhancing trade policies. Trade protection also often encourages wasteful rent seeking.

Besides serving as independent policy instruments, exchange and trade measures can complement or substitute each other. Governments may resort to exchange controls to support trade policy instruments; for instance, the administrative allocation of foreign exchange through foreign exchange budgets tends to accompany import monopolies. Trade measures can be effected through the exchange system, for example, through multiple exchange rates and exchange-based taxes and subsidies. In turn, trade restrictions and licensing can be used to facilitate the management of exchange controls and the administrative allocation of foreign exchange. As policy substitutes, exchange controls are more often used for macroeconomic purposes, such as to protect the level of foreign exchange reserves, while trade measures have more often the objective of protecting or promoting individual industries. As regards fiscal purposes, exchange controls may affect government revenue indirectly depending on whether they help preserve the domestic tax base; in contrast, trade taxes are used directly as a taxation instrument.

Exchange and trade liberalization can both enhance welfare and promote economic growth by reducing distortionary intervention and thus improving the efficiency of the inter- and intratemporal allocation of resources.[25] A policy challenge lies in sequencing and coordinating various phases of exchange and trade reforms so as to maximize net welfare gains from these interrelated reforms.

Exchange liberalization contributes to the success of trade reform in the following ways. First, the removal of binding exchange controls reduces distortions in the exchange and trade systems, leading to a more efficient allocation of resources. Without exchange reform, the welfare gains from trade reform are likely to be limited. Exchange controls tend to raise the domestic relative price of imports, thereby reducing imports and distorting consumption, production and investment.[26] Trade reform needs to be accompanied by the dismantling of binding exchange controls to promote production and trade in accor-dance with comparative advantage.[27] In particular, the unification of the exchange rates for current account transactions prior to the liberalization of commodity trade could help ensure that exporters and importers face the same effective price of foreign exchange.[28]

Second, exchange liberalization fosters the development of liquid, continuous and efficient foreign exchange markets, thereby lowering transaction costs and uncertainty associated with international transactions. The settlement of trade payments becomes easier because exchange reform stimulates the development of modern payment instruments with lower processing time and higher reliability of payments (for instance, checks, debit and credit cards, and automated clearinghouse transfers, and large-value transfer systems). Last but not least, the cost and flexibility of business operations improve as exchange liberalization reduces incentives for the evasion of controls and rent seeking.

Third, exchange liberalization can help establish the preconditions to reform the trade system. Disequilibria in the foreign exchange market and the system of administrative allocation of foreign exchange may be key factors that gave rise to quantitative import restrictions. The removal of these restrictions hinged on exchange reforms, which helped to eliminate disequilibria in the foreign exchange market.[29] However, in some countries with serious balance of payments problems, exchange liberalization might slow down trade reform where in the aftermath of exchange liberalization the country increased reliance on trade measures, for example, quantitative restrictions or countervailing duties, for balance of payments reasons.[30] On the other hand, where depreciation or devaluation accompanies exchange liberalization, it is likely to stimulate exports and thus support trade reform.[31]

Exchange liberalization can also make trade reform more credible by enhancing its political feasibility and signaling precommitment to market opening. Exchange liberalization is often more feasible politically than trade reform.[32] Unlike most trade measures, exchange controls are not specific to individual products, firms, or sectors, and therefore, dismantling exchange barriers does not require overriding powerful lobbies in protected sectors as much as trade reform does, and exchange reform can thus be implemented faster than trade reform. Issues concerning exchange

[25]In a recent study, Sachs and Warner (1995) found that openness and economic growth are positively related in developing countries.

[26]Greenwood and Kimbrough (1987) showed that the economic effects of exchange controls are similar to those of an import quota, and multiple exchange rates for imports and exports are equivalent to exchange controls. For an analysis of exchange controls in the presence of sophisticated financial markets, see Stockman and Hernandez (1988).

[27]See Krueger (1986); and Pritchett (1993).

[28]See also McKinnon (1993).

[29]IMF (1994).

[30]Trade restrictions are rarely an appropriate response to balance of payments difficulties, even in the short term.

[31]Thomas, Nash, and associates (1991); Papageorgiou, Choksi, and Michaely (1990).

[32]On a related topic, see the comparative analysis of the political economy of capital account and trade liberalization in Helleiner (1994).

controls have lower political visibility than those concerning trade barriers. Furthermore, export expansion stimulated by exchange liberalization often strengthens political coalitions supporting trade reforms, thereby increasing the sustainability of trade reform. Finally, in this context, the fundamental mobility and fungibility of money makes it difficult to control payments and transfers. As exchange controls become less effective over time, their liberalization becomes more feasible politically.

Both exchange and trade reforms may need to be coordinated with fiscal reform to avoid excessive reliance on trade and exchange taxes for fiscal purposes while achieving budget objectives. The impact of exchange liberalization on government revenues and expenditure is generally ambiguous. Exchange liberalization may involve the direct elimination of certain taxes or subsidies from the budget (e.g., multiple currency practices that apply a preferential rate to official transactions). This might encourage greater reliance on trade taxes to compensate for the lost tax revenue and thus might inhibit progress in trade liberalization.[33] On the other hand, exchange liberalization can help reduce capital flight and thus the erosion of the tax base.

Exchange and capital controls tend to act as a barrier to trade, and thus increasing trade requires liberalizing both trade barriers and exchange and capital controls. This conclusion emerges from an empirical model, in which bilateral exports depend on the wealth and size of countries, the distance between them, tariff barriers, and exchange and capital controls.[34] In a cross-sectional sample of 40 industrial, developing and transition countries for 1996, exchange and capital controls are found to reduce bilateral exports. The negative coefficient on the index of exchange and capital controls is significant at the 95 percent level for the entire sample and the subsample of developing and transition countries, but not for the subsample of industrial countries. The latter have relatively few exchange and capital controls, which affect trade negligibly. In contrast, in developing and transition countries exchange and capital controls are more widespread and tend to reduce bilateral exports significantly. The results suggest that the liberalization of exchange and capital controls can complement

trade liberalization, leading to a noticeable expansion of trade.

In sum, exchange liberalization preceding or at least accompanying trade liberalization can enhance efficiency gains from and the sustainability of trade liberalization. By reducing distortions and entry barriers, exchange liberalization promotes competition. It also improves allocative and productive efficiency by helping foster a more market-based exchange system and the development of modern payments instruments. Furthermore, by allowing the exchange rate to move closer to its market equilibrium level, exchange liberalization stimulates exports and thus increases the sustainability of trade reform. However, to maximize the net gains from liberalization, trade and exchange system reforms must be part of a comprehensive package of economic reforms, including appropriate monetary, fiscal, and exchange rate policy.[35]

Selected Countries' Experience with Exchange and Trade Liberalization

This section analyzes the phasing of exchange and trade liberalization in five countries—China, India, Korea, Mexico, and Russia—to 1997. The countries are selected to reflect various experiences with exchange and trade liberalization in terms of sequencing and results. The progress in reforms is illustrated by an array of measures. For trade liberalization, these measures include the mean tariff rate, the dispersion of tariffs, and the coverage of tariff lines by nontariff barriers. For exchange liberalization, the measures focus on the presence of individual exchange controls, such as multiple currency practices, special payments arrangements, foreign exchange budgets, and repatriation or surrender requirements.

China

Prior to 1979, China's exchange and trade regimes were subject to administrative control and central planning.[36] Trade rights were limited to a modest number of specialized foreign trading companies (FTCs). The trade plan set import targets to cover domestic shortages in raw materials and capital goods, and the corresponding export targets to obtain foreign exchange to pay for imports. Foreign exchange was allocated administratively according to the foreign

---

[33]Although fiscal considerations are often cited as impediments to more rapid trade reform, a recent IMF study did not find a correlation between indicators of fiscal difficulty and citation of fiscal constraints on trade reform (see IMF (1998) for more details). To mitigate the fiscal impact of trade reform, revenue-enhancing or neutral elements of trade reform may be implemented first (such as issuing tariffs of quantitative trade restrictions or elimination of customs duty exemptions). It might also be possible to develop alternative tax instruments that do not distort international trade.

[34]See the appendix to this section for more details on the empirical study and Section VII for the description of the indices of exchange and capital controls.

[35]The liberalization of controls on current international payments and transfers opens more opportunities for the circumvention of capital controls and thus makes it harder to control the capital account. Thus, following exchange liberalization, monetary and fiscal discipline became particularly crucial for achieving balance of payments objectives.

[36]Thomas, Nash, and associates (1991); Dean, Desai, and Riedel (1995); Mehran and others (1996); and World Bank (1993).

Table 15. Phases of Exchange and Trade Reforms in China, 1979–97

Main Phases of Exchange Liberalization	Main Phases of Trade Liberalization
1979–84	
• A system of foreign exchange retention quotas was introduced (1979). • Foreign exchange swaps were allowed (1980). • Multiple internal settlement rates for transactions between foreign trading companies and enterprises were unified (1981).	• Import tariff rates were revised. • Export duties were abolished (1980) and then reintroduced (1982). • The scope of export licensing was expanded (1984).
1985–93	
• Experimental swap centers were established (1985). • All enterprises were granted access to swap centers (1988). • Retention quotas were relaxed (1985–88) and unified (1991). • The internal settlement rate was abolished (1985).	• Foreign trade reform aimed at decentralizing trade began (1985). • An import regulatory tax was imposed (1985). • Import tariffs were reduced (1992). Import quotas and licensing were scaled back. A new tariff schedule in accordance with the Harmonized System was introduced (1992). • The scope of export licensing was expanded (1990). Export subsidies were eliminated (1991). Mandatory planning for exports was abolished (1991).
1994–97	
• The retention quota system was abolished (1994). • Exchange rates were unified at the prevailing swap rate. • Foreign exchange certificates were discontinued. • Foreign exchange accounts were allowed. • Purchase of foreign exchange no longer required approval. • The China Foreign Exchange Trading System was established. • Regulations on current payments and transfers were eased (1995–96). • Article VIII was accepted (1996). • Surrender requirements were eased (1997).	• The mandatory import plan was abolished (1994). • Import tariffs lowered. • Import quotas and licensing were reduced. • Transparency of trade regulations improved owing to the reduction of the number of internal documents. • The tendering system for exports of 24 items that were subject to restrictions by destination countries was introduced.

Sources: Chinese authorities; and IMF, *Annual Report on Exchange Arrangements and Exchange Restrictions* (various years).

exchange plan. In 1979, China started a gradual economic transformation aimed at the decentralization of economic decision making, and the introduction of market incentives in the economy. Exchange and trade liberalization were the cornerstone of China's reforms.

1979–84

Exchange liberalization was a prelude for trade reform, alleviating the severest foreign exchange constraints of enterprises (Tables 15 and 16). As early as 1979, the system of foreign exchange retention quotas and the associated trading mechanisms were introduced. Domestic enterprises were granted access to foreign exchange in an amount equal to the share of their foreign exchange earnings at the official exchange rate. Foreign-funded enterprises (FFEs) had an option of retaining their foreign exchange earnings di-

rectly in foreign exchange accounts. In selected localities an experimental trading system for foreign exchange was initiated, allowing enterprises to swap excess foreign exchange obtained through their retention quotas. Transactions were executed through the Bank of China at multiple internal settlement rates fluctuating within a tight band around the official rate. The rates were subsequently unified into a single internal settlement rate that was more depreciated than the official exchange rate. However, the remaining restrictions on the trading and use of accumulated retention quotas continued to inhibit the growth of swap trading.

1985–93

The introduction and proliferation of foreign exchange centers led to the emergence of a segmented

Table 16. Individual Indicators of the Extent of Liberalization for China

Period	Exchange Rate	Foreign Exchange Budget	Surrender Requirement	Average Unweighted Import Tariffs	Standard Deviation of Tariffs	Share of Imports Covered by Nontariff Barriers	Export Taxes, Quotas, and Licensing
Prior to 1979	Multiple	Yes	Yes	Not available	Not available	Not available	Yes
1979–84	Dual	Yes	Yes	Not available	Not available	Not available	Yes
1985–93	Dual	Yes	Yes	38% (1986) 43% (1992)	27.4% (1992)	50% (1989)[1] 25% (1992)[1] 51.4% (1992)[2] 33% (1992)[3]	Yes 67% (1987) 50% (1989) 15% (1992)[4]
1994–96	Unitary	No	Yes	23% (1996) 17.6% (1997)[6]	16.7% (1996) 13.0% (1997)	32.5% (1996)[5] 18% (1996)[3]	Yes [7]

Sources: Chinese authorities; IMF, *Annual Report on Exchange Arrangements and Exchange Restrictions* (various years); and Dean, Desai, and Riedel (1995).

[1]Import licensing.

[2]All nonoverlapping nontariff measures, including "canalization" under state and designated trading; licenses, quotas, and controls; and import tendering.

[3]"Canalization" (i.e., state or designated trading).

[4]Export licensing.

[5]All nonoverlapping nontariff measures, including "canalization" under state and designated trading; licenses, quotas, and controls; and import tendering.

[6]United Nations Conference on Trade and Development. Trade-weighted average rate was 18.2 percent (end-1997).

[7]About 15 percent of exports were covered by nontariff barriers in 1996.

foreign exchange market. In 1985–86, independent swap centers—foreign exchange adjustment centers (FEACs)—were established as an experiment for trading retention quotas and retained foreign exchange earnings, primarily by foreign-funded enterprises. The incipient foreign exchange market was nurtured through the progressive expansion of entry rights and the relaxation and eventual unification of retention quotas. In 1988, all enterprises with retention quotas were granted access to the centers, and concurrently the swap exchange rate was decontrolled. In addition, all domestic residents were permitted to sell foreign exchange at the swap rate at designated bank branches. Purchases remained subject to approval by the State Administration of Exchange Control (SAEC) according to a priority list, which covered key imports and foreign debt-service payments.

The fostering of a market-based exchange system was accompanied by a decentralization of trade and a cutback of mandatory planning. In 1985, provincial branches of national FTCs became independent financial entities and each province was permitted to establish its own, causing a proliferation of them. In addition, FTCs were granted greater autonomy to trade on own account. The range of products they were allowed to trade expanded as mandatory planning was scaled back. In 1991, enterprises and local authorities were rendered more independent in setting trade targets. Mandatory trade planning was abolished in 1991 for exports and in 1994 for imports.

The retrenchment of administrative regulation resulted in a perplexing system of trade controls, involving tariffs, quantitative restrictions, licensing and other nontariff barriers on exports and imports. Direct trade controls were frequently overlapping; import licensing was used to allocate quotas and to influence imports in accordance with domestic and balance of payments objectives; import controls in the form of obligatory approval were adopted to protect domestic producers in selected sectors, inter alia, electronics and machinery; export licenses and quotas were applied to fulfill agreements with trading partners; import tariff rates were high and dispersed; and export taxes were widespread. A system of duty exemptions was in place, mainly for imports related to export production, imports by foreign-funded enterprises, and border trade.

1994–97

Exchange liberalization was largely completed during 1994–96. In 1994, exchange rates were unified at the prevailing swap rate and the retention quota system was abolished. The wholesale foreign exchange market was unified and integrated with the establishment of China's Foreign Exchange Trading System (CFETS)—a national electronic trading system, which connected regional swap centers with the interbank market.[37] Domestic enterprises remained subject

---

[37]The rules for participation in CFETS varied for domestic and foreign entities. Domestic enterprises only had access to the bank retail market, which was subject to different settlement arrangements than the wholesale market, while FFEs could trade directly, through their banks, in the wholesale market.

to surrender requirement for foreign exchange receipts. Nonetheless, they were permitted to open foreign exchange accounts for selected transactions, such as foreign borrowing, stock issues, and approved debt-service payments. Approval requirements for access to the foreign exchange market for most trade and trade-related transactions was abolished, and purchases of foreign exchange could be made at designated financial institutions upon presentation of appropriate documents. SAEC approval was still needed for non-trade-related current payments by Chinese nationals, such as travel expenses, and for FFEs that wished to access the swap market. The use of foreign exchange certificates for foreign nationals was discontinued, and the multiple currency practice arising from the conversion of unused foreign certificates at the old official rate was eliminated. The remaining controls on access to foreign exchange for FFEs and limits on the availability of foreign exchange for certain non-trade-related current international transactions were abolished. Following these measures, in December 1996, China accepted the obligations of Article VIII, Sections 2, 3, and 4 of the Fund's Articles of Agreement.

In parallel with the abolition of exchange controls on current international payments and transfers, trade liberalization accelerated. The Trade Package of April 1, 1996 stipulated the selective reduction of tariff and nontariff barriers. In 1997, import tariffs were lowered further. As a result, the average import tariff rate fell from about 40 percent at the end of 1992 to 17.6 percent at the end of 1997. In addition, tariff dispersion fell and duty exemptions were scaled back. The scope of export licensing and export taxes was also lowered. Also, the share of imports subject to nontariff barriers declined from more than one-half in 1992 to about one-third in 1996. Producers received larger access to trading rights as the share of imports subject to "canalization" declined from about one-third in 1992 to 18 percent in 1996. Furthermore, joint-venture foreign trading companies were permitted on an experimental basis in selected localities. Notwithstanding the recent progress, as of 1997, China's trade regime continued to be characterized by numerous nontariff barriers, restricted trading rights, and high and dispersed tariffs.

India

India initially maintained highly restrictive exchange and trade regimes.[38] To protect agriculture and to encourage industrial development, most imports were banned, except for goods not produced domestically (mainly raw materials and certain machinery items). Although import restrictions on certain intermediate and capital goods and inputs for export industries were eased in the late 1970s, the external regime remained extremely distorted with stringent exchange controls, high and dispersed tariff rates, widespread quantitative and licensing restrictions, and an intricate system of export controls and incentives. For example, imports of many goods were chaneled through parastatal monopolies, commodities for import were classified into 26 lists and subject to ten different types of import licenses, and imports of most consumer goods were prohibited. Some of these trade restrictions were maintained for balance of payments reasons under the General Agreement on Tariffs and Trade.

1991–92

A balance of payments crisis in 1990–91 spurred trade liberalization, and major trade liberalization measures were taken during 1991–92 (Tables 17 and 18). The level and dispersion of import tariff rates were substantially reduced in a succession of tariff cuts. The tariff structure was streamlined by reducing the number of tariff bands and eliminating special tariff exemptions. Import licensing requirements were eased, and quantitative restrictions on imports of most capital and intermediate goods were removed. The number of restricted items subject to "canalization" (i.e., those that can be imported only by the public sector) was also reduced. Goods- and sector-specific schemes with more general incentive schemes accessible to all exporters were streamlined, and many export taxes and direct export subsidies were abolished. Also, a system of EXIM scripts—special tradable import licenses—was introduced, allowing imports of production inputs up to a value equivalent to 30 percent of exporters' foreign exchange earnings. The remaining goods (mostly agricultural and consumer items) were transferred to a unified negative list and subject to either import licensing or "canalization," except for a few prohibited items. Items were gradually moved to a positive list or were issued open general licenses. In 1992, special import licenses (SIL) were introduced in preparation for relaxing restrictions on consumer goods imports. These tradable licenses were issued to exporters up to 15 percent of their export or foreign exchange earnings and could be used to import a few consumer goods, which had previously been on the negative list.

At the onset of trade liberalization in 1991, the exchange rate was devalued by about 20 percent, and a free market exchange rate was introduced for many permitted transactions in 1992.[39] Under the dual ex-

---

[38]See Thomas, Nash, and associates (1991); Dean, Desai, and Riedel (1995) for a general discussion on India's regime.

[39]Previously, the exchange rate was set on the basis of a basket of exchange rates of India's major trading partners.

Table 17. Phases of Exchange and Trade Reforms in India, 1991–97

Main Phases of Exchange Liberalization	Main Phases of Trade Liberalization
1991–92	
• A dual exchange rate system was introduced to facilitate transition to a more market-based exchange rate (1992). • Authorized dealers were permitted to offer forward cover for all transactions permitted under the exchange control regulations (1992). • Payments for some invisible transactions were liberalized (1992).	• The EXIM Script scheme was introduced, under which exporters received tradable import entitlement equivalent to 30 percent of the value of their exports (1991). The EXIM Script scheme was subsequently replaced by a dual exchange rate structure (1992). • Import tariffs were substantially lowered. Quantitative restrictions on imports of most capital and intermediate goods were removed. A single negative list was introduced. A number of nontariff barriers were abolished, including actual user policy, phased manufacturing program, and government purchase preferences. On a limited scale, import of consumer goods was allowed through open general license, special import license scheme, and as luggage. • Direct export subsidies were eliminated. Sector specific subsidies were replaced by duty exemption schemes, including advance licensing, duty drawback and other schemes, and tax exemptions. • The coverage of export taxes substantially narrowed and remained only on a few selected items—for example, tea. • The scope of import and export "canalization" was narrowed.
1993–94	
• Exchange rates were unified (1993). • Limits on payments for many invisibles were liberalized (1994). • The scope of an exchange guarantee scheme for interest payments on nonresident foreign currency deposits, which resulted in a multiple currency practice, was narrowed to cover only deposits with a maturity of three years (1994). • Article VIII was accepted (1994); however, a number of exchange restrictions remained in place.	• The level and dispersion of import tariffs were substantially reduced. • The scope of import and export "canalization" was narrowed. • Export controls were substantially relaxed.
1995–97	
• Payments for and remittances of proceeds from some invisibles were liberalized (1995). • Restrictions on the repatriation of current investment income were eliminated (1997). • The multiple currency practice associated with existing exchange rate guarantees on nonresident deposits was phased out (1997). • Ceilings were liberalized on a range of current account transactions and authorized dealers were permitted to conduct transactions—without seeking prior approval—on a bona fide basis (1997).	• Import tariff rates were substantially lowered. • Import quantitative restrictions were eased through the expansion of the negative list.

Sources: Indian authorities; and IMF, *Annual Report on Exchange Arrangements and Exchange Restrictions* (various years).

change rate system, the official rate applied only to imports by government, crude oil, fertilizers, and life-saving drugs; all other permissible transactions were executed at a free market rate. Exporters were allowed to sell 60 percent of their earnings at a free market rate. Along with the changes in the exchange arrangement, payments for some invisible transactions were liberalized.

Table 18. Individual Indicators of the Extent of Liberalization for India

Period	Exchange Rate	Foreign Exchange Budget	Surrender Requirement	Average Unweighted Import Tariff	Standard Deviation of Import Tariffs	Share of GDP Covered by Nontariff Barriers	Export Taxes, Quotas, and Licensing
Prior to 1991	Unitary	No	Yes	128% (1990)	41% (1990)	93% (1990, in terms of tradable value added)	Yes (export controls on 439 items)
1991–92	Dual	No	Yes	128% (1991) 94% (1992)	41% (1991) 34% (1992)	75% (1992, same as above)	Yes (export controls on 296 items)
1993–94	Unitary	No	Yes	71% (1993) 55% (1994)	30% (1993) 25% (1994)	Not available	Yes
1995–97	Unitary	No	Yes	41% (1995) 39% (1996) 34% (1997)	19% (1995–96) 17% (1997)	66% (1995, same as above)	Yes (export controls on 152 items)

Sources: Indian authorities; and IMF, *Annual Report on Exchange Arrangements and Exchange Restrictions* (various years).

1993–94

During 1993–94, India made important steps toward current account convertibility. In March 1993, the exchange rates were unified, and most restrictions on payments and transfers for current international transactions were eliminated. Additionally, rules for repatriation of income and investment earnings were liberalized, and foreign exchange dealers were allowed to enter into forward transactions. Following these changes, in August 1994, India accepted the obligations of Article VIII, Sections 2, 3, and 4 of the Fund's Articles of Agreement. However, some exchange restrictions remained in place, including those on nonresident deposits, income transfers by nonresident Indians, bilateral payment and debt agreements, and a dividend-balancing requirement.

Along with the unification of exchange rates, the trade regime was substantially liberalized. Tariff and nontariff barriers were lowered further. Notably, auxiliary duties involving differential rates that were applied on top of the basic tariff schedule were simplified and eventually discontinued. Quantitative import restrictions on capital goods and intermediate inputs were abolished, and maximum tariff rates dramatically reduced. In addition, licensing requirements for many export goods were eliminated.

1995–97

During 1995–97, exchange and trade liberalization continued, albeit at a slower pace. Restrictions on repatriating current investment income were eliminated, starting with income earned during the 1996–97 tax year. The multiple currency practice associated with the existing exchange rate guarantees on nonresident deposits was phased out as deposits under the scheme matured. In 1997, authorized dealers were permitted to conduct a broader range of current account transactions without seeking prior approval on a

bona fide basis. In addition, the authorities began to prepare new legislation to streamline foreign exchange regulations. At the same time, import tariff rates were reduced, and import restrictions on consumer goods were partially liberalized. Although duty exemption schemes remained in place, they were streamlined in 1997 by discontinuing value-based advance license schemes.

Notwithstanding the progress in trade liberalization, as of 1997, India's trade regime remained restrictive. The tariff structure was complex with 11 tariff bands and a 34 percent average tariff rate. Quantitative import restrictions and licensing continued to cover most consumer goods. Export controls, including quotas, prohibitions, and minimum prices, were extensive enough to keep domestic prices below the world level (particularly for agricultural exports, such as cotton, wheat, and rice). Furthermore, state enterprises retained monopoly control over trade in key goods, including some petroleum products, medicines, and cereals.

Republic of Korea

From 1953 to 1960, Korea's economic development was based on an import substitution strategy, resulting in highly protectionist exchange and trade regimes.[40] Multiple exchange rates and taxes on sales of foreign exchange for imports were in place. Exporters and others with foreign exchange earnings were given transferable rights to use their foreign currency proceeds for importing under an import-export linking system. Foreign exchange to finance imports that were not paid for with foreign exchange earned from exports was allocated by auctions. Residents were re-

---

[40]See Thomas, Nash, and associates (1991); Dean, Desai, and Riedel (1995); and Kim (1994) for a general discussion of Korea's regime.

56

quired to surrender foreign exchange in full to the Bank of Korea at the official banking rate. Upon surrender, residents received nontransferable exchange certificates, which could be used to repurchase foreign exchange within three months from the time of surrender.

Like the exchange system, the trade regime was severely distorted. Import tariff rates were high and dispersed. In 1960, for example, the unweighted average tariff rate was about 30 percent; and allowing for the foreign exchange tax, tariff equivalents, and exemptions, the actual tariff rate reached about 46 percent.[41] Import commodities were differentiated into two categories: those paid for with Korean foreign exchange (so-called KFX imports) and those paid for with U.S. aid funds. KFX imports were classified into those subject to automatic approval, semirestricted, restricted (i.e., subject to quotas), unspecified, or prohibited items. While imports were extensively controlled, exports were promoted through multiple exchange rates and export subsidies.

1961–83

Exchange liberalization played a central role in the transition from import substitution to an export-oriented development strategy (Tables 19 and 20). Foreign exchange taxes were abolished in 1961, and multiple exchange rates were unified in 1964. By eliminating the severest disincentives for exports, these measures stimulated export growth. Between 1965 and 1980, exports as a share of GNP increased from 5.8 percent to 23.9 percent.[42] Trade liberalization started in 1964 with the easing of some quantitative import restrictions and licensing. Export subsidies were revised several times and eventually abolished in 1965. The gradual reduction of tariffs began in 1973.

1984–97

Since 1984, broad trade reform has been implemented in Korea, proceeding at a faster pace in manufacturing than in agriculture. By the end of 1991, most quantitative and licensing controls on manufactured imports were removed. Import tariff reductions were accelerated and by 1996, the unweighted average rate was less than 8 percent, and 93.4 percent of tariff rates were below 10 percent. The average tariff rate on nonagricultural imports was lowered to that of industrial trading partners. Import licensing became automatic, except for a narrow list of products with potentially adverse health or security effects. In response to bilateral trade frictions, Korea introduced an import diversification program aimed at alleviating signifi-

cant bilateral trade imbalances. As a result, foreign producers gained access to service sectors, and some nontariff barriers, particularly for agricultural imports and automobiles, were removed.[43] Exports were free of restrictions and were promoted through preferential credits and duty-drawback schemes.[44]

Exchange liberalization proceeded more rapidly than trade reform. During 1985–87, exchange restrictions on current payments and transfers were removed. In 1988, Korea formally accepted the obligations of Article VIII, Sections 2, 3, and 4 of the IMF's Articles of Agreement. Subsequently, foreign exchange controls were eased further, notably those relating to documentation requirements, the foreign exchange position of banks, and capital controls. Exchange regulations were modified to improve the efficiency of spot and forward foreign exchange markets. Steps were taken to facilitate the settlement of external transactions by reducing documentation requirements and streamlining processing. Surrender requirements were maintained until 1995, and repatriation requirements still remained in place, as of 1997.

Mexico

After World War II, Mexico followed import substitution policies, and, as a result, its trade regime was characterized by a substantial anti-export bias.[45] Import tariff rates were high, particularly on agricultural and consumer goods, and dispersed, and import licensing and quantitative restrictions were widespread. Traditionally, export restrictions were less pervasive than import ones. Export taxes, licensing, quotas, and prohibitions applied to a narrow range of items, mostly petroleum and agricultural products. In the aftermath of the balance of payments crisis of 1982, trade restrictions were tightened further, and by late 1982 import licensing requirements covered almost all imports. At the same time, the damaging consequences of extensive protection became evident as balance of payments problems mounted.

In contrast to the trade regime, Mexico's exchange regime was relatively liberal, following the adoption of the obligations of Article VIII, Sections 2, 3, and 4

[41]See Kim (1994).
[42]Ibid.

[43]Adjustment tariffs and special safeguard duties were levied on a small number of commodities (about 1 percent of total imports) and were within the bindings of the World Trade Organization (WTO). Korea's developing country status under the WTO allows it 10 years to fulfill the WTO commitments.
[44]In response to the currency and financial crisis of late 1997, the Korean authorities expressed their intention to implement additional trade liberalization measures, including, inter alia, the reform of trade-related subsidies, import licensing, and import diversification program. A detailed consideration of these recent developments lies beyond the scope of this study.
[45]See Thomas, Nash, and associates (1991); Dean, Desai, and Riedel (1995); and Loser and Kalter (1992) for a discussion of Mexico's regime.

Table 19. Phases of Exchange and Trade Reforms in Korea, 1961–97

Main Phases of Exchange Liberalization	Main Phases of Trade Liberalization
1961–83	
• Foreign exchange taxes were abolished (1961).	• The system of export subsidies was revised (1961–64) and was abolished (1965).
• The issuance of exchange certificates against the surrender of foreign exchange was discontinued.	• The import-export linking system was expanded (1963). Some quantitative restrictions were relaxed or converted into tariffs, or both (1964).
• The foreign exchange for all authorized purposes was to be sold without requesting the surrender of certificates (1961).	• Most goods previously requiring an individual import license were brought under the automatic approval procedure (1964).
• The retention quota system for export proceeds was abolished (1961).	• Import restrictions were relaxed. The number of items authorized for import was increased from 694 to 1,431.
• Qualified banks and dealers were permitted to conduct exchange operations, except in respect of foreign aid (1962).	• Import procedures were simplified (1965).
• A major exchange reform was announced that substantially liberalized the exchange system.	
• Exchange rate was unified (1964).	
• Restrictions on payments for invisibles were relaxed. Licenses for payments for invisibles connected with foreign trade were granted automatically (1965).	
• Restrictions pertaining to resident and nonresident accounts were liberalized (1964, 1980).	
• Foreign exchange certificates were abolished (1980).	
1984–97	
• Restrictions on payments for and proceeds from invisibles and current transfers were liberalized (1985, 1987).	• Import controls were liberalized, as the number of automatically approved import items increased. Higher elastic tariffs were introduced for some of the newly liberalized import items (1985). The number of items of the elastic tariff list, including adjustment and emergency tariffs, was reduced (1984, 1985). The number of items on the import surveillance list was reduced (1987–88). Import tariff rates were reduced (1988).
• The use of the Foreign Exchange Supply and Demand Plan was discontinued (1988).	
• Article VIII of the IMF's Articles of Agreement was accepted (1988).	
• The requirement of advance import deposits was eliminated (1990).	
• Documentation requirements for foreign exchange transactions and foreign currency deposits were liberalized (1991, 1995).	• A new Foreign Trade Act entered into effect, which, inter alia, liberalized a system of safeguards against import surcharges, by creating a special Trade Commission authorized to judge whether imports harmed domestic industries and reducing the reliance on import surveillance lists and adjustment tariffs (1987).
• The prohibition on sales of foreign currencies from accounts for making domestic payments was abolished (1991).	
• The regulations on forward exchange transactions were liberalized (1992–93).	• Export restrictions were eased (1984).
• The regulations on resident foreign exchange accounts were liberalized (1992).	• The import surveillance list, which required approval of the Korean Foreign Traders' Association before an import license could be granted, was abolished (1989).
• The limit on the amount of Korean banknotes allowed to be exported was increased (1995).	• The system of emergency tariffs was abolished (1989).
• Documentation requirements for payments and transfers abroad were simplified (1995).	• Import tariff rates were reduced (1989–92).
• Residents were allowed to hold foreign exchange without registering with banks (1995).	• Imports controls on 93 items, mostly agricultural products, were liberalized (1991).
• The prescription of currency requirements was abolished (1996).	• Tariff quotas were introduced to replace import quotas in agriculture (1995). Tariff quotas also applied to crude oil.
	• A number of trade-related subsidies, for example, reserves for export losses, were abolished (1997).

Sources: Korean authorities; and IMF, *Annual Report on Exchange Arrangements and Exchange Restrictions* (various years).

Table 20. Individual Indicators of the Extent of Liberalization for Korea

Period	Exchange Rate	Foreign Exchange Budget	Surrender Requirement	Average Weighted Import Tariffs	Standard Deviation of Import Tariffs	Number of Items Covered by Nontariff Barriers[1]	Export Taxes, Quotas, Licenses
Prior to 1961	Multiple	No	Yes	30% (1960)[2]	Not available	Not available	Yes
1961–83	Unitary (since 1964)	No	Yes	23.7% (1982)	Not available	Not available	Yes
1984–97	Unitary	No	No (since 1995)	21.9% (1984) 18.1% (1988) 10.1% (1992) 7.9% (1996)[3]	6% (1992)	15.2% (1984) 4.6% (1988) 2.3% (1992) 0.7% (1996)	Yes

Sources: Korean authorities; and IMF, *Annual Report on Exchange Arrangements and Exchange Restrictions* (various years).

[1]Percentage of tariff lines covered by licensing requirements, import restrictions, and so forth.
[2]If the foreign exchange tax, tariff equivalents, and exemptions are accounted for, the actual tariff rate was about 46 percent (Kim, 1994).
[3]Unweighted.

of the IMF's Articles of Agreement in 1946. Foreign exchange accounts were permitted, and payments for invisible transactions were virtually free of restrictions. However, the foreign exchange market was segmented into controlled and free markets. Proceeds from exports of goods and services were subject to repatriation and surrender requirements. Special payments arrangements were in place, mostly with respect to other Latin American countries.

1983–85

During 1983–85, trade restrictions were selectively removed (Tables 21 and 22). The coverage of import licensing requirements was somewhat narrowed. The import permit requirement was abolished on intermediate and capital goods that were not manufactured domestically. The tariff schedule was rationalized, and, as a result, trade dispersion decreased. The coverage of official import reference prices was also narrowed. Nevertheless, these measures were limited, and trade restrictions continued to cover about three-fourths of imports and most goods that could be produced domestically.

1985–91

In 1985, along with a broader growth-oriented stabilization and adjustment program, Mexico started comprehensive trade reforms. The following year it joined the General Agreement on Tariffs and Trade and signed a number of bilateral free trade agreements. Trade regimes were substantially liberalized. Quantitative import restrictions were replaced with tariffs, which were lowered subsequently. The coverage of quantitative restrictions fell from 92.2 percent of domestic production in 1985 to 19.9 percent in 1990. Imports of intermediate and capital goods became virtually free of quantitative restrictions. The average production-weighted tariff rate was reduced from 23.5 percent in 1985 to 12.5 percent in 1990;

however, tariff escalation remained. Official import prices were gradually phased out during 1985–87 (previously, about one-fourth of imports was subject to official import prices). In addition to import liberalization, many export controls were removed. The coverage of production by export licenses declined from 48.9 percent in 1985 to 17.6 percent in 1991; the remaining export licensing requirements applied mostly to agricultural and agro-industrial products. Export taxes were eliminated in 1989. Trade reform was supported by the phasing out of the controlled foreign exchange market and surrender requirements. Surrender requirements were eased and then eliminated in 1991. At the same time, the controlled exchange rate market was abolished.

1992–97

During 1992–97, the exchange regime did not change significantly, while trade liberalization proceeded further, albeit at a slower pace. The average import tariff rate remained stable at about 13 percent; however, tariff dispersion increased from 4.5 percent in 1992 to about 7.4 percent in 1995. The phasing-out of import licenses continued, and the coverage of licensing requirements declined from 10.5 percent of imports in 1992 to 7.2 percent in 1995. Export licensing requirements were also liberalized. Mexico continued to participate in regional trade liberalization; notably, the North American Free Trade Agreement among Mexico, the United States, and Canada entered into force in 1994.

Russia

The Soviet economic paradigm stood on the pillars of state property, central planning, administrative regulation, and import substitution.[46] Imports mainly ac-

---

[46]See Tamirisa (1998).

Table 21. Phases of Exchange and Trade Reforms in Mexico, 1983–97

Main Phases of Exchange Liberalization	Main Phases of Trade Liberalization
1983–mid-1985	
• All imports subject to import duty became eligible for access to foreign exchange at the controlled market rate.	• The prior import permit requirement was relaxed
• Foreign exchange financing of royalty payments for technology transfer was shifted from the free to the controlled market (1984).	• Tariffs were raised, and the tariff structure was rationalized.
• Surrender requirements were eased (1984).	• The coverage of official import reference prices was narrowed.
Mid-1985–91	
• Surrender requirements were eased further (1985–86, 1991) and were eliminated (1991).	• Import licensing requirements were liberalized and were replaced with tariffs (1985, 1986). Temporary import licensing requirements were imposed on selected items (1990). The requirement of import permits was eased (1985).
• The controlled exchange rate market was eliminated (1991).	• A new tariff structure was introduced (1985). Import tariffs were reduced (1986, 1990) and were increased on selected items (1989).
	• Export subsidies were expanded (1985, 1991).
	• Export licensing was reduced (1990–91). Export duties were lowered (1990). Registration requirements for exporters and importers were introduced (1989).
1992–97	
• An over-the-counter market in forward and options in foreign exchange was introduced (1995).	• Import duties were lowered (1993). Import tariffs on selected items were raised (1994–95). Import licensing requirements were liberalized (1992–93).
	• Export licensing requirements were further liberalized (1992, 1994).
	• The North American Free Trade Agreement was signed (1992) and came into force (1994).

Sources: Mexican authorities; and IMF, *Annual Report on Exchange Arrangements and Exchange Restrictions* (various years).

quired foreign technology and goods not available domestically, while exports provided foreign exchange to pay for imports. The right to engage in foreign trade and foreign exchange transactions was largely monopolized by the state. Foreign exchange was allocated administratively, while payments and transfers for international transactions were severely restricted.

1987–91

During 1987–91, trading rights were decentralized (Tables 23 and 24). In 1987, state monopoly on foreign trade was dismantled. Four years later, in 1991, producers were allowed to engage in international trade without registration. Simultaneously, the first interbank foreign exchange market, Moscow Interbank Foreign Currency Exchange (MICEX), opened in the capital. Decentralization of foreign trade paved a way for comprehensive exchange and trade liberalization,

which accelerated after the breakup of the Soviet Union in December 1991.

1992–97

As a result of the sweeping exchange reform of 1992–96, Russia moved from an administrative exchange regime closer to current account convertibility. Following the unification of exchange rates in July 1992, a new foreign exchange law was adopted in November 1992, which introduced current account convertibility for residents. By 1993, current account controls pertaining to nonresidents were substantially liberalized, and the frequency of foreign exchange auctions was increased. Some exchange restrictions remained in place, including those in the form of delays in settling outstanding net debit balances under inoperative bilateral payments agreements with Bulgaria, Egypt, and the Syrian Arab Republic under the

Table 22. Individual Indicators of the Extent of Liberalization for Mexico

Period	Exchange Rate	Foreign Exchange Budget	Surrender Requirement	Average Unweighted Import Tariffs	Standard Deviation of Import Tariffs	Share of Imports Covered by Nontariff Barriers	Export Taxes, Quotas, and Licensing.
Prereform	Dual	No	Yes	Not available	Not available	Not available	Yes
1985–91	Dual	No	Yes	23.5% (1985)[2] 12.5% (1990)[2] 13.1% (1989–91)	4.4% (1989) 4.5% (1991)	60% (1981)[3] 100% (1982)[3] 92.2% (1985)[4] 19.9% (1990)[4] 18.3% (1989) 8.9% (1991)	Yes
1992–97	Unitary	No	No	13.1% (1992) 13.0% (1993) 12.5% (1994) 13.5% (1995)	4.5% (1992) 4.7% (1993) 6.0% (1994) 7.4% (1995)	10.5% (1992) 21.8% (1993) 10.6% (1994) 7.2% (1995)	Yes

Sources: Mexican authorities; and IMF, *Annual Report on Exchange Arrangements and Exchange Restrictions* (various years).
[1]Weighted by imports. Refers to licensing.
[2]Weighted by domestic production.
[3]Import quantitative restrictions.
[4]Share of domestic production.

transitional arrangements of Article XIV, Section 2. Following their elimination, in 1996, Russia formally accepted the obligations of Article VIII, Sections 2, 3, and 4 of the IMF's Articles of Agreement.

In parallel with the liberalization of restrictions on current payments and transfers, surrender requirements were eased, and other measures to prevent capital flight were introduced. In 1992, exporters were permitted to surrender foreign exchange at market rates rather than below as previously. After 1994, the authorities monitored repatriation of foreign exchange export proceeds through a "passport" system of exchange registration. Under this system, an exporter had to present a breakdown of all financial transactions related to export to customs prior to shipment, thereby allowing ex post verification that export proceeds had been repatriated. A similar scheme existed for the prepayment of imports.

Along with the development of a more market-based exchange system, trade liberalization proceeded gradually. During 1992–93, a key objective of trade reform was achieved, as Russia shifted to relying on world market prices in trade with other countries, including the Baltic and other countries of the former Soviet Union. As a result, implicit price subsidies to the former members of the Council for Mutual Economic Assistance and to the Baltic and other countries of the former Soviet Union were eliminated. Prices of export goods, mainly energy and raw materials, started to rise gradually to the world market levels. Furthermore, Russia dismantled most bilateral payment arrangements with countries other than those of the former Soviet Union. Settlement began to take place in convertible currencies for most transactions, except barter and countertrade.

Trade reform resulted in a relatively liberal import regime by 1997. In 1992, a relatively uniform import tariff schedule was introduced for fiscal reasons with an average rate of about 15 percent. Despite repeated revisions, the average trade-weighted duty (excluding specific duties on alcohol) remained stable at around 13 percent, while the dispersion declined since mid-1995. Tariff rates above 30 percent were lowered to at least 30 percent, except tariffs on alcoholic beverages. The import regime was almost free of quantitative and licensing restrictions, and only a few items remained subject to licensing controls, mostly for health and security reasons. Although the practice of discretionary duty exemptions was discontinued in 1995, some legal exemptions were preserved, albeit at a smaller scale since 1996 (for instance, humanitarian aid and contributions to the charter capital of joint ventures). Persisting protectionist pressures resulted in the introduction of an import licensing requirement for ethyl alcohol and vodka in 1997. Under the requirement, the prepayment of all customs duties was needed for an import license request to be satisfied.

In contrast to import liberalization, the removal of export controls, such as taxes, quotas, licensing, and other nontariff barriers, proceeded slowly and intermittently. Export restrictions centered on strategic commodities (including raw materials, energy, and precious metals) and were aimed mainly at halting domestic inflation, preventing illegal exports and capital outflows, and improving tax collection. During 1994–95, export taxes were gradually reduced, and, in 1996, the remaining export duties on strategic commodities were abolished. The fiscal impact of tariff reform in Russia could be illustrated briefly as follows. In 1993, trade taxes represented the third largest

61

Table 23. Phases of Exchange and Trade Reforms in Russia, 1992–97

Main Phases of Exchange Liberalization	Main Phases of Trade Liberalization
1987–91	
• The first and largest of the interbank currency exchanges, Moscow Interbank Foreign Currency Exchange (MICEX), commenced daily trading of the U.S. dollar (1991).	• The state monopoly on foreign trade was abolished (1987). • Enterprises and associations were allowed to engage in foreign trade without any special registration (1991).
1992–97	
• Exchange rates were unified (July 1992). • The new foreign exchange law introduced current account convertibility for residents (November 1992). Current account convertibility was extended to nonresidents (1992–93). • Surrender requirements were eased from 100 percent to 50 percent (1992). The requirement that exporters subject to the 50 percent surrender requirement must sell 30 percent of export proceeds to the Central Bank of Russia was abolished; the entire amount of the surrendered foreign exchange should be sold to the auction exchange market through authorized banks (1993). • Export earnings of joint ventures were made subject to the 50 percent surrender requirement (1993). • The direct interbank foreign currency market developed as the largest authorized banks began to open credit lines for authorized commercial banks and to carry out regular operations to trade foreign currencies on a contractual basis (1993). • Authorized banks holding general licenses were permitted to import and export foreign currency banknotes, treasury notes, coins in circulation, and securities without restrictions, provided that customs regulations were observed (1993). • Regulations on procedures for nonresidents to open and maintain Russian ruble accounts were issued (1993). • A new system of controlling repatriation of export proceeds based on domiciliation in authorized Russian banks came into effect (1994). • The use of foreign currency banknotes in the domestic retail trade was banned (1994). • Article VIII was accepted (1996).	• A relatively uniform import tariff schedule was introduced (1992). Import tariff rates were reduced for foodstuffs, medicines, and medical equipment, etc., and increased for alcohol and delicatessens (1993). Import tariff rates were increased by 5 percent on average (1994). • Special import tax of 3 percent was introduced (1994). A value-added tax of 20 percent and excise taxes (ranging from 10 percent to 250 percent) were introduced for most imports (1993). Import tariff rates were increased mainly on foodstuffs and agricultural products. An excise tax of 10 percent was introduced on imported foodstuffs (1995). Import subsidies were discontinued (1994). The remaining import licensing requirements were mostly abolished (1992). Import licensing requirements were introduced for ethyl alcohol and vodka (1997). Safety, quality, and certification procedures were introduced for most imports (1993). • Export taxes were reduced (1994–95) and abolished (1996). Uniform procedures for licensing and export quotas were introduced (1993). Export quotas and licensing were abolished (1994–95). The institution of special exporters existed (1992–95). Preshipment contract registration and mandatory certification procedures were in place (1994–96). A "passport" system of exchange registration was introduced (1994). • Discretionary duty exemptions were eliminated (1994); however, some exemptions remained to promote foreign investment in certain sectors (e.g., autos).

Sources: Russian authorities; and IMF, *Annual Report on Exchange Arrangements and Exchange Restrictions* (various years).

source of revenue for the federal government, accounting for about 23.0 percent of federal government total revenue. In 1996, trade taxes became the fifth largest source of revenue and covered about 10.3 percent of total revenue. Export licensing and quantitative restrictions were harmonized in 1993 and abolished during 1994–95. Nonetheless, other nontariff barriers remained in place. For example, during 1994–96, exports of strategic commodities were subject to the mandatory registration of preshipment contracts and the certification of quality, quantity, and price. Additionally, in 1993, about one-fourth of exports was recentralized to provide the government with access to foreign exchange to pay for centralized imports. Other centralized exports continued to include arms and defense-related equipment. In 1992, rights to export strategic commodities were given to approved intermediaries, also known as special exporters; following the abolition of this system in 1995, all enterprises became eligible to export. However, access to oil pipelines remained subject to government regulation.

Table 24. Individual Indicators of the Extent of Liberalization for Russia

Period	Exchange Rate	Foreign Exchange Budget	Surrender Request	Average Unweighted Import Tariffs	Standard Deviation of Import Tariffs	Share of Imports Covered by Nontariff Barriers	Export Taxes, Quotas, and Licensing
Prior to 1987	Multiple	Yes	Yes	Not available	Not available	Not available	Yes
1987–91	Multiple	Yes	Yes	Most imports were exempt from taxes but subject to quotas and licensing.	Not available	Not available	Yes
1992–97	Unitary	Yes	Yes	15% (1992) 14% (1994) 15% (1995) 12.7% (1995)[1] 13.3% (1996)[1]	9.6% (1995)[2] 9.1% (1996)[2]	Less than 3% (health and security reasons)	Taxes: Yes (until 1996) Quotas and licensing: No (since 1994–95)

Sources: Russian authorities; and IMF, *Annual Report on Exchange Arrangements and Exchange Restrictions* (various years).

[1]Trade-weighted. Weights are based on 1994 data collected by the State Customs Committee on imports from non-CIS countries. Rates include for some products specific duties, which have been converted into ad valorem equivalents.

[2]Measured over the list of individual items (over 1,300) to which statutory rates apply.

Summary of Country Experiences and Conclusions on Phasing Exchange and Trade Liberalization

The review of countries' experiences suggests that while there is no universal approach to phasing external liberalization, exchange system liberalization has often been a critical early element of such liberalization.

Summary of Country Experiences

The study examined the experience of five countries—China, India, Korea, Mexico, and Russia—in phasing exchange and trade liberalization. For each country, the relative timing of exchange and trade liberalization can be summarized in a reform sequence matrix. The matrix focuses on certain benchmarks or milestones in the reform process. For exchange liberalization, these benchmarks include the unification of exchange rates, the elimination of foreign exchange budgets, the abolition of surrender requirements, and the acceptance of obligations of Article VIII, Sections 2, 3, and 4 of the IMF's Articles of Agreement. For trade liberalization, the focus is on the abolition of import quotas and licensing, the reduction of import tariffs to the 10 percent level of the average unweighted import tariff rate, and the joining of the WTO. Each element of the matrix represents the number of years by which the exchange liberalization benchmark in the respective row preceded the trade liberalization benchmark in the respective column. A positive number in the matrix means that the exchange liberalization measure was completed earlier than the respective trade liberalization measure. A negative number means that the exchange liberalization measure occurred after the trade liberalization measure. Zero in-

dicates that the respective exchange and trade measures were implemented in the same year. The entry in the matrix is indeterminate if neither the exchange measure nor the respective trade measure have been liberalized yet. For instance, in China, abolishing import quotas and licensing was still ongoing, as of 1997, although it started in 1993. The earliest, in principle, when import quotas and licensing could be abolished was 1998. Hence, the unification of exchange rates, which occurred in 1994, would precede the abolition of import quotas and licensing by at least four years.

In *China,* exchange reform tended to lead and was completed earlier than trade liberalization (see Table 25). The transition to a market-based exchange system began with the introduction of exchange retention quotas and arrangements for their trading, which eventually developed into a nascent foreign exchange market. By the mid-1990s, exchange rates had been unified and the remaining restrictions on payments and transfers for current international transactions had been eliminated. Although trade reform accelerated in the late 1990s, many tasks remain: inter alia, lowering import tariffs and nontariff barriers, and expanding the rights to trade. Trade reform is proceeding gradually, instigated partly in the process of China's accession to the WTO.

India implemented exchange and trade reforms as part of broader efforts aimed at liberalizing the restrictive economic regime. During 1991–94, substantial trade reforms took place (especially when evaluated from the starting point of the regime). After 1994, trade reforms continued, albeit at a slower pace. Exchange liberalization proceeded concurrently, starting in 1991 with the devaluation of the exchange rate and a subsequent introduction of a free market exchange

Table 25. Reform Sequence Matrix for China

Phases of Liberalization	Abolition of Import Quotas and Licensing (since 1993)	Reduction of Import Tariffs (since 1992)	Joining the World Trade Organization (no)
Unification of exchange rates (1994)	At least +4	At least +4	At least +4
Elimination of foreign exchange budgets (1994)	At least +4	At least +4	At least +4
Abolition of surrender requirements (no, as of 1997)	—	—	—
Acceptance of Article VIII (1996)	At least +2	At least +2	At least +2

Sources: Chinese authorities; and IMF, *Annual Report on Exchange Arrangements and Exchange Restrictions* (various years).

rate for many permitted transactions (see Table 26). Exchange rates were unified in 1993, and the obligations of Articles VIII, Sections 2, 3, and 4 of the IMF's Articles of Agreement were accepted in 1994. Notwithstanding notable achievements, trade liberalization remained only partial.

In *Korea,* exchange liberalization was a pivotal factor in the transition from import substitution to an export-oriented industrialization policy and in stimulating export growth. Exchange reform started in the early 1960s with the abolition of foreign exchange taxes and the unification of the exchange rates. Though some nontariff barriers were lowered during the 1960–70s, concerted trade reforms began only in 1984. Controls on current payments and transfers, including prescription of currencies, import and export payments, and payments for and proceeds from invisible trade, were liberalized gradually and tended to lead the liberalization of the trade system (Table 27).

Since the end of World War II, *Mexico* had a relatively liberal exchange regime (Table 28). Trade liberalization began in the early 1980s within a broader context of macroeconomic stabilization. In concert with comprehensive trade reforms, Mexico unified exchange rates by eliminating the controlled foreign

exchange market. Surrender requirements were gradually eased and eventually abolished. As a result of reforms, Mexico's exchange and trade regimes became virtually free of restrictions.

Russia, in contrast to the other countries surveyed, implemented a "big bang" rather than a gradualist approach to external liberalization. Exchange liberalization followed the abolition of the state monopoly on foreign trade and proceeded in tandem with trade reform (Table 29). After the interbank foreign exchange market was established, most restrictions on payments and transfers related to current account transactions were removed. Transition from an administrative exchange system to current account convertibility was largely completed during 1992–96. Likewise, Russia has made considerable progress in trade liberalization: tariff rates remained relatively low and uniform, most quantitative and licensing restrictions were eliminated, and export taxes were lowered. A number of trade-related barriers, however, remained in place, and discussions on Russia's accession to the World Trade Organization currently focus on market access issues, protection of intellectual property rights, government procurement, preferential trade, and investment measures.

Table 26. Reform Sequence Matrix for India

Phases of Liberalization	Abolition of Import Quotas and Licensing (since 1991)	Reduction of Import Tariffs (since 1980s)	Joining the World Trade Organization (1994)
Unification of exchange rates (1993)	At least +5	At least +5	+1
Elimination of foreign exchange budgets (did not exist in 1990)	Not applicable	Not applicable	Not applicable
Abolition of surrender requirements (no, as of 1997)	—	—	At least –4
Acceptance of Article VIII (1994)	At least +4	At least +4	0

Sources: Indian authorities; and IMF, *Annual Report on Exchange Arrangements and Exchange Restrictions* (various years).

Table 27. Reform Sequence Matrix for Korea

Phases of Liberalization	Abolition of Import Quotas and Licensing (since 1964)	Reduction of Import Tariffs (1973–92)	Joining the World Trade Organization (1994)
Unification of exchange rates (1964)	At least +34	+28	+30
Elimination of foreign exchange budgets (1988)	At least +10	+4	+6
Abolition of surrender requirements (1995)	At least +3	−3	−1
Acceptance of Article VIII (1988)	At least +10	+4	+6

Sources: Korean authorities; and IMF, *Annual Report on Exchange Arrangements and Exchange Restrictions* (various years).

Conclusions on the Phasing of Exchange and Trade Liberalization

There is no universal approach to the phasing of exchange and trade reforms, and the evolution of the national regulatory regime largely depends on country-specific macroeconomic and institutional conditions. Nonetheless, the analysis of experience in the five countries suggests some general principles concerning initial conditions, phasing, speed, and outcome of exchange and trade liberalization.

Exchange liberalization generally started prior to or concurrently with trade reform and proceeded in tandem with it with the objective of fostering trade and economic growth by eliminating restrictive trade barriers, and controls on current payments and transfers. Most binding exchange controls tended to be abolished early in the reform process, while trade liberalization and institution-building measures were often implemented more gradually. Surrender and repatriation requirements were abolished at the later stages of reforms as part of a more gradual liberalization of the capital account. (See Section VI for a discussion of the sequencing of capital account liberalization.)

In Korea, the multiple currency practice and foreign exchange taxes were eliminated at the beginning of

the reforms, and other controls on current payments and transfers were liberalized later. Gradual trade liberalization began after the first major exchange reform and continued after the introduction of current account convertibility. In India, the exchange rate devaluation and the dual exchange rate system were used as transitional steps in a successful movement to a unified exchange rate system and current account convertibility. In parallel, trade regime was liberalized step-by-step, with major trade reforms implemented at the outset. In Mexico, the main distortion in the exchange system was eliminated with the unification of exchange rates at the beginning of exchange and trade reforms. Current account convertibility was achieved prior to the successful completion of trade reform.

The phasing of exchange liberalization depended on the extent of initial government intervention. Transition economies faced a daunting challenge of transforming a command economic system into a market-based one, and therefore, their exchange liberalization was coordinated with the decentralization of trade and the creation of basic market institutions. In Russia, exchange reform followed the elimination of the state monopoly on foreign trade. The first step in exchange liberalization was the establishment of the interbank foreign exchange market, followed by the removal of

Table 28. Reform Sequence Matrix for Mexico

Phases of Liberalization	Abolition of Import Quotas and Licensing (since 1985)	Reduction of Import Tariffs (1985–91)	Joining the World Trade Organization (1994)
Unification of the exchange rate (1991)	At least +7	−1	+3
Elimination of foreign exchange budgets (did not exist in 1946)	Not applicable	Not applicable	Not applicable
Abolition of surrender requirements (1991)	At least +7	−1	+3
Acceptance of Article VIII (1946)	At least +52	+44	+48

Sources: Mexican authorities; and IMF, *Annual Report on Exchange Arrangements and Exchange Restrictions* (various years).

Table 29. Reform Sequence Matrix for Russia

Phases of Liberalization	Abolition of Import Quotas and Licensing (1992)	Reduction of Import Tariffs (1992)	Joining the World Trade Organization (no, as of 1997)
Unification of exchange rates (1992)	0	0	At least +6
Elimination of foreign exchange budgets (1992)	0	0	At least +6
Abolition of surrender requirements (no, as of 1997)[1]	At least −6	At least −6	—
Acceptance of Article VIII (1996)	−4	−4	At least +2

Sources: Russian authorities; and IMF, *Annual Report on Exchange Arrangements and Exchange Restrictions* (various years).

[1]The surrender requirement is to the Interbank Foreign Exchange Market and not the Central Bank of Russia.

the remaining restrictions on current payments and transfers for residents and then nonresidents. In parallel, quantitative and licensing restrictions on imports were converted into a relatively uniform tariff structure, quantitative and licensing restrictions on exports were abolished, and export taxes were reduced. In China, early establishment of the exchange retention quota system paved a way for the development of a rudimentary foreign exchange market and was followed by the unification of exchange rates, integration of foreign exchange markets, and elimination of the remaining restrictions on current payments and transfers. In parallel, the decentralization of trade and scaling back of mandatory planning proceeded gradually. Notwithstanding the significant progress in trade liberalization, the lowering of import tariffs and nontariff barriers and the expansion of trading rights remain on the reform agenda.

Exchange liberalization tended to proceed at a faster speed and to be completed earlier than trade reform. Trade liberalization often took longer to implement because it had to be closely coordinated with industrial and fiscal policies. In particular, the speed of tariff reductions sometimes reflected the availability of alternative sources of tax revenues for achieving fiscal objectives. Furthermore, most trade measures were specific to individual industries and even firms, and, as a result, political economy factors influenced the speed and extent of trade reform. Trade reform was often implemented gradually to give domestic industries time to adjust to more competitive economic conditions.

The duration of reforms varied across countries, reflecting, inter alia, the overall strategy of economic reform. China, for example, pursued a gradual approach to economic liberalization, including external sector reform. Current account convertibility was achieved after about 17 years of continual institutional transformation. In contrast, exchange and trade reforms in Russia proceeded at a much faster pace, partially be-

cause Russia followed the "big bang" approach to liberalization. The main steps of exchange liberalization were largely completed within two years.

The outcome of exchange liberalization was more similar across the countries than that of trade liberalization. As a result of exchange liberalization, all countries have achieved a high degree of current account convertibility and adopted the obligations of Article VIII, Sections 2, 3, and 4 of the IMF's Articles of Agreement. India continued to maintain some exchange restrictions after adopting the obligations of Article VIII, Sections 2, 3, and 4. In contrast to exchange liberalization, outcomes of trade reform varied dramatically across countries. As of 1997, trade liberalization remained incomplete in China and India, which maintained relatively high and dispersed import tariffs and numerous nontariff barriers. Korea, Mexico, and Russia had largely completed major tasks in trade reforms and established relatively liberal trade regimes.

The foregoing analysis suggests that exchange liberalization can be an important catalyst and complement to trade liberalization. Exchange liberalization preceding or accompanying trade liberalization can contribute to the success of trade liberalization. The elimination of binding exchange controls and the development of a market-based exchange system tends to reinforce efficiency gains from, and the sustainability of, trade reform. Thus, exchange and trade reforms need to be coordinated to create a policy framework for an orderly development of an open, neutral, and transparent external sector regime.

As a final point, the empirical analysis discussed in the appendix to this section finds that in view of the extent to which exchange systems have been liberalized for payments and transfers for current international transactions, controls on capital movements are now the more significant nontariff barrier to trade, and that capital account liberalization could support trade liberalization. As discussed elsewhere in the volume, capital account liberalization should also be coordinated with financial sector reforms in view of the critical importance of using and allocating efficiently international financial resources.

Appendix. Exchange and Capital Controls as a Trade Barrier

This appendix briefly describes the methodology, data, and results of an empirical study that examined how important exchange and capital controls are as a barrier to international trade.[47] The analysis is based on the gravity-equation framework, in which bilateral exports depend on the distance between countries, the countries' size and wealth, tariff barriers, and exchange and capital controls. The extent of exchange and capital controls is measured by unique indices.[48] Overall, exchange and capital controls are found to represent a noticeable barrier to trade. The specific impact of exchange and capital controls on trade, however, varies depending on the level of development of a country and the type of control. In view of the degree to which countries have liberalized their exchange systems, controls on current payments and transfers are found to be a minor impediment to trade. Capital controls are also found to be a minor impediment to trade for the industrial countries, while they significantly reduce exports into developing and transition economies. An implication of this study is that further liberalization of exchange and capital controls could discernibly foster trade for the developing and transition economies.

An Empirical Model of Trade with Exchange and Capital Controls

According to the gravity model, bilateral trade is determined by the wealth and size of countries, the distance between them, and other factors distorting trade. This parsimonious and flexible general equilibrium framework has been successfully and extensively used in empirical studies of international economics since the 1960s. Recently, the theoretical foundations of the model have been based on the theory of trade under imperfect competition and have been integrated recently with the factor-proportions and demand-based theories of international trade.[49] The basic gravity equation is given by

$$X_{ij} = \alpha_0 (Q_i/N_i)^{\alpha_1} (N_i)^{\alpha_2} (Q_j/N_j)^{\alpha_3}$$
$$(N_j)^{\alpha_4} (D_{ij})^{\alpha_5} (A_{ij})^{\alpha_6} e_{ij}, \qquad (1)$$

where X_{ij} are exports from country i to country j; (Q_i/N_i) and (Q_j/N_j) are per capita incomes of countries i and j; N_i and N_j are populations of countries i and j; D_{ij} is the geographical distance between countries i and j, which represents a proxy for transportation and other transaction costs; A_{ij} denotes factors distorting/augmenting trade, and e_{ij} is a log normally distributed error term.

For the empirical analysis, the above equation is modified by taking natural logs and defining tariffs, and exchange and capital controls as trade distortions, that is,

$$\ln X_{ij} = \alpha_0 + \alpha_1 \ln(Q_i/N_i) + \alpha_2 \ln N_i +$$
$$\alpha_3 \ln(Q_j/N_j) + \alpha_4 \ln N_j + \alpha_5 \ln D_{ij} +$$
$$\alpha_6 \ln(1+T_{ji}) + \alpha_7 E_j + \varepsilon_{ij}, \qquad (2)$$

where T_{ji} is the import duty imposed by country j on imports from country i, and E_j denotes an aggregate measure of exchange and capital controls in country j. Given the computational difficulty of obtaining the data on bilateral import duties, an average measure of import duties in country j, T_j, is typically used as an approximation of T_{ji}; thus, for estimation purposes, $T_{ji} = T_j$. The intercept accounts for the effect of unmeasured trade distortions on bilateral exports.

Data

The model is estimated using the ordinary-least-squares method for a sample of 40 industrial, developing, and transition economies for 1996. The sample includes 15 industrial countries (Australia, Canada, Denmark, France, Germany, Greece, Israel, Italy, Japan, the Netherlands, New Zealand, Norway, Spain, United Kingdom, and the United States), 19 developing countries (Argentina, Brazil, Chile, China, Egypt, India, Indonesia, Kenya, Republic of Korea, Mexico, Morocco, Pakistan, the Philippines, Saudi Arabia, South Africa, Thailand, Tunisia, Turkey, and Uruguay), and 6 transition economies (Czech Republic, Hungary, Kazakhstan, Latvia, Poland, and Russia). Thirty-eight of the 40 countries in the sample have accepted the obligations of Article VIII, Sections 2, 3, and 4 of the IMF's Articles of Agreement. Brazil and Egypt maintained exchange restrictions under Article XIV. For comparison, as of the end of 1996, 138 out of 181 members have accepted obligations of Article VIII, Sections 2, 3, and 4 of the IMF's Articles of Agreement. Summary statistics and correlations are presented in Tables 30 and 31, respectively. The extent of national exchange and capital controls is captured in three aggregate measures: the indices of controls on current payments and transfers (denoted by CCI), capital controls (KCI), and exchange and capital controls

---

[47]For a more detailed discussion of the empirical model, data, and estimation results, see Tamirisa (1998).

[48]See Section VI for more details on the indices of exchange and capital controls.

[49]For more details on the gravity model, see Anderson (1979); Bergstrand, (1985), (1989), and (1990); and Helpman and Krugman (1985).

Table 30. Summary Statistics

	EX	DIST	POPEX	POPIM	GDPEX	GDPIM	1+TAR	CCI	KCI	ECI
All countries										
Mean	1,897.73	4,880	107	107	10,674	10,730	1,14.0	0.13	0.38	0.25
Standard deviation	8,268.54	3,873	235	235	7,485	7,491	13.5	0.10	0.30	0.19
Minimum	0.01	137	2	2	1,380	1,380	100.0	0.01	0.01	0.03
Maximum	16,4761.40	79,635	1,222	1,222	26,980	26,980	156.3	0.33	0.95	0.62
Count	1519	1519	1,519	1,519	1,519	1,519	1,519	1,519	1,519	1,519
Industrial countries										
Mean	3,806.80	4,795.85	107	53	10,416	19,467	105.3	0.05	0.12	0.09
Standard deviation	12,689.60	4,478.18	236	67	7,414	3491	3.5	0.04	0.12	0.07
Minimum	0.01	187	2	4	1,380	11,710	100	0.01	0.01	0.03
Maximum	16,4761.40	79,635	1,222	267	26,980	26,980	110.5	0.16	0.54	0.35
Count	580	580	580	580	580	580	580	580	580	580
Developing and transition countries										
Mean	718.54	4,931.58	107	141	10,834	5,334	119.3	0.17	0.54	0.35
Standard deviation	2,757.08	3,448.21	235	290	7,528	2,635	14.6	0.10	0.26	0.17
Minimum	0.01	137	2	2	1380	1,380	100.0	0.03	0.10	0.10
Maximum	56,760.80	62,333	1,222	1,222	26,980	18,940	156.3	0.33	0.95	0.62
Count	939	939	939	939	939	939	939	939	939	939

in their entirety (ECI). The indices summarize information on 142 individual types of national exchange and capital control from the IMF's *Annual Report on Exchange Arrangements and Exchange Restrictions* (*AREAER*) and primarily reflect the de jure incidence of controls (see Section III).

Data on exports of goods and services (denoted by "EX") are from the IMF's *Direction of Trade Statistics Yearbook*. GDP per capita ("GDPIM" and "GDPEX" for importing and exporting countries, respectively) are adjusted according to the purchasing power parity and come from the World Bank's *World Debt Tables*. Population data ("POPIM" and "POPEX" for importing and exporting countries, respectively) are for 1996 or the latest available year, as published in the IMF's *International Financial Statistics*. The geographic distance ("DIST") is measured as the direct-line distance between the capital cities of countries.[50] Trade restrictions are repre-

sented by mean tariff rates ("TAR") by country. The tariff data for 1995 or the latest available year come from the World Bank's *World Development Indicators Database* and are adjusted to take into account free trade agreements, as reported in the *Annual Report* of the World Trade Organization.

Estimation Results

Equation (2) is estimated with three alternative measures of exchange and capital controls, CCI, KCI, and ECI, and the respective equations are denoted as 2a, 2b, and 2c in Table 32.[51] Estimation results are summarized in the table. The estimated intercept is negative, implying that unmeasured trade distortions tend

---

[50]See Fitzpatrick and Modlin (1986).

[51]The adjusted R-squares are above 0.70, and F-statistics are significant at the 99 percent level. Since heteroskedasticity may be a problem owing to differences in country size, standard errors and covariances are calculated on the basis of the White heteroskedasticity-consistent matrix.

Table 31. Correlations

	EX	DIST	POPEX	POPIM	GDPEX	GDPIM	1+TAR	CCI	KCI	ECI
EX	1.000									
DIST	−0.113	1.000								
POPEX	0.036	0.009	1.000							
POPIM	0.037	0.014	−0.028	1.000						
GDPEX	0.231	−0.002	−0.238	0.001	1.000					
GDPIM	0.230	0.009	0.001	−0.239	−0.032	1.000				
1+TAR	−0.136	0.097	0.028	0.554	−0.057	−0.608	1.000			
CCI	−0.103	−0.009	−0.006	0.428	0.021	−0.631	0.615	1.000		
KCI	−0.125	−0.006	−0.005	0.340	0.022	−0.661	0.583	0.829	1.000	
ECI	−0.124	−0.007	−0.005	0.374	0.023	−0.675	0.611	0.901	0.990	1.000

Table 32. Estimation Results

	All Countries			Industrial Countries			Developing and Transition Countries		
	Eq. (2a)	Eq. (2b)	Eq. (2c)	Eq. (2a)	Eq. (2b)	Eq. (2c)	Eq. (2a)	Eq. (2b)	Eq. (2c)
C	−37.13*	−37.34*	−37.11*	−33.56*	−33.27*	−33.73*	−38.69*	−38.03*	−38.91*
ln DIST	−0.91*	−0.91*	−0.91*	−0.59*	−0.60*	−0.58*	−1.06*	−1.04*	−1.07*
ln POPIM	0.94*	0.94*	0.94*	0.94*	0.95*	0.93*	0.96*	0.95*	0.96*
ln POPEX	1.03*	1.03*	1.03*	0.99*	0.99*	0.99*	1.06*	1.06*	1.06*
ln GDPIM	1.37*	1.39*	1.37*	0.97*	0.93*	0.99*	1.48*	1.40*	1.51*
ln GDPEX	1.90*	1.90*	1.90*	1.77*	1.77*	1.77*	1.99*	1.98*	1.99*
ln (1+*TAR*)	−0.73	−0.83	−0.73	−7.14	−6.69	−7.30	−0.21	−0.64	−0.10
ECI	−0.66**			−1.20			−0.75**		
CCI		−0.89			−2.21			−0.65	
KCI			−0.42**			−0.71			−0.53**
Number of observations	1519	1519	1519	580	580	580	939	939	939
R-squared	0.76	0.76	0.76	0.80	0.80	0.80	0.72	0.72	0.72
F-statistic	697.05*	694.76*	697.26*	318.81*	318.52*	318.59*	334.31*	332.47*	334.82*

Notes:
* Denotes coefficient that is significant at the 99 percent level.
** Denotes coefficient that is significant at the 95 percent level.

to reduce bilateral exports. Distance has a significant negative effect on bilateral exports, in part because trade costs (e.g., transportation and communication) tend to increase with distance. Tariff barriers in the importing countries have a negative, albeit insignificant, effect on exports into these countries. GDP per capita and population, on the other hand, have significant positive effects on bilateral exports. The insignificance of the coefficient on tariff barriers, although not uncommon in studies based on an aggregate gravity model, could be explained as follows. First, the measure of tariff barriers—the mean tariff rate adjusted for the free trade agreements—does not capture the full variation in tariff barriers across trading partners. Second, in developing countries, nontariff barriers are often more important than tariff barriers. The effect of

nontariff barriers (other than exchange and capital controls) is reflected in the intercept, which is significant.

Exchange and capital controls are a barrier to exports to developing and transition economies but not to industrial countries. This finding can be attributed to capital controls, which noticeably reduce bilateral exports to developing and transition economies and have only a minor negative impact on bilateral exports to industrial countries. The reason is that industrial economies have relatively liberal regimes for international capital movements, while many developing and transition economies continue to maintain various capital controls. Controls on current payments and transfers represent only a minor barrier to bilateral exports to all countries, since these controls have been substantially liberalized worldwide.

VI

Capital Account Liberalization in Selected Asian Crisis Countries

Capital account liberalization is generally seen as a beneficial move for an economy. In opening the capital account it is also necessary, however, to anticipate and minimize the risks that such liberalization may pose. For example, both the 1994 Mexico crisis and the recent crises in Asian countries were preceded by a sizable buildup of short-term foreign liabilities. A substantial amount of work, inside and outside the IMF, has been undertaken already, or is under way, on the Asian crisis. This section investigates one aspect of the events leading up to the Asian crisis—namely, whether the nature of regulation of capital movements and, in particular, the sequencing of the liberalization of the capital account, contributed to the buildup of short-term debt in the three main Asian crisis countries, Indonesia, Korea, and Thailand. It discusses implications for the management of capital inflows, and notes in particular that capital account liberalization must be seen as part of a broader strategy of economic liberalization, achieved in conjunction with the strengthening of key institutions and appropriate macroeconomic and exchange rate policies. An appendix provides a chronology of developments in the exchange systems of five Asian economies—the three main Asian crisis economies plus Malaysia and the Philippines—from June 1997 to March 1998.

Overview of Liberalization in Indonesia, Korea, and Thailand

Boxes 4–6 depict the sequencing of the liberalization of capital inflows since 1985 and the regulatory framework for such flows as at mid-1997, in Indonesia, Korea, and Thailand.[52] An important general point to note first is that, contrary to some perceptions, Indonesia, Korea, and Thailand adopted markedly different approaches to the liberalization of their capital account regimes in the years leading up to the crisis.

Indonesia liberalized outflows relatively early, and liberalized inflows relatively gradually. After 1985, liberalization of capital account movements pro-

ceeded steadily: successive measures progressively liberalized foreign investments in Indonesian companies (both listed and unlisted in the Stock Exchange), and widened the range of opportunities available to foreign direct investments. Regulation of commercial credit was progressively eased, while financial borrowing remained broadly restricted for both banks and corporations. Bank borrowing was liberalized in 1989, but tightened again in 1991 after concerns emerged about the excessive buildup of foreign liabilities. However, there is no strong indication that regulations favored any particular maturity, especially shorter over longer maturities. In some instances (e.g., Presidential Decree No. 39 in 1991), ceilings were imposed on foreign commercial borrowing, except for financing of long-term projects.

Korea followed a very gradual approach to liberalizing the capital account regime beginning with capital outflows, and only in the mid-1990s began the cautious liberalization of capital inflows into its security markets.[53] Restrictions were progressively removed on a range of transactions and operations, including forwards and futures, currency options, and various forms of bonds and loans. Most transactions, however, remained subject to the approval of the Ministry of Finance and Economy or the Bank of Korea. In 1992, nonresidents were permitted limited access to the stock market, and the types of securities that residents could issue abroad were expanded. Foreign exchange banks were authorized to borrow abroad, but direct foreign borrowing by corporations was controlled. While some forms of trade credit were deregulated (and trade credits grew rapidly), beginning in 1994, the ceiling on banks' foreign currency loans was lifted, but the Bank of Korea applied window guidance in the form of ceilings on banks' medium- and long-term borrowings from international financial markets. One explanation that has been offered for the maintenance of controls on longer-term external borrowing by banks is that the Ministry was seeking to prevent a loss of control over financial institutions through possible debt-equity swaps. The letter of the law, however, did not entail preferential treatment for short-term inflows, per se. Frequently the law estab-

---

[52]For a more detailed discussion of the sequencing experience in these three countries, along with Chile, see Johnston and others (1997).

[53]For some further detail, see Park (1998).

Box 4. Indonesia: Capital Account Liberalization, 1985–96, and Capital Controls, 1997

Sequence of Capital Inflow Liberalization, 1985–96

1985 *FDI:* Procedures and requirements for foreign direct investments (FDI) projects are somewhat eased.

1986 *FDI/PI:* Rules on foreign ownership of firms are relaxed in a number of sectors and some foreign companies become eligible for treatment equivalent to the domestic investment scheme.

1987 *FDI:* Rules on foreign ownership are further eased and more sectors are open to FDI.

1988 *FDI/PI:* Foreign investors are allowed to establish joint ventures in financial companies, banks, and insurance companies where they have the majority of the capital.

1989 *FDI:* More sectors are opened to FDI and rules are again eased.
PI: Foreign investors are allowed to purchase up to 49 percent of listed companies.
OIF: Direct ceilings on offshore borrowing by foreign exchange banks are replaced with a limit on open foreign exchange net position of 25 percent of capital.

1991 *OIF:* Limits on banks' foreign currency swaps are increased from 20 percent to 25 percent of capital. Ceilings on foreign commercial borrowing by major banks and companies are established. Trade-related credit, private project financing, and transactions below $20 million are exempted. Banks' foreign exchange short-term liabilities (less than two years) are limited to 30 percent of capital. The limit on banks' foreign currency net open positions (including off-balance sheet items) is lowered to 20 percent of capital. At least 80 percent of the total foreign loans is to be allocated to business earning foreign exchange.
FDI: More sectors are opened to FDI while regulations on FDI are loosened.

1992 *OIF:* Foreign participation in the capital of banks' is raised to 49 percent and in the capital of nonbanks financial companies to 85 percent.
FDI: Rules are once again slackened and more sectors are opened.

1993 *FDI/PI:* Licensing and procedures for FDI are simplified while rules on foreign ownership are eased.

1994 *OIF:* The limit on banks' foreign currency net open positions (including off-balance sheet items) is increased to 25 percent of capital and the limits on individual foreign currencies are eliminated.
FDI/PI: Further liberalization of FDI and foreign ownership is enacted.

1995 *OIF:* Dealing by banks in foreign exchange derivatives is allowed.
1996 *PI:6* Foreign ownership of corporations is raised to 85 percent of capital. Mutual funds can be totally foreign owned.

A Synopsis of Capital Inflows Regulation in Mid-1997
The system of controls on capital inflows is pervasive. The inflows are de jure strictly controlled by the Bank of Indonesia and specifically by the Commercial Offshore Loan Team (COLT).

Capital markets: No restrictions on issues abroad; if securities are listed on the Indonesia stock exchange, they should comply with the Capital Market Act. Purchase of shares by nonresidents is limited to 49 percent of the capital.

Money market instruments: Approval by COLT is required for offshore issues with maturities over two years or for amounts exceeding $20 million a year, and in any case total issuance cannot exceed 30 percent of the bank's capital.

Derivatives: Derivatives transactions other than those associated with foreign exchange and interest rates are forbidden unless permission from Bank Indonesia is granted.

Commercial credits from nonresidents are supervised by COLT and must be reported periodically. Prior approval is necessary for foreign loans taken by any public enterprise, commercial bank, or public sector bodies. Authorization is required for (1) certain borrowing related to development projects; (2) borrowing related to development projects with financing based on build-operate-transfer, build-and-transfer, and similar schemes; (3) borrowing related to government or state-owned companies.

Financial credits from nonresidents to residents are restricted.

Foreign exchange operations by banks have limits: (1) the weekly average total net open position (including off-balance sheet items) cannot exceed 25 percent of the bank's capital; (2) the average weekly off-balance sheet net open position cannot exceed 25 percent of the bank's capital.

Foreign direct investments are subject to a host of requirements and ownership regulations and investments in several key sectors are restricted.

Note: FDI = foreign direct investments; OIF = other capital inflows; PI = portfolio investments.
Sources: Johnston and others (1997); IMF, *Annual Report on Exchange Arrangements and Exchange Restrictions.*

lished detailed quantitative limits on the amount of the transaction or on the size of the firms that were allowed to trade on international markets. Indeed, on joining the OECD in 1996, the authorities expressed their reluctance to ease capital controls further and ex-

plicitly stressed that they wished to maintain controls over short-term capital inflows that may "hamper macroeconomic and financial market stability." For this reason the authorities resisted the liberalization of access by nonresidents to domestic money market in-

Box 5. Korea: Capital Account Liberalization, 1985–96, and Capital Controls, 1997

Sequence of Capital Inflow Liberalization, 1985–96

1985 *OIF/PI:* Currency swap operations between domestic and foreign entities are permitted. Regulations on foreign loans taken by shipping companies are eased.

OIF/PI: Korean companies are allowed to issue warrants and depository notes up to 15 percent of their outstanding share volume provided that no single foreign entity can acquire more than 3 percent of the capital by exercising conversion rights.

FDI: The number of sectors where foreign direct investments are admissible is substantially raised.

1986 *OIF:* More liberal regime for swaps is enacted. Regulations on foreign currency loans are tightened.

1987 *OIF:* Futures and option contracts on foreign exchange are allowed. The limit on the forward contract period is eliminated. The ceiling on foreign banks' swap operations is lowered by 10 percent. The government directs financial institutions to repay foreign short-term borrowing and bank loans that bear "unfavorable conditions." Special deposits by the central bank are made at Korean foreign exchange banks for this purpose.

PI: Inward remittances greater than $20,000 are monitored to discourage investments in the stock exchange. Nine additional foreign banks are allowed to enter the trust investment business.

FDI: 26 manufacturing sectors are opened to FDI; tax breaks on FDI are reduced.

1988 *OIF/PI:* Limits on banks' foreign exchange loans to small and medium-sized enterprises and export firms are strictly enforced. Nonresidents are prohibited from converting in won amounts withdrawn from their accounts. The limit on swaps by foreign banks is lowered again by 10 percent. Sales by nonresidents of foreign currency to domestic banks is limited to $10,000.

FDI: Advertising and motion pictures sectors and, to some extent, the insurance industry are opened to FDI.

1989 *OIF:* A limit of $200 million is set on special foreign currency loans granted to a firm during a year. The ceilings on swap operations by foreign banks are lowered by another 10 percent. The amount of foreign currency allowed in the country without notification to the tax authorities is raised in two steps to $10,000. A U.S. dollar call market is opened. Currency loans are now admissible for investment operations abroad, subject to a ten year maturity limit and ceilings of 60 percent and 80 percent of the investment for large and small firms respectively. Foreign exchange banks are allowed to issue foreign currency bonds offshore and to underwrite and trade foreign currency bonds issued by nonresidents. The limit on investments by foreign security firms was raised to 40 percent.

PI: Foreigners are allowed to trade among themselves. Korean shares acquired through the exercise of bond conversion rights.

FDI: Other six manufacturing sectors are opened to FDI and the limit on automatic approval is raised to $5 million from $3 million.

1990 *OIF/PI:* Central bank loans for the redemption of the foreign currency loans by banks and firms are abolished. The government allows each of the three domestic investment trusts to set a $100 million fund (of which $60 million to be raised abroad) to invest in Korean companies (70 percent of the capital) and foreign securities.

FDI: The limit on automatic approval is raised to $100 million from $3 million. Two other sectors are opened to FDI.

1991 *OIF:* Limits on foreign currency loans for investments abroad are reduced to 40 percent and 60 percent of the total for large and small enterprises respectively.

PI: Nonresidents are allowed to convert in won up to $100,000 to invest in development trusts with a maturity of more than 2 years. Securities in foreign currencies can be issued by residents to finance import of inputs and machinery for which no domestic substitute is available. Nonresidents who had acquired Korean shares through convertible bonds are allowed to trade them in the stock exchange.

FDI: Only a notification is required for projects with foreign participation of less than 50 percent. Exemptions are granted to foreign firms on corporate profit taxes and to their foreign employees on income taxes for three years, while a 50 percent exemption is established for the two successive years. Restrictions on foreign ownership of retail businesses are relaxed.

1992 *OIF/PI:* The range of forward exchange contracts admissible is extended. The maximum amount of loans for overseas investments is increased to 60 percent and 70 percent for large and small enterprises, respectively. Residents can issue abroad negotiable certificates of deposits and commercial papers. The authorization for the issuance of these securities, as well as bonds, callable bonds, warrants, and stock depository receipts, is simplified and funds can be maintained in accounts abroad.

PI: Investments in stocks by resident foreign financial institutions are subjected to the same limits as those of institutions owned by nationals. The stock exchange is opened to nonresidents subject to quantitative limitations.

FDI: The general approval requirement is replaced by a notification system for investments in most business sectors.

1993 *OIF:* Nonresidents are allowed to hold won accounts. The central bank raises the amount of foreign exchange reserves earmarked for supporting foreign currency loans by domestic banks from $1 billion to $4 billion. Regulations on forward foreign exchange transactions are relaxed; ceilings held on foreign exchange deposits payable in domestic currency are abrogated. Overseas branches of domestic banks are allowed to supply loans to residents who trade commodities futures and financial futures. Issues of securities denominated in foreign currency are not subject to permission but only to a reporting requirement; the class of eligible issuers is widened to include those with positive cumulative profits over the past three years. Manufacturing companies can obtain loans in foreign currencies for all imports of inputs and equipment; the Bank of Korea earmarks some foreign exchange reserves to support these loans.

1994 *PI:* Nonresidents can purchase up to 12 percent of Korean firms' capital, up from 10 percent. Ceilings held are abolished on borrowing by resident corporations and their foreign branches from nonresident financial institutions located abroad. Foreign-financed general manufacturing companies are eligible for short-term overseas borrowing, while the overseas borrowing by foreign-financed, hi-tech firms is raised to 100 percent of the foreign capital share.
FDI: The Foreign Capital Inducement Act is amended to streamline application procedures and facilitate stock acquisition and sales by foreigners. Rules on land ownership are relaxed.

1995 *OIF:* Issuance of exchangeable bonds overseas is permitted provided that they do not exceed 15 percent of the firm's capital. Eight leasing companies are allowed to undertake medium- and long-term borrowing offshore without intermediation from foreign exchange banks. Limits on offshore security issuance by small and medium-sized companies are lowered. Direct foreign borrowing by enterprises engaged in social projects and foreign-financed, hi-tech firms is allowed up to 100 percent of capital (90 percent for large corporations) for redemption of import-related debts. Ratio of foreign currency loans taken by large companies for import of inputs and machinery is lowered to 70 percent of total cost.
PI: Nonresidents can hold up to 15 percent of private Korean firms' capital and 10 percent (up from 8 percent) of public corporations. Brokers are allowed to engage in foreign exchange transactions related to nonresident investments in the stock market.
FDI: Investment in 101 sectors is permitted or greatly liberalized.

1996 *OIF/PI:* Documentation requirements for forward and futures transaction are eliminated, but transactions still need to be based on real demand. The ceiling on swaps facility provided to foreign banks is lowered by 10 percent. Swaps are allowed for portfolio investments abroad by financial and insurance companies. The yen-won spot

and forward market is established. For certain small and medium-sized firms restrictions on foreign borrowing are eliminated.
PI: Foreign currency derivative transactions are opened to nonresidents on the basis of real demand. Nonresidents are allowed to open won accounts in overseas branches of domestic banks. Limits on foreign ownership of listed Korean firms is raised to 20 percent and to 15 percent for public enterprises; individual ownership is increased to 5 percent. Investment in domestic bonds by foreigners is allowed through a country fund as the $100 million Korea Bond Fund is listed in London. Up to 50 percent of won-denominated securities issued by nonresidents can be sold abroad.

A Synopsis of Regulation on Capital Inflows in Mid-1997

The system of capital controls is pervasive. All settlements with other countries can be made in any convertible currency except the won. Foreign exchange banks can conduct all form of transactions in the foreign currency market, including swaps, options, forwards and futures but the terms of forward transaction between banks and nonbank customers must be based on bona fide transactions. Export earnings exceeding $50,000 must be repatriated within six months.

Capital market securities. (1) Foreign ownership of listed companies is limited to 20 percent of the capital, with individual stakes limited to 5 percent of a listed firm. Foreigners can collectively purchase only 30 percent of convertible bonds issued by small and medium-sized companies and only 5 percent individually. The purchase of other securities is subject to the approval by the Ministry of Finance and Economy (MOFE); (2) The issue abroad of won-denominated securities requires approval by the MOFE. The issue of foreign currency denominated securities must be reported to the MOFE.

Money market instruments. (1) Foreign investment funds approved by the MOFE can purchase domestic money market instruments. Other foreign institutions and individuals require the prior approval of the MOFE, (2) The issuance abroad of other securities like certificates of deposit in foreign currency denominations require the MOFE's approval.

Mutual funds and collective investment securities. Purchases in the domestic market by residents are subject to the same rules as capital market securities. All other transactions between residents and nonresidents and issuance domestically or abroad is subject to the MOFE's approval.

Derivatives. Foreign investment funds and foreign banks may purchase domestic instruments in Korea. Other transactions require MOFE's approval. Residents can purchase derivatives through a foreign exchange bank, but issuance abroad requires MOFE's approval.

Commercial credit. Certain forms of trade credits are allowed without prior approval; however, deferred pay-
(*continued on next page*)

Box 5 (*concluded*)

ments for the imports of goods and export advances (except those by small and medium-sized firms) are subject to binding value limits. Export down payments up to 80 percent of the value are allowed for ships and plant building during production.

Financial credit. Foreign exchange banks can borrow from abroad. Credits from nonresidents to nonbank residents require prior approval by the MOFE. Foreign-financed, hi-tech companies can borrow up to 100 percent of the foreign invested capital with maturity limited to three years. Foreign borrowing with a maturity less than three years is governed by the Foreign Exchange Act. Residents cannot lend abroad without the approval of the MOFE.

Foreign direct investments. The establishment of foreign companies and bank branches is subject to approvals by the Bank of Korea and the MOFE. Inward investments are allowed subject to a notification requirement in all industries except those specified in a

negative list accounting for 5 percent of all industrial sectors and 1 percent of the manufacturing sectors.

Provisions regarding commercial banks activities. Foreign exchange banks need to report foreign borrowing to the MOFE when the maturity exceeds one year and for amounts over $10 million. Open positions in foreign currencies are subject to the following limits: (1) the overall overbought position must be lower than 15 percent of the equity capital and the oversold position lower than 10 percent of the equity capital or $20 million, whichever is larger; (2) the spot oversold positions cannot exceed 3 percent of the equity capital or $5 million, whichever is larger.

Note: FDI = foreign direct investments; OIF = other capital inflows; PI = portfolio investments.

Sources: Johnston and others (1997); and IMF, *Annual Report on Exchange Arrangements and Exchange Restrictions.*

---

struments during the accession to the OECD. The Korean regulations did, however, favor foreign borrowing (and onlending) by banks, over direct access by corporations to international capital markets: credits from nonresidents to nonbank residents—with the exception of trade credits—were subject to prior approval, which apparently discouraged this kind of operation.

Thailand adopted a quite aggressive policy of attracting foreign inflows, including through the provision of tax incentives, but liberalized capital outflows more gradually. The Thai authorities liberalized capital movements and exchange restrictions in successive waves from 1989 to 1992, including promoting access to Thai security markets. In Thailand's case too, the general thrust of the regulatory framework did not differentiate between the maturity of the capital flows, per se, but did tend to favor inflows directly intermediated by the domestic banking system. With the establishment of the Bangkok International Banking Facility (BIBF) in 1992, the government tried to improve the access of domestic entities to international capital markets through the banking system, and this helped to channel short-term inflows through the banking system. The Bangkok International Banking Facility is a government-sponsored umbrella organization through which Thai banks can conduct their foreign borrowing and lending operations. While restrictions on foreign direct investment remained in place (as indeed they do for defined sectors in most OECD countries), significant liberalization, nevertheless, occurred in this area, especially for Indonesia and Thailand. In the latter case, tax incentives were available for majority foreign investments approved by the

Board of Investment. The authorities subsequently pursued a policy of promoting foreign investments into the country, and security markets were also liberalized. Nevertheless, the inflows of foreign capital through the capital and money markets, controlled by the Security and Exchange Commission (SEC), lagged behind those intermediated through the banking sector.

Growth of Short-Term Liabilities

The overall picture from the above discussion is that the capital account regulations in the three countries were not *directly* biased toward short-term external borrowing to any great extent, except in one respect in the case of Korea. With that exception, where credit from or securities sales to nonresidents were permitted, the capital account regulations did not directly favor shorter-term over longer-term fundings. Perhaps more important, however, is the fact that the commercial banking system played a key role in channeling foreign capital inflows, in Korea and Thailand in particular; and that in these two countries, the capital account regulations did bias flows toward the local banking system. As noted above, the restrictions on direct external borrowing by nonbank residents in Korea, and the preferential treatment of the BIBF in Thailand are major examples of these biases. This institutional bias seems to have *indirectly* favored short-term borrowing rather than longer-term flows, since banking institutions normally tend to rely on shorter-term finance. The heavy reliance on short-term flows also reflected inadequacies of risk assessment, management, and control.

The emphasis on bank-intermediated flows was, on the surface at least, consistent with the existing financial structure in these economies. Commercial banks dominated financial intermediation in all three countries, and the development of other financial markets was more gradual. For example, the bond markets in Indonesia and Thailand barely reach 10 percent of GDP, while in Korea it is currently equivalent to 50 percent of GDP, but with most corporate bonds guaranteed by financial institutions.[54] Moreover, foreign lenders may have generally preferred to channel their loans through the banking sector to the extent that they saw it as less risky, and in view of the difficulty in assessing individual corporations because of more limited information on their balance sheets and prospects. Perhaps even more important in this regard is the possibility that banks were seen to be not just supervised, but backed more directly by the authorities.

As a number of economists have stressed, there may well have been a strong element of implicit government guarantee associated with banks in these countries.[55] To the extent such a perception was indeed held, both by the banks themselves and lenders to banks, this may have been an important factor in the lack of adequate currency and liquidity risk management in the banking sector. It is likely that the institutional biases in the capital account regulations interacted with these factors to exacerbate the buildup of inadequately managed short-term liabilities. The nature of the Basle capital adequacy requirements for OECD creditor banks might also have played some role here. While lending to other OECD banks is given a risk weight of 20 percent for capital adequacy purposes, irrespective of the term of the loan, lending to non-OECD banks carries this weight only for loans of under one year, while longer-term loans carry the full 100 percent risk weight. Since all lending to corporations also carries the same 100 percent weight, there is also an incentive to favor (short-term) loans to banks, rather than nonbanks in non-OECD countries.

A second factor behind the buildup of short-term debt is that the underlying riskiness of the investments in these countries may have led to some preference by lenders for shorter maturities. Inter alia, the lack of well-developed bond markets probably made pricing of longer-term debt more difficult, while residual uncertainty about the legal and financial infrastructure and relatively costly monitoring of local developments are typical factors that would tend to encourage external creditors to favor shorter-term investments over longer-term ones. To some extent, this effect might have declined over time, as apparently robust

macroeconomic trends continued to obscure underlying weaknesses. Nevertheless, as the outlook for either the specific borrowing institution or the country more generally became more uncertain, the tendency to prefer shorter-term exposure would have reasserted itself. In such a situation, the interest rates charged by lenders typically increase to reflect the higher risk or uncertainty premium, but the premium itself typically tends to rise more than proportionally with the maturity of the loan. This is particularly so when hedging instruments for foreign exchange risks are limited to very short-term maturities.

In these circumstances, the borrower would be squeezed into progressively shorter-term contracts, and could face difficulties in rolling over its obligations should conditions continue to deteriorate. Such a buildup of short-term liabilities can occur regardless of the regulatory environment, in view of the scope to effectively redenominate longer-term contracts into shorter-term ones, through derivative and other transactions. Though it is clear that relatively new and innovative instruments such as credit derivatives and options can be used to achieve this effect, it can also be done in much more basic ways. For example, as the IMF's 1995 *International Capital Markets* report noted (p. 96), a "synthetic sale" of direct investments can be created relatively quickly and cheaply by obtaining a bank loan in domestic currency.

Developments in Indonesia seem to confirm a general market preference for shorter-term credit, except perhaps for the strongest and most sizable borrowers. Indonesia's capital account regulations contained neither an obvious direct bias toward shorter-term rather than longer-term flows nor a bias toward bank-intermediated inflows (bank borrowing was more restricted than private corporate borrowing, in fact). Nevertheless, to the extent that larger private Indonesian corporations had close links of various sorts with the authorities, moral hazard issues (a perception of official support) may well have played a role in the excessive and inadequately managed external borrowing, similar to that in the buildup of bank debt in Korea and Thailand.

Beyond the underlying reasons for market preferences for shorter-term or bank-intermediated external borrowing, or both, and beyond any additional biases that may have been created by capital account regulations, a third important factor in the buildup of shorter-term external debt in the Asian crisis countries has been the incentives created by the macroeconomic environment. The three countries considered here all quite actively pursued either nominal or real exchange rate targets (a de facto peg in Thailand's case), while orienting interest rates toward internal stability objectives (see Johnston, Darbar, and Echeverria, 1997). This resulted in significant periods of relatively high interest rate differentials, especially at the shorter end, which encouraged capital inflows that

---

[54]By comparison, the bond market accounts for 110 percent of GDP in the United States, 90 percent in Germany, and 75 percent in Japan.

[55]See, among others, Krugman (1998).

Box 6. Thailand: Capital Account Liberalization, 1985–96, and Capital Controls, 1997

Sequence of Capital Inflow Liberalization, 1985–96

1985 *OIF:* The Bank of Thailand requires every individual to declare within seven days every loan obtained from abroad.

1986 *OIF:* Tax on dividends and capital gains earned by nonresidents on mutual funds investments is lowered.

1989 *OIF:* The first round of foreign exchange liberalization is enacted. In addition to a more liberal regime on small foreign exchange transaction, the law allows commercial banks to sell foreign exchange and transfer bahts into transferable nonresidents' baht accounts. They can be held by foreign investors and foreign borrowers registered with the Bank of Thailand to deposit funds originated from sales of shares or dividend receipts.

1990 *OIF:* The second round of liberalization gives commercial banks the authority to approve the repatriation of interest payments, transfers for the repayment of foreign loans, and transfers into and from nonresidents' baht accounts. The limit on daily transfers to nonresidents' accounts is increased to B 5 million.
PI: Three new closed-end mutual funds are approved to attract foreign capital with a maturity of 25 years.

1991 *PI:* The repatriation of investment funds, loan repayments, and interest payments by foreign investors is admitted without restrictions. The tax on dividends remitted abroad is lowered from 20 percent to 15 percent.
FDI: The Investment Promotion Act is amended to stimulate foreign investments. One hundred percent foreign ownership of export firms is permitted. Joint ventures and foreign ownership in certain projects is limited to 49 percent.

1992 *OIF:* The government establishes the Bangkok International Banking Facility (BIBF); participating commercial banks are allowed to accept deposits or borrow in foreign currencies from abroad and lend in Thailand. Moreover the banks participating in the BIBF are allowed, among other things, to conduct cross-currency operations, guarantee debt or letters of credit in foreign currencies, and manage offshore loan procurement. BIBF commercial banks are granted a corporate tax reduction from 30 percent to 10 percent, as well as other breaks.
PI: To promote foreign investments in the stock market, several taxes on dividends, interests, and capital gains obtained by nonresidents are reduced.
FDI: Requests for foreign ownership are delegated to ministries that decide on a case-by-case basis. Tax incentives are granted to projects in special sectors.

1993 *OIF:* Rules governing the issuance of debentures in foreign countries are set with the intent of attracting funds.

1994 *OIF/PI:* Foreign currency borrowed by residents through the BIBF and by nonresidents through authorized banks can be deposited in foreign currency accounts.

1995 *OIF:* The Provincial International Banking Facility (PIBF) is established under the same conditions as the BIBF, but with the possibility of lending domestically in baht. Restrictions are imposed on foreign currency bank lending for nonpriority projects. A 7 percent reserve requirement is imposed on nonresident baht accounts and on finance companies' promissory notes.
PI: The Bank of Thailand requires banks to submit detailed information on risk control mea-

---

were substantially short term, and in particular in the form of foreign currency borrowing. The latter was largely unhedged because of expectations that relatively stable exchange rates would be maintained indefinitely.

The main implications of the above are, first, that the sustainability of inflows depends on the efficient use of the funds, not least as regards the prudent management of the risks involved with external funding. Specifically, the channeling of funds through banking sectors where risk management was relatively weak and unsophisticated, and where there were distorted incentive structures associated with excessive lending to interrelated entities and moral hazard, ultimately brought this efficiency into question. The rapid bank credit expansions strained credit assessment procedures and resulted in banks channeling newly bor-

rowed funds into unprofitable or speculative activities such as real estate lending, while the prudential supervision framework was not strong enough to curtail these trends effectively. And where external borrowing by corporations is guaranteed by financial institutions (as in Korea), much the same issues arise. A major concern is, therefore, to ensure that commercial banks comply with appropriate prudential standards, including procedures for the management of asset and liability (liquidity) risks, and that banks face appropriate incentive structures (e.g., moral hazard is avoided as much as possible, and appropriate controls on lending to interrelated entities exist). Overall, currency mismatches (open foreign exchange positions) were not a significant issue in Asian banks, but liquidity mismatches (arising from excessive maturity transformation) and inadequate credit assessment were.

sures on foreign exchange operations including derivatives. Finance and securities firms' daily net long and short open positions on exchange rates are lowered to 25 percent and 20 percent of capital, respectively. These limits for commercial banks are 20 percent and 15 percent of the capital or $5 million, whichever is larger. Criteria for the calculation of the net open positions are toughened.

1996 *OIF:* A 7 cash percent reserve requirement is imposed on nonresident baht accounts with maturities of less than one year and on foreign borrowing by commercial banks and BIBF banks (reduced to 6 percent in 1997). Exceptions include international trade financing, nonresident deposits at BIBF banks, overdrafts and liabilities from currency and derivatives trade. The Bank of Thailand tightens the limits on banks net open foreign exchange positions by excluding loans to high-risk sectors from banks' assets. The preferential tax rate on BIBF profits is reduced. The BIBF is allowed to manage liquidity risks through buying forward or option contracts against the baht.

A Synopsis of Regulation on Capital Inflows in Mid-1997

Thailand's system of capital controls is subject to numerous limitations.

Capital and money market instruments. The sale or issue of long-term and short-term securities in the domestic market is under the jurisdiction of the Security and Exchange Commission (SEC) whose approval is required. Nonresidents are subject to the same rules as residents. Foreign equity participation is limited to 49 percent of Thai corporations and 25 percent of the paid-up capital of financial institutions, banks, and asset-management companies. Stricter limits apply to individual stakes. The issue abroad of capital market securities by residents is subject to SEC approval and securities cannot be traded domestically. Money market instruments cannot be sold or issued abroad.

Collective investments. Nonresidents can freely buy mutual funds domestically, but the launch of mutual funds in domestic and offshore markets is subject to the SEC approval.

Derivatives. A security company cannot trade in derivatives unless explicitly allowed by the SEC. Other subjects need the approval by the Bank of Thailand. Issues by nonresidents of equity-related instruments and bonds are subject to SEC approval.

Commercial credits. The regime is rather liberal.

Financial credit. Residents can freely take loans from abroad.

Direct investments. Projects exceeding $10 million are subject to approval by the Bank of Thailand. Foreign capital can be freely imported into the country, but proceeds must be surrendered to authorized banks or deposited in foreign currency accounts within 15 days.

Regulations regarding commercial banks' activities. Only 50 percent of commercial lending in foreign exchange to particular sectors can be counted in the banks' assets. Nonresident baht accounts with less than one year maturity are subject to a 7 percent reserve requirement. Negative balances on foreign currencies positions cannot exceed 15 percent of the capital and positive positions cannot exceed 20 percent.

Note: FDI = foreign direct investments; OIF = other capital inflows; PI = portfolio investments

Sources: Johnston and others (1997); and IMF, *Annual Report on Exchange Arrangements and Exchange Restrictions.*

Second, appropriate risk-management incentives are also fundamental to avoiding excessive direct external borrowing by nonbank corporations. Prudential measures applied to financial institutions may have some indirect effect here (to the extent that corporations borrowing offshore also borrow from local banks). But more central is the need to avoid implicit government guarantees of corporations and associated moral hazard, as with the banks themselves. In addition, exchange rate regimes that avoid excessive rigidity tend to create a much greater awareness, both among banks and nonbanks, of the need to manage exchange rate risk.

Third, increasing recourse to shorter-term debt can be an indicator of growing uncertainty about economic prospects. The monitoring and disclosure of such debt is, therefore, important, both as a guide to domestic macroeconomic management and as an input into better informed decision making by international financial markets. However, because of the scope to redenominate longer-term debt as short-term debt, statistical measures of short-term liabilities may not always be easy to interpret, particularly in the lead up to a crisis when private lenders may seek to change quickly the composition of their assets.

Fourth, where restrictions remained on capital market issues abroad by resident corporations and on nonresident purchases of securities on the local market, it might well have been desirable to speed up the development of the longer-term security markets both through domestic capital market reforms (including greater disclosure of information by borrowers), and by removing the capital controls. With an appropriate public sector and private sector relationship that avoids moral hazard, allowing corporations access to the international bond markets could have an important market disciplining effect, since such access would require meeting higher financial disclosure standards. More broadly, policymakers need to be careful when liberalizing capital flows so that they do not unduly favor some types of channels or instruments over others—a less-than-level playing field could skew the incentives for different groups in ways that are unhelpful for prudent competition and sound risk management.

Fifth, it is not clear that the reintroduction of controls helped much, either before the crisis, or especially once the crisis had begun. Thailand and Indonesia resorted to capital controls in an effort to reduce inflows before the crisis, and to restrict outflows during the crisis (see appendix at the end of this section). Outside the three main crisis countries, the Philippines took a number of successive measures to tighten certain capital controls from mid-1997, while Malaysia took one measure to tighten nonresident access to swap transactions. The Phillippines measures are seen as temporary, and the authorities have indicated they would be phased out. The more recent controls generally aimed to restrict forward or derivative transactions and their financing, but during the crisis they sent a negative signal to the market discouraging further capital inflows at a critical juncture. It is notable that most of the new controls introduced in Thailand were removed again in early 1998, while in Korea the emphasis was solely on liberalizing measures throughout the crisis. In Indonesia too, additional liberalization measures were taken in addition to the single restrictive measure. As regards capital controls that seek to shift the composition of capital inflows to longer-term inflows, Chile is often cited as a country that has successfully used capital controls to limit short-term inflows. While the assessment of the effectiveness of controls is difficult, these particular controls, like others, appear to have been effective mainly only as a temporary measure: short-term inflows for Chile declined in the year that such measures were introduced or intensified, only to increase in the following year. The different performance in Chile compared with East Asia may be attributable to the fact that (1) Chile had already addressed serious banking sector weaknesses following an earlier banking crisis; and (2) Chile's somewhat more flexible exchange rate policy was rather more attuned to dealing with significant capital inflows (see Johnston, Darbar, and Echeverria, 1997).

Conclusion

The Asian country experiences confirm that it is necessary to approach capital account liberalization as an integral part of more comprehensive programs of economic reform, coordinated with appropriate macroeconomic and exchange rate policies, and including policies to strengthen financial markets and institutions. The question is not so much one of the capital liberalization having been too fast, since some of the countries in Asia have followed a very gradualist approach. Rather, it is more to do with the appropriate sequencing of the reforms and, more specifically, what supporting measures need to be taken.

The liberalization of inflows through the banking system clearly needed to be more fully supported with reforms to encourage stronger management and supervision in that sector. There was also clearly a need to avoid moral hazard problems as much as possible for corporations as well as banks; and, in the more liberal market environment, to have adequate transparency and improved information flows so that there could be informed market decision making, which would in turn reduce the risks of sharp shifts in market sentiment in response to uncertainties. There was also a need to develop the markets for hedging and managing risks, which are an essential part of efficient market-based financial systems, and which were notably lacking in many Asian economies.

Finally, it is also necessary for policymakers to recognize that with more open capital accounts, a country's interest rate policy will be constrained by its choice of exchange arrangement and vice versa. Greater attention has to be given to an appropriate, internally consistent mix of macro policies to avoid creating incentives for excessive short-term capital inflows, and the risk of subsequent sharp reversals.

Appendix. Changes in the Exchange System in Five Asian Economies, June 1997–March 1998

Indonesia

- Bank Indonesia widened its dollar-rupiah intervention band to 12 percent from 8 percent, creating a wider band at 2,374–2,678 rupiah, compared with the previous band of 2,430–2,622 rupiah. *(July 11, 1997)*
- Forward foreign currency trading by domestic banks with nonresidents was limited to $5 million a customer. Each bank's net open position in the forward market was also limited to $5 million. *(July 1997)*
- The authorities abandoned the policy of maintaining the currency within a set trading exchange rate band and adopted a free floating exchange rate arrangement. *(August 14, 1997)*
- The 49 percent limit on foreign holdings of listed shares was abolished. *(September 1997)*
- The government removed all formal and informal barriers to foreign investment in palm oil planta-

tions. At the end of March 1998, the ban on exports of crude palm oil was replaced with an export tax of 40 percent. As a temporary measure aimed at stabilizing domestic prices, the authorities asked government producers to direct their output to the domestic market and that four major, private producers reserve a proportion of their production for the domestic market. *(February 1, 1998)*

- The authorities lifted restrictions on branching of foreign banks. *(February 1, 1998)*
- The authorities lifted restrictions on foreign investment in retail trade and wholesale trade. *(March 15 and April 15, 1998)*

Korea

- Foreign investors were allowed access to nonguaranteed bonds of small and medium-sized companies (maturities over three years and up to 50 percent of the amount listed) and of conglomerates (up to 30 percent limit of issue or a 6 percent individual limit). *(June 1997)*
- The Ministry of Finance and Economy abolished regulations on the usage of long-term loans with maturities of over five years, brought into the country by foreign manufacturers. *(July 1997)*
- The debt limits on corporations making overseas direct investments, whereby 20 percent of investments exceeding $100 million had to be financed by a firm's own capital, were abolished. *(August 1997)*
- The ceiling on export advances was raised from 20 percent to 25 percent in February 1997 and was abolished in August 1997. *(August 1997)*
- The period for importing on a deferred payments basis was lengthened by 30 days for raw materials used in manufacturing exports commodities for SMEs in April 1997. The period was extended for large enterprises as well in August 1997. *(August 1997)*
- Authorities raised the ceiling on aggregate foreign ownership of listed Korean shares from 26 percent to 50 percent and the individual ceiling from 7 percent to 50 percent; eliminated all limits on foreign investment in nonguaranteed bonds issued by small and medium-sized companies; and allowed foreign investment in the guaranteed corporate bond market (for maturities greater than three years) with limits at 10 percent and 30 percent for individuals and in aggregate, respectively. *(December 11, 1997)*
- Authorities raised aggregate limits for foreign investment in nonguaranteed corporate (convertible) bonds from 30 percent to 50 percent. *(December 12, 1997)*
- Korea abandoned the fluctuation margins for the exchange rate maintained under the managed floating system and floated the won. Previously, the exchange rate against the U.S. dollar was allowed to float within specified margins around the previous day's weighted average exchange rate in the interbank market. The margins were widened five times between March 1990 and November 1997, with the most recent margin at ±10 percent. *(December 16, 1997)*
- Authorities allowed foreigners to invest in government and special bonds, up to the aggregate ceiling of 30 percent, and eliminated all individual limits for foreign investment in corporate bonds. *(December 23, 1997)*
- Restrictions on commercial bank ownership have been eased to encourage foreign investment in domestic financial institutions. The financial sector legislation passed on December 29, 1997 abolished the 4 percent ownership limit for commercial banks. Purchase of bank equity by foreign banks is now permitted without limit, but requires approval at three stages: 10 percent, 25 percent, and 31 percent. Domestic ownership above 4 percent is permitted provided that an equal or larger share is held by a foreign bank. *(December 29, 1997)*
- Authorities eliminated all foreign investment ceilings for the government, special, and corporate bond markets, including for maturities of less than three years; lifted the restriction on foreign borrowing of over three years' maturity; and raised the aggregate ceiling on foreign investment in Korean equities to 55 percent. *(December 30, 1997)*
- Authorities removed restrictions on corporate borrowing from abroad up to $2 million for venture companies. Authorities opened up money market instruments issued by nonfinancial institutions (commercial papers, commercial bills, and trade bills) to foreigners without limits. *(February 16, 1998)*
- Authorities allowed foreign banks and brokerage houses to establish subsidiaries. *(March 31, 1998)*

Malaysia

- The Bank Negara imposed a $2 million limit on outstanding noncommercial ringgit offer-side swap transactions per nonresident customer to limit speculators' access to the ringgit.[56] *(August 4, 1997)*
- The government raised the quota on sales of high-end condominiums to foreigners from 30 percent to 50 percent. In addition, foreigners were allowed to acquire 2 units of condominiums (up from 1 previously). *(October 1997)*

[56]The Malaysian authorities see the intention of this measure to allow domestic interest rates to be more reflective of domestic conditions rather than to curb speculative pressures.

Philippines

- The 30 percent cover requirement for foreign currency liabilities of foreign currency deposit units (FCDUs) may be maintained in the following liquid assets: (1) due from other banks; (2) interbank loans maturing within one year; (3) unmatured export bills purchased, except those classified by the Central Bank of the Philippines (BSP) as bad or uncollectible; and (4) readily marketable debt instruments denominated in foreign currency. *(June 6, 1997)*
- The authorities announced a new exchange arrangement under which they will float the peso to allow the peso-dollar rate initially to find its own level, and then move within a target band sufficiently large to permit market forces to operate fully. Soon after the floating of the peso, the market was unexpectedly closed when the Bankers' Association of the Philippines invoked an old rule that trading would stop when the exchange rate moves by more than 1.5 percent. This rule was eliminated on July 14, 1997. *(July 14, 1997)*
- The central bank modified the allowable net open foreign exchange positions of banks. The overbought limit was reduced from 20 percent of capital to 5 percent or $10 million (whichever is lower) and the oversold limit was raised from 10 percent to 20 percent of capital. *(July 22 and July 30, 1997)*
- All forward contracts to sell foreign exchange to nonresidents (including offshore banking units) with no full delivery of principal, including cancellations, rollovers or renewals thereof, shall be submitted for prior clearance to the central bank. *(July 22, 1997)*
- Banks are required to submit an inventory of outstanding forward contracts with nonresidents (including offshore banking units) to sell or purchase foreign exchange with no full delivery of principal. *(July 22, 1997)*
- The central bank announced a three-month suspension of the local right to sell dollars through nondeliverable forward contracts[57] (NDFCs) from onshore banks to offshore counterparties. *(July 22, 1997)*
- Stock dividends accruing to BSP-registered foreign investments would no longer be issued a new Bangko Sentral Registration Document (BSRD). Whenever the stock dividends are sold and the proceeds are outwardly remitted through a remitting bank other than the custodian bank, the BSRD of the mother shares, to which the stock dividends accrued, shall be the BSRD quoted in the BSRD letter-advise required to be issued under existing rules. *(July 24, 1997)*
- Banks whose unencumbered foreign currency cover for liabilities in the FCDU fell below the minimum 30 percent were given a period of six months to comply. *(July 25, 1997)*
- The central bank temporarily restricted access of six foreign banks to the spot foreign exchange market. These banks were permitted limited reentry on August 13, 1997. *(July 28, 1997)*
- The amount of foreign exchange that can be sold (over-the-counter) without documentation and prior approval was reduced from $100,000 to $25,000. Foreign exchange subsidiaries were exempted from this ruling from September 18, 1997, provided that they sell dollars only to authorized agent banks. *(July 30, 1997)*
- The central bank met foreign currency needs of foreign banks and banks with maturing NDFCs on a forward basis. These contracts have maturities of 30–90 days. *(July/August/December 1997)*
- On August 20, 1997, the central bank stopped providing peso liquidity through the overnight lending window. After October 8, 1997, only banks with a reserve deficiency and squared foreign exchange positions can tap the facility. On November 5, 1997, the criteria were relaxed to allow banks with slight overbought positions (2.5 percent) to borrow from this window. *(August 20, 1997)*
- Foreign exchange subsidiaries and affiliates of banks are considered as part of the banking system and, therefore, subject to all foreign exchange rules and regulations applicable to all banks. *(September 5, 1997)*
- The central bank required commercial banks to submit daily their foreign exchange position, including transactions made by their respective subsidiaries and affiliates. *(September 10, 1997)*
- An applicant's income tax return is required to be submitted to support an application to purchase foreign exchange not exceeding $6 million for outward investment that does not require prior central bank approval. *(September 11, 1997)*
- An investment funded by foreign exchange deposited in an investee's FCDU account for investment purposes shall be issued a Bangko Sentral Registration Document as evidence of central bank registration only after the amount deposited had been converted into pesos as certified by the bank maintaining the said FCDU account. *(September 16, 1997)*
- Foreign exchange subsidiaries and affiliates of banks are discouraged from taking net foreign exchange positions. Whatever net foreign exchange positions are maintained by them are to be con-

---

[57]Nondeliverable forward contracts are similar to regular forward contracts, with the exception that they are rolled over at maturity, with net settlement of mark-to-market value in peso at the date of maturity so that no foreign currency changes hands.

solidated into the total net foreign exchange position of the respective banks with whom they are affiliated. Foreign exchange corporations, subsidiaries, and affiliates shall not (1) sell foreign exchange to nonresidents; and (2) sell foreign exchange to resident financial institutions other than authorized agent banks of the central bank and bank-affiliated foreign exchange corporations. *(September 17, 1997)*

- As a general rule, foreign exchange subsidiaries and affiliates of banks may sell foreign exchange to residents. However, they cannot sell foreign exchange to resident financial institutions other than authorized agent banks of the central bank and bank-affiliated foreign exchange corporations. *(October 2, 1997)*
- The Bankers' Association of the Philippines, which operates the foreign exchange market, introduced a 4 percent volatility band (comprising three tiers) in an attempt to stabilize the market. The first band was set at ±2 percent of the reference rate for the peso/U.S. dollar exchange rate of the previous day. If the limit of the band is reached, trades cannot be executed outside the band during the following half hour. Thereafter, the band is widened to ±3 percent. If the limit of the wider band is reached, trades cannot be executed outside the band for one hour. Finally, the width of the band is extended to ±4 percent. If this limit is reached, trades cannot be executed outside the 4 percent band for the remainder of the day. In the first week of operation the limits were reached on several occasions, and in both directions. *(October 7, 1997)*
- Banks are required to submit, to the Foreign Exchange Department of the central bank, a report of all forward sales contracts entered into with nonresidents. *(October 9, 1997)*
- All commercial banks are required to report to the Foreign Exchange Department of the central bank all cancellations or nondelivery of outstanding forward sales contracts. The cancellations will have to pass the following tests: (1) eligibility, (2) frequency, (3) counter party, and (4) mark-to-market. Failure to satisfy the enumerated tests will result in the exclusion of the forward sales contracts in the computation of the consolidated daily foreign exchange position of banks, where sanctions or monetary penalties, or both will be imposed in the event commercial banks should exceed the prescribed limits in the overbought-oversold position as a result of the recomputation. *(October 24, 1997)*
- The central bank and commercial banks agreed to set up a pool of $150 million or more a day to restore supply in the interbank market. Banks contribute a minimum of $50 million in the morning (at the previous day's rate), and the central bank matches that on a 2-for-1 basis. The pooled resources are then sold back to banks at market rates during the day, for sale to banks' corporate clients. *(December 17, 1997)*
- A temporary onshore nondeliverable forward (NDF) facility was set up to ease the pressure on the spot market. Corporations with future foreign exchange obligations can enter into a NDF contract with a bank, which in turn covers the forward contract with the central bank. The central bank takes the foreign exchange risk, while the bank takes the credit risks. *(December 17, 1997)*
- All companies that have central bank registered foreign exchange obligations that are unhedged are able to enter regular forward contract or NDFCs with commercial banks. In such cases, banks can enter an NDFC with the central bank to cover their position. The provision was extended in January 1998 to (1) exporters; (2) commercial banks who bring foreign currency from offshore and use this currency to buy pesos; and (3) oil companies, up to an amount equivalent to their oil imports. *(December 22, 1997)*
- Banks are required to maintain at all times a 100 percent cover for their FCDU liabilities, where at least 30 percent of the cover requirement shall be in the form of liquid assets. *(December 24, 1997)*
- Two additional FCDU asset accounts may be included as among the eligible asset cover: (1) foreign currency notes and coins on hand, and (2) foreign currency checks and other cash items. *(December 24, 1997)*
- Authorities introduced a 7.5 percent tax on interest income of foreign currency deposits of residents. *(December 1997)*
- A law was passed that enables investment houses to open up further to foreign investment by raising the foreign equity participation from 49 percent to 60 percent voting shares. *(Late 1997)*
- The authorities allowed the peso to float more freely against the dollar by lifting the volatility band system that was introduced on October 8, 1997, in an attempt to stabilize the market. The band was widened to ±6 percent on January 7, 1998, with the base changed from the afternoon weighted average to the closing rate in the previous day. *(March 16, 1998)*

Thailand

- The Bank of Thailand introduced a series of measures with respect to transactions with foreign financial institutions to limit capital outflows. The temporary measures, which did not apply to foreign exchange transactions with genuine underlying business related to the export and import of goods and services, direct investment, and various types of portfolio investment in Thailand, included measures (1) to limit transactions with nonresidents that could facilitate the buildup of baht positions in the offshore market, including direct loans, overdrafts, currency swaps, interest rate swaps, forward rate agreements, currency options, and interest rate options; (2) to limit outright forward transactions in baht with nonresidents; (3) to limit selling baht spot against foreign currencies to nonresidents; (4) to require payment in U.S. dollars for any purchase from nonresidents before maturity of baht-denominated bills of exchange, promissory notes, certificates of deposit, and other debt instruments such as debentures and bonds, at the exchange rate prevailing in the domestic market on the purchase date; and (5) to submit daily reports of foreign exchange transactions with nonresidents, including all spot, forward, and swap transactions, as well as purchase of debt instruments from nonresidents, to the Bank of Thailand. *(May–June 1997)*

- Thailand tightened exchange restrictions by temporarily requiring that the baht proceeds from sales of stocks by nonresidents be converted into foreign currency at the onshore exchange rate. *(June 1997)*
- The Thai authorities announced that the baht's exchange rate will be managed within an unpublished band, whereby the value of the baht would be determined by market forces within the newly established band. The authorities also announced that they will try to keep the exchange rate within this band centered on a new, wider currency basket and that a baht-dollar reference rate would be announced daily, and it would be based on the baht's trading average of the previous day. In addition, authorities introduced a two-tier currency market that creates separate exchange rates for investors who buy baht in domestic markets and those who buy it overseas. *(July 2, 1997)*
- The exchange control regulation was modified as follows: (1) foreign exchange earners were allowed to deposit their foreign exchange received in their foreign currency deposit account only if they have obligations to pay out such amounts to nonresidents abroad within three months from the deposit date;[58] and (2) exporters receiving packing credit from the Bank of Thailand through the Export-Import Bank of Thailand were required to sign a forward contract to sell their foreign exchange with a commercial bank selling promissory notes to the Export-Import Bank. The forward contract must specify the amount of foreign currencies in terms of baht, which cannot be less than 50 percent of the face value of the promissory note. *(September 8, 1997)*
- The authorities announced the liberalization of foreign ownership rules. Foreign investors were allowed full ownership of local financial institutions for up to 10 years. *(October 2, 1997)*
- The authorities unified the on- and off-shore exchange markets by lifting the exchange and capital controls that were imposed in mid-1997 to stem speculative pressures on the baht. The authorities replaced the outright prohibition on baht lending to nonresidents with a B 50 million limit per counterparty not having an underlying trade or investment transaction. *(January 1998)*

---

[58]Under the previous regulation, deposits in the foreign currency account could be made irrespective of the proof of obligation. The limits on the outstanding balances of all foreign currency accounts remained at $500,000 for individuals and $5,000,000 for corporations.

VII

Indices of Exchange and Capital Controls and Relationships with Economic Development

Evaluating the restrictiveness of exchange regimes is a complex task, but in recent years it has been regarded as an important element of reaching a better analytical understanding of the impact of exchange systems on economic performance. This section presents indices of controls on current payments and transfers (denoted by CCI), capital controls (KCI), and exchange and capital controls (ECI). The latter index is an average of the two former indices and represents an overall measure of controls. These indices provide a concise yet comprehensive measure of the prevalence of a member's exchange and capital controls for policy and research and allow for cross-country comparisons of the relative degree of openness and neutrality of members' exchange systems. The indices aggregate information from the IMF's *Annual Report on Exchange Arrangements and Exchange Restrictions*. In 1997, the *AREAER* information[59] was presented in a new tabular format, which has allowed for the development of these more complete measures.

The indices are estimated for a sample of 41 industrial, developing, and transition economies, with close to complete data for 1996. On average, capital controls are more prevalent and vary more widely across countries than controls on current payments and transfers. Sensitivity analysis demonstrates the general robustness of the indices to the different treatment of specific types of control, for example, international security restrictions and controls on direct foreign investment, and to different weights. The extent of exchange and capital controls, as measured by the indices, is found to be positively related to the size of the parallel, black, or free market premium; volatility of the exchange rate; and the level of trade barriers. Lower levels of exchange and capital controls are found to be associated with a higher level of economic development, higher efficiency and depth of the financial sector, larger trade and capital flows, and greater openness of the economy.

The indices of exchange and capital controls and the index of trade regime restrictiveness characterize

the respective aspects of the external sector regime.[60] The indices of exchange and capital controls are a useful analogue and counterpart to the index of trade regime restrictiveness, which was developed at the Fund in 1997. Despite its limitations, the trade restrictiveness index was considered to represent a useful tool for classifying the relative restrictiveness of trade regimes and analyzing the progress in trade liberalization.

Literature Review

One conventional approach to measure the restrictiveness of exchange regimes focuses on the assessment of the observable effects of exchange controls, including onshore-offshore interest differentials, the size of the black market premium, deviations from covered interest parity, and capital flows.[61] Such measures, however, require a minimum development of financial markets, and measures of the black market premium are not always available or reliable. In addition, the measures might be misleading to the extent that prices are affected by nonpolicy factors, for example, the size of the economy. Likewise, an index of capital mobility, such as, for example, the absolute value of the current account deficit relative to GDP,[62] is a useful, albeit imperfect, proxy of the extent of the liberalization of capital controls, partially because it reflects net, rather than gross, capital flows.

An alternative approach is to develop measures of the prevalence of exchange controls on the basis of government regulations. The existence of exchange and capital controls can be indicated by a dummy variable, which is set equal to 1, if the respective control(s) is (are) in place, and zero otherwise. On the basis of *AREAER* summary tables, Grilli and Milesi-

---

Note: This section was prepared primarily by Natalia Tamirisa.
[59]Data in the 1997 issue of *AREAER* refer to 1996.

[60]See Sharer and others (1998). The indices characterize the two aspects of the regulatory regime pertaining to the external sector: trade and exchange. The trade restrictiveness index evaluates the restrictiveness of trade regimes on the 10-point integer scale, taking into account information on the average tariff rate, the number of sectors covered by nontariff barriers, and the percent of production or trade covered by nontariff barriers.
[61]See, for example, Dooley and Isard (1980).
[62]See Taylor (1996).

Ferretti (1995) construct dummy variables for restrictions on current account and capital account transactions, and multiple currency practices and empirically analyze the effects of exchange and capital restrictions on inflation, real interest rates, and growth, as well as the factors determining the use of capital controls.[63] Loungani, Razin, and Yuen (1997) use Grilli and Milesi-Ferretti's data to examine the effects of capital controls on the output-inflation trade-off. Lewis considers the effects of exchange and capital restrictions, as measured by dummy variables, on the consumption-smoothing behavior.[64] Although parsimonious dummy variables are convenient, they reflect the presence only of a particular type or types of control. A potentially more fruitful approach is to develop aggregate indicative measures describing the regulatory regime.

Bartolini and Drazen (1997) suggest aggregating dummy variables into a simple index of capital controls. They base their index on three types of measures: restrictions on payments for capital transactions, multiple exchange rates, and restrictions on repatriation of export proceeds. They assign values to these variables on the basis of AREAER for 73 developing countries. The index of capital controls in developing countries is the sum of dummy variables for individual countries normalized by three times the number of countries. Bartolini and Drazen's methodology was recently applied to the analysis of capital flows to emerging markets.

Another aggregate measure of exchange and capital controls is presented in the IMF's review of experience under arrangements supported by the Extended Structural Adjustment Facility (ESAF). The measure used is a simple average of two individual indicators: the level of premium in the parallel exchange market, and the extent of surrender requirements and nonmarket allocation of foreign exchange. Each indicator measures the extent of policy distortions on a six-point scale, whereby higher scores correspond to better policies or fewer distortions.[65]

Johnston and Ryan (1994) suggest a refined version of the dummy variable technique in an empirical study of the effectiveness of controls in protecting the private capital accounts of countries' balance of payments. Complementing AREAER information with the OECD Code of Liberalization of Capital Movements, the authors classify capital control regimes into liberal or restrictive, depending on the existence of direct and indirect restrictions on capital movements. The corresponding dummy variable is an improvement over conventional binary measures, as it implicitly incorporates the scope and intensity of capital controls. Moreover, for time-series analysis the authors introduce four additional dummy variables to measure changes in the coverage and intensity of regulations.

Methodological Approach and Data

Data on exchange and capital controls maintained by individual countries are contained in the AREAER. In 1997, the information in the AREAER was presented in a new tabular format, which classified and standardized the information on members' exchange systems and expanded the coverage of capital controls. Classification of the information in this new tabular format has made it possible to develop and apply more comprehensive indices of the pervasiveness of exchange and capital controls. Like AREAER, the indices consider the restrictiveness of the exchange and capital control regime from an economic rather than the IMF's jurisdictional perspective.

Specifically, the AREAER's tabular presentation identifies 142 individual types of exchange and capital controls. These are aggregated hierarchically into 16 categories; these categories are aggregated into the indices, which measure the pervasiveness of controls on current payments and transfers, capital controls, and exchange and capital controls in their entirety. Individual types of exchange and capital controls and aggregation in categories are shown in Box 7.

Mathematically, the structure of the indices can be described as follows. The existence of control i in country j is represented by a dummy variable D_{ij}, which equals 1 when an *individual* type of control is in place, and zero otherwise. The index of controls in category k, denoted by CI_{kj}, is defined as the actual number of controls normalized by the total feasible number of controls:[66]

$$CI_{kj} = \frac{1}{N_k} \sum_1^{N_k} D_{ij}, \qquad (1)$$

where N_k denotes the number of controls in category k.

The indices of controls on current payments and transfers and capital controls, denoted by CCI_j and KCI_j respectively, are defined as averages of the indices of the respective categories, that is,

$$CCI_j = \frac{1}{N_{CCI}} \sum_1^{N_{CCI}} CI_{kj}, \qquad (2)$$

---

[63]A similar approach has been used to describe the presence of capital controls in the member countries in Mathieson and Rojas-Suárez (1993).

[64]See Lewis (1996) and (1997).

[65]See Gwartney, Lawson, and Block (1996) for a similar approach of rating the freedom to engage in international capital transactions.

[66]For an analogous approach applied to the evaluation of the extent of market access commitments under the General Agreement on Trade in Services see Hoakman (1995).

Box 7. Structure of Indices of Exchange and Capital Controls

Index of Controls on Current Payments and Transfers		Index of Capital Controls

Exchange arrangement
Exchange rate structure
  Dual
  Multiple
Exchange tax
Exchange subsidy
Forward exchange market
  Prohibited
  Official cover of forward
    operations required
**Arrangements for payments
and receipts**
*Prescription of currency
  requirements*
*Bilateral payments
  arrangements*
  Operative
  Inoperative
Other payments arrangements
  Regional agreements
  Clearing agreements
  Barter agreements and
    open accounts
*International security
  restrictions*
  In accordance with IMF
    Executive Board
    Decision No. 144-(52/51)
  Other
  In accordance with UN
    sanctions
Payments arrears
  Official
  Private
*Controls on trade in gold
  (coins and/or bullion)*
  Controls on domestic
    ownership and/or trade
  Controls on external trade
*Controls on exports and
  imports of banknotes*
  On exports
    Domestic currency
    Foreign currency
  On imports
    Domestic currency
    Foreign currency
Resident accounts
Foreign exchange accounts
  Held domestically
    Prohibited
    Approval required
  Held abroad
    Prohibited
    Approval required
Nonresident accounts
Foreign exchange accounts
  Prohibited
  Approval required
Domestic currency accounts
  Prohibited
  Approval required
Blocked accounts

**Payments for invisible transactions
and current transfers**
Freight/insurance
  Prior approval
  Quantitative limits
  Indicative limits/bona fide test
Unloading/storage costs
  Prior approval
  Quantitative limits
  Indicative limits/bona fide test
Administrative expenses
  Prior approval
  Quantitative limits
  Indicative limits/bona fide test
Commissions
  Prior approval
  Quantitative limits
  Indicative limits/bona fide test
Interest payments
  Prior approval
  Quantitative limits
  Indicative limits/bona fide test
Profit/dividends
  Prior approval
  Quantitative limits
  Indicative limits/bona fide test
Payments for travel
  Prior approval
  Quantitative limits
  Indicative limits/bona fide test
Medical costs
  Prior approval
  Quantitative limits
  Indicative limits/bona fide test
Study abroad costs
  Prior approval
  Quantitative limits
  Indicative limits/bona fide test
Subscriptions and membership fees
  Prior approval
  Quantitative limits
  Indicative limits/bona fide test
Consulting/legal fees
  Prior approval
  Quantitative limits
  Indicative limits/bona fide test
Foreign workers' wages
  Prior approval
  Quantitative limits
  Indicative limits/bona fide test
Pensions
  Prior approval
  Quantitative limits
  Indicative limits/bona fide test
Gambling/prize earnings
  Prior approval
  Quantitative limits
  Indicative limits/bona fide test
Family maintenance/alimony
  Prior approval
  Quantitative limits
  Indicative limits/bona fide test
Credit card use abroad

Proceeds from exports, invisibles, and current transfers
  Repatriation requirements for export proceeds
  Surrender requirements for export proceeds
  Repatriation requirements for proceeds from
    invisibles and current transfers
  Surrender requirements for proceeds from
    invisibles and current transfers
  Restrictions on use of funds
Controls on capital and money market instruments
On capital market securities
  Purchase in the country by nonresidents
  Sale or issue locally by nonresidents
  Purchase abroad by residents
  Sale or issue abroad by residents
On money market instruments
  Purchase in the country by nonresidents
  Sale or issue locally by nonresidents
  Purchase abroad by residents
  Sale or issue abroad by residents
On collective investment securities
  Purchase in the country by nonresidents
  Sale or issue locally by nonresidents
  Purchase abroad by residents
  Sale or issue abroad by residents
Controls on derivatives and other instruments
Purchase in the country by nonresidents
Sale or issue locally by nonresidents
Purchase abroad by residents
Sale or issue abroad by residents
Controls on credit operations
Commercial credits
  By residents to nonresidents
  To residents from nonresidents
Financial credits
  By residents to nonresidents
  To residents from nonresidents
Guarantees, sureties, and financial backup facilities
  By residents to nonresidents
  To residents from nonresidents
Controls on direct foreign investment
Outward direct investment
Inward direct investment
Controls on liquidation of direct investment
Controls on real estate transactions
Purchase abroad by residents
Purchase locally by nonresidents
Sale locally by nonresidents
**Provisions specific to commercial banks and
  other credit institutions**
Borrowing abroad
Maintenance of accounts abroad
*Lending to nonresidents (financial or commercial
  credits)*
Lending locally in foreign exchange
*Purchase of locally issued securities denominated in
  foreign exchange*
*Differential treatment of nonresident deposit accounts
  and/or deposit accounts in foreign exchange*
  Reserve requirements
  Liquid asset requirements
  Interest rate controls
  Investment regulations
  Credit controls

(continued on next page)

Box 7 (*concluded*)

Index of Controls on Current Payments and Transfers		Index of Capital Controls
Imports and import payments *Foreign exchange budget* *Financing requirements* *for imports* Minimum financing requirements Advance payments requirement Advance import deposits *Documentation requirements for* *release of foreign exchange* *for imports* Domiciliation requirements Preshipment inspection Letters of credit Import licenses used as exchange licenses Other *Import taxes collected through* *the exchange system* **Exports and export proceeds** *Documentation requirements* Letters of credit Guarantees Domiciliation Preshipment inspection Other *Export taxes collected through* *the exchange system*	Prior approval Quantitative limits Indicative limits/bona fide test	Open foreign exchange position limits **Provisions specific to institutional investors** *Limits (max.) on portfolio invested abroad* *Limits (min.) on portfolio invested locally* *Currency matching regulations on assets/liabilities* *composition*

$$KCI_j = \frac{1}{N_{KCI}} \sum_1^{N_{KCI}} CI_{kj}, \qquad (3)$$

where N_{CCI} and N_{KCI} denote the number of categories in CCI and KCI, respectively. The index of exchange and capital controls, denoted by ECI_j, is the average of CCI_j and KCI_j, that is,

$$ECI_j = \frac{1}{2}(CCI_j + KCI_j). \qquad (4)$$

Each index ranges from zero (the lowest extent) to 1 (the highest extent). *CCI* measures the extent of controls on current payments and transfers, and *KCI* reflects the pervasiveness of direct controls on capital movements. *ECI* comprises controls on payments and transfers for current and capital transactions and thus reflects the overall incidence of exchange controls (see Tables 33 and 34 for the list of categories included in the indices).

Values of the dummy variables are assigned on the basis of the following conventions. The value of 1 corresponds to prohibitions, quantitative limits, approval and registration requirements,[67] restrictions on in-

vestors' opportunity set (e.g., the type of securities), and cases where the respective markets are lacking. The value of zero is assigned for statistical measures, administrative verification, optional official cover of forward operations, liberal granting of licenses, and the lack of access to the formal market for foreign exchange transactions. Under the IMF's jurisdiction, registration or licensing used to monitor rather than restrict payments and verification requirements, such as a requirement to submit documented evidence that a payment is bona fide do not constitute an exchange restriction, unless the process results in undue delays. With indicative limits, authorities approve all requests for foreign exchange for bona fide current international transactions in excess of limits or for transactions for which there is no basic allocation of foreign exchange. If the public is made aware of such a policy, indicative limits do not constitute a restriction.

The above methodology is applied to a cross-sectional sample of 41 industrial, developing, and transition countries, all of which, except two (Brazil and Egypt) have accepted the obligations of Article VIII of the IMF's Articles of Agreement. The countries are selected to represent various geographical regions and levels of economic development. On average, 99 percent of the relevant data is available for the countries in the sample. The baseline indices are defined as av-

---

[67]Similarly, registration requirements are treated as restrictions in World Bank (1997).

Table 33. Indices of Categories of Controls on Current Payments and Transfers, 1996

	Exchange Arrangement	Arrangements for Payments and Receipts	Resident Accounts	Nonresident Accounts	Imports and Import Payments	Exports and Export Proceeds	Payments for Invisibles and Current Transfers
Argentina	0.0	0.2	0.0	0.0	0.0	0.0	0.0
Australia	0.0	0.1	0.0	0.2	0.0	0.0	0.0
Brazil	0.5	0.5	0.0	0.0	0.5	0.3	0.4
Canada	0.0	0.2	0.3	0.2	0.0	0.0	0.0
Chile	0.5	0.1	0.0	0.0	0.2	0.7	0.0
China	0.3	0.3	0.5	0.4	0.4	0.0	0.5
Côte d'Ivoire	0.0	0.4	0.5	0.2	0.3	0.6	0.5
Czech Republic	0.0	0.1	0.3	0.0	0.0	0.0	0.0
Denmark	0.0	0.1	0.0	0.0	0.0	0.0	0.0
Egypt	0.0	0.6	0.3	0.0	0.0	0.0	0.0
France	0.0	0.1	0.0	0.0	0.1	0.1	0.0
Germany	0.0	0.1	0.0	0.2	0.0	0.0	0.0
Greece	0.0	0.2	0.0	0.0	0.0	0.0	0.2
Hungary	0.0	0.4	0.3	0.0	0.1	0.0	0.0
India	0.0	0.5	0.3	0.0	0.0	0.0	0.8
Indonesia	0.0	0.3	0.0	0.0	0.4	0.6	0.0
Israel	0.3	0.2	0.3	0.0	0.2	0.0	0.3
Italy	0.0	0.5	0.0	0.2	0.0	0.0	0.0
Japan	0.0	0.1	0.5	0.0	0.0	0.0	0.0
Kazakhstan	0.0	0.2	0.3	0.0	0.5	0.7	0.4
Kenya	0.0	0.1	0.0	0.0	0.2	0.0	0.0
Korea, Republic of	0.0	0.2	0.0	0.2	0.0	0.0	0.3
Latvia	0.3	0.2	0.0	0.2	0.0	0.0	0.0
Mexico	0.0	0.2	0.0	0.2	0.0	0.0	0.0
Morocco	0.0	0.6	0.5	0.0	0.2	0.1	0.5
Netherlands	0.0	0.1	0.0	0.2	0.0	0.0	0.0
New Zealand	0.0	0.1	0.0	0.0	0.0	0.0	0.0
Norway	0.0	0.1	0.0	0.0	0.0	0.0	0.0
Pakistan	0.3	0.3	0.3	0.2	0.4	0.3	0.5
Philippines	0.0	0.4	0.0	0.0	0.3	0.1	0.4
Poland	0.0	0.4	0.3	0.0	0.0	0.0	0.2
Russia	0.0	0.6	0.5	0.0	0.3	0.1	0.3
Saudi Arabia	0.0	0.2	0.0	0.0	0.0	0.0	0.0
South Africa	0.0	0.4	0.5	0.4	0.2	0.1	0.4
Spain	0.0	0.3	0.0	0.0	0.0	0.0	0.0
Thailand	0.0	0.2	0.5	0.2	0.1	0.1	0.0
Tunisia	0.0	0.4	0.3	0.0	0.2	0.3	0.3
Turkey	0.0	0.5	0.0	0.0	0.0	0.6	0.0
United Kingdom	0.0	0.2	0.0	0.0	0.0	0.0	0.0
United States	0.0	0.1	0.0	0.2	0.0	0.0	0.0
Uruguay	0.3	0.4	0.0	0.0	0.0	0.0	0.0
Summary statistics							
Mean	0.1	0.3	0.2	0.1	0.1	0.1	0.1
Standard deviation	0.1	0.2	0.2	0.1	0.2	0.2	0.2
Minimum	0.0	0.1	0.0	0.0	0.0	0.0	0.0
Maximum	0.5	0.6	0.5	0.4	0.5	0.7	0.8

erages of the indices calculated under two alternative assumptions about missing data: controls and no controls. The average error margin due to missing data does not exceed 0.01. However, the interpretation of results for some countries requires caution. The error margins for Poland's KCI and ECI are 0.07 and 0.04, respectively, and Russia's KCI is 0.04.

The present approach has a number of advantages over earlier ones. The measures reflect the prevalence of a broad array of individual types of control, and capture a variety of changes in the regulatory regime. The transparent structure of the indices simplifies their interpretation. The indices are also easy to update and to modify by including or excluding individual types of control. Finally, the indices are based on the documented evidence on exchange and capital controls and reflect the minimum subjectivity possible in this type of study.

The indices should be interpreted as indicative measures of the prevalence of exchange and capital controls. The measures do not explicitly take into account the monitoring and enforcement of exchange and capital controls and thus reflect primarily the de jure rather than de facto incidence of controls. There-

Table 34. Indices of Categories of Capital Controls, 1996

	Proceeds from Invisibles, Exports, and Current Transfers	Capital and Money Market Instruments	Derivatives and Other Instruments	Credit Operations	Direct Foreign Investment	Liquidation of Direct Foreign Investment	Real Estate Transactions	Operations of Commercial Banks and Other Credit Institutions	Operations of Institutional Investors
Argentina	0.0	0.1	0.0	0.0	0.5	0.0	0.3	0.1	0.7
Australia	0.0	0.3	0.3	0.0	0.5	0.0	0.3	0.1	0.0
Brazil	0.8	0.4	1.0	1.0	1.0	0.0	0.0	0.5	0.3
Canada	0.0	0.0	0.0	0.0	0.5	0.0	0.0	0.0	0.0
Chile	0.6	1.0	1.0	0.8	1.0	1.0	1.0	0.9	0.3
China	1.0	1.0	1.0	0.8	1.0	0.0	0.7	0.7	0.0
Côte d'Ivoire	0.8	0.8	1.0	0.8	1.0	1.0	0.7	0.4	1.0
Czech Republic	0.4	0.6	0.8	0.3	0.0	0.0	0.3	0.3	0.3
Denmark	0.0	0.0	0.0	0.0	0.0	0.0	0.7	0.0	0.0
Egypt	0.0	0.1	0.0	0.2	0.5	1.0	0.7	0.3	0.0
France	0.0	0.6	0.0	0.0	0.5	0.0	0.0	0.0	0.3
Germany	0.0	0.4	0.0	0.0	0.0	0.0	0.0	0.2	0.0
Greece	0.0	0.0	0.0	0.0	0.5	0.0	0.0	0.0	0.0
Hungary	0.8	0.7	1.0	0.2	0.5	0.0	0.3	0.6	1.0
India	1.0	1.0	1.0	1.0	1.0	1.0	0.7	0.7	0.0
Indonesia	0.2	0.3	1.0	0.5	0.5	0.0	0.7	0.6	0.3
Israel	1.0	0.7	0.5	0.5	1.0	0.0	0.3	0.2	0.3
Italy	0.0	0.1	0.0	0.0	0.0	0.0	0.0	0.1	0.3
Japan	0.0	0.2	0.0	0.2	0.5	0.0	0.0	0.3	0.3
Kazakhstan	0.6	1.0	1.0	1.0	1.0	1.0	1.0	0.9	1.0
Kenya	0.0	0.6	0.5	0.0	0.0	0.0	0.3	0.1	0.0
Korea, Republic of	0.8	0.8	1.0	1.0	1.0	0.0	1.0	0.4	0.3
Latvia	0.0	0.0	0.0	0.0	0.5	0.0	0.3	0.1	0.0
Mexico	0.0	0.3	1.0	0.5	0.5	0.0	0.3	0.4	0.3
Morocco	0.8	0.9	0.8	0.8	0.5	1.0	0.7	0.6	0.3
Netherlands	0.0	0.0	0.0	0.0	0.0	0.0	0.0	0.1	0.0
New Zealand	0.0	0.0	0.0	0.0	0.5	0.0	0.3	0.0	0.0
Norway	0.0	0.0	0.0	0.0	0.0	0.0	0.0	0.1	0.3
Pakistan	0.8	0.6	1.0	0.7	1.0	0.0	1.0	0.9	0.0
Philippines	0.0	0.5	1.0	0.8	0.5	0.0	1.0	0.1	0.3
Poland	0.4	0.8	1.0	0.5	1.0	0.0	1.0	0.2	0.0
Russia	0.8	1.0	1.0	0.8	1.0	1.0	0.7	0.5	0.7
Saudi Arabia	0.0	0.4	0.3	0.7	0.0	0.0	0.3	0.2	0.0
South Africa	1.0	0.6	1.0	0.5	0.5	0.0	0.3	0.8	0.3
Spain	0.0	0.0	0.0	0.0	0.5	0.0	0.0	0.2	0.3
Thailand	0.8	0.9	1.0	0.2	1.0	0.0	1.0	0.5	0.3
Tunisia	1.0	1.0	1.0	0.7	1.0	0.0	1.0	0.5	1.0
Turkey	0.4	0.3	0.0	0.3	1.0	0.0	0.3	0.5	0.3
United Kingdom	0.0	0.0	0.0	0.0	0.5	0.0	0.0	0.1	0.0
United States	0.0	0.2	0.0	0.2	0.5	0.0	0.3	0.0	0.0
Uruguay	0.0	0.0	1.0	0.0	0.0	0.0	0.0	0.2	0.0
Summary statistics									
Mean	0.3	0.4	0.5	0.4	0.6	0.2	0.4	0.3	0.3
Standard deviation	0.4	0.4	0.5	0.4	0.4	0.4	0.4	0.3	0.3
Minimum	0.0	0.0	0.0	0.0	0.0	0.0	0.0	0.0	0.0
Maximum	1.0	1.0	1.0	1.0	1.0	1.0	1.0	0.9	1.0

fore, an estimate of exchange and capital control's restrictiveness is biased upward for countries with weak enforcement of controls or that developed informal markets to help circumvent controls at a relatively low cost. Beyond the question of enforcement and supervision, there is a different question of the welfare effects of exchange and capital controls. These effects are clearly very difficult to measure. Although a rigorous estimation of the welfare effects of exchange and capital controls is beyond the scope of this study, it examines the robustness of the cross-country rankings to different weightings (see below for more details). As with all measures constructed on the basis of regulations, selection and classification of individual types of control, and coding of information are subjective.[68] The indices do not distin-

---

[68]See, for example, Grilli, Masciandaro, and Tabellini (1991) and Cukierman, Webb, and Neyapti (1992) for examples of indices of central bank independence.

guish individual types of exchange and capital control beyond the *AREAER*'s classification. Although individual types and categories of control are given equal weighting in the indices and thus the intensity of exchange and capital controls is not taken into account explicitly, the indices are found to be robust to weighing by subjective intensity measures (see below).

Country Indices

Indices of exchange and capital controls are calculated for 41 countries for 1996 (see Table 35 and Figures 9–11). On average, controls on current payments and transfers are less widespread and less variable across countries than capital controls. The breakdown of the source of the exchange restrictiveness by individual categories of controls is presented in Tables 33–34. The latter depend on the actual number of exchange and capital controls normalized by the total feasible number of measures in the respective category.

Controls on Current Payments and Transfers

The prevalence of controls on current payments and transfers varies across countries. In industrial countries, regulatory regimes on current payments and transfers are virtually free of controls. However, the index CCI is not equal to zero, partly because many industrial countries selectively restrict current payments to selected countries on security grounds. Such measures are included for completeness, since the indices describe exchange controls in general rather than focusing on motivation. Norway has the most liberal regime with a single exchange measure in place: international security restrictions in accordance with United Nations' sanctions. The United States and Germany impose international security restrictions and have blocked accounts. In the United Kingdom, external trade in some types of gold is subject to licensing and there are international security restrictions. In addition to international security restrictions, Japan maintains controls on exports and imports of banknotes. Foreign exchange resident accounts held domestically are prohibited, and there are controls on foreign exchange resident accounts held abroad. The latter controls were lifted in April 1998 as part of the financial "Big Bang" reform. The indices, however, refer to 1996 and thus reflect the presence of the control in Japan at that time.

In developing and transition economies, controls on current payments and transfers are more prevalent. Of the sample, Côte d'Ivoire has the highest CCI of 0.34, reflecting approval requirements for resident foreign exchange accounts, documentation requirements on exports and export proceeds, prescription of currency

requirements, clearing agreements, payments arrears, controls on trade in gold and exports of banknotes, and controls on payments for invisibles and current transfers (Table 33). The CCI for China of 0.33 reflects approval requirements for resident and nonresident accounts, controls on payments for invisible transactions and transfers, and documentation and financing requirements for imports. Likewise, the CCI for Brazil of 0.31 captures the existence of a dual exchange rate structure, exchange taxes, financing and documentation requirements for imports, prescription of currency requirements, bilateral and clearing payment arrangements, international security restrictions, private payment arrears, controls on trade in gold, controls on exports and imports of banknotes, and controls on payments for invisible transactions and current transfers.

Capital Controls

The indices measuring the extent of capital controls are higher on average than those of current controls, ranging from 0.01 to 0.95 (Table 35). About 46 percent of countries have KCIs below 0.25. Among these countries are industrial economies and some developing and transition economies—Argentina, Kenya, Latvia, and Uruguay—which have liberalized their capital accounts. Chile, Côte d'Ivoire, India, Kazakhstan, Russia, and Tunisia have KCIs above 0.75, indicating that they maintain relatively restrictive regimes for capital movements. Table 34 provides a breakdown of the source of the exchange restrictiveness by categories of controls.

Within the sample, Kazakhstan has the highest KCI of 0.95. Capital controls are used extensively for regulating capital and money market transactions, derivatives, credit operations, direct foreign investment and its liquidation, real estate transactions, and provisions specific to institutional investors. Chile's KCI of 0.89 reflects controls on such categories of transactions as capital and money market instruments, derivatives and other instruments, direct investment and its liquidation, real estate transactions, operations of commercial banks and other credit institutions, and credit operations. Likewise, Russia maintains extensive controls on capital and money market instruments, derivatives and other instruments, direct foreign investment and its liquidation.

Of the sample, the Netherlands has the most liberal regime pertaining to capital movements with the KCI equal to 0.01. The only measure is open foreign exchange position limits for commercial banks; such prudential measures are included in the database for completeness and are generally not considered capital controls. The KCI of the United States is 0.13 owing to controls on capital market securities (purchased locally by nonresidents, and sold and issued by nonres-

Table 35. Indices of Exchange Controls, 1996

	Exchange and Capital Controls (ECI)	Current Payment and Transfers (CCI)	Capital Controls (KCI)
Netherlands	0.03	0.05	0.01
Norway	0.03	0.01	0.05
United Kingdom	0.05	0.03	0.07
Denmark	0.05	0.02	0.07
Germany	0.05	0.04	0.07
New Zealand	0.05	0.02	0.01
Greece	0.06	0.06	0.06
Canada	0.07	0.09	0.06
Italy	0.08	0.10	0.06
Spain	0.08	0.04	0.11
United States	0.09	0.05	0.13
France	0.10	0.04	0.16
Latvia	0.10	0.10	0.10
Kenya	0.11	0.05	0.17
Uruguay	0.11	0.09	0.13
Argentina	0.11	0.03	0.19
Australia	0.12	0.04	0.20
Saudi Arabia	0.12	0.03	0.21
Japan	0.12	0.09	0.16
Czech Republic	0.19	0.04	0.33
Mexico	0.21	0.05	0.36
Egypt	0.21	0.12	0.30
Turkey	0.26	0.16	0.36
Philippines	0.32	0.16	0.47
Hungary	0.33	0.10	0.57
Indonesia	0.34	0.18	0.50
Israel	0.35	0.16	0.54
Thailand	0.40	0.17	0.63
Poland	0.40	0.12	0.69
Korea, Republic of	0.40	0.10	0.70
South Africa	0.43	0.29	0.56
Brazil	0.46	0.31	0.60
Pakistan	0.48	0.31	0.66
Morocco	0.49	0.27	0.72
Tunisia	0.51	0.21	0.81
China	0.53	0.33	0.73
India	0.55	0.22	0.87
Chile	0.56	0.22	0.89
Côte d'Ivoire	0.58	0.34	0.82
Russia	0.59	0.27	0.91
Kazakhstan	0.62	0.30	0.95
Summary statistics			
Mean	0.26	0.13	0.39
Standard deviation	0.20	0.10	0.30
Minimum	0.03	0.01	0.01
Maximum	0.62	0.34	0.95

idents), money market securities (sold or issued locally by nonresidents), financial credits (by residents to nonresidents), inward foreign direct investment, and real estate transactions (purchased locally by nonresidents). Japan's KCI reflects measures on capital market securities, financial credits (by residents to nonresidents), inward direct foreign investment, and provisions specific to commercial banks and other credit institutions (Table 34).

Correlation Analysis

Correlations between the indices of exchange and capital controls and indicators of economic development, trade and investment, trade regime, and financial sector development are presented in Table 36. Data and sources for correlation analysis are described in Table 37. Exchange and capital controls tend to exist in countries with a large parallel, black,

Figure 9. Index of Controls on Current Payments and Transfers, 1996

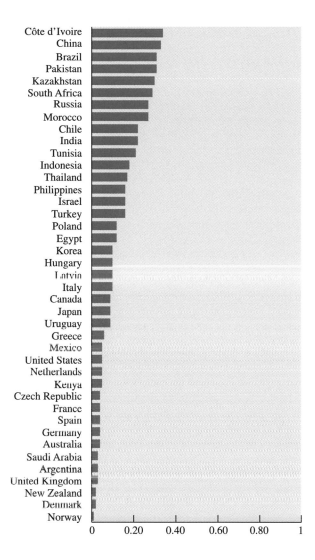

Figure 10. Index of Capital Controls, 1996

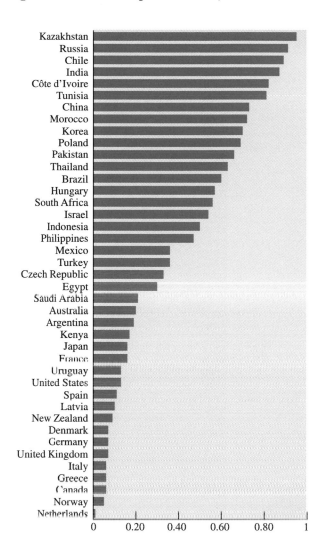

or free market premium; a low level of economic development; high volatility of the exchange rate; small trade and investment flows; restrictive trade regime; and an inefficient financial system. Relatively high correlations are found with the parallel, black, or free market premium and the level of tariff barriers; and negative correlations with the degree of economic development and inward portfolio investment as a share of GDP. In addition, extensive controls on current payments and transfers tend to be associated with widespread capital controls. Correlation coefficients measure how strongly the indices and the respective variables are linearly related and do not necessarily imply a causality relation between the indices and these variables.

On average, the more extensive are restrictions on current account transactions, the more extensive are capital controls.[69] The indices are highly and positively correlated with each other, with correlation (Figure 12) coefficients ranging from 0.84 to 0.99. One possible explanation of this result is that controls on current payments and transfers may be imposed in an attempt to manage capital flows. For instance, controls on payments for invisible transactions and current transfers are often introduced when limiting capital flight.

The extent of exchange and capital controls is inversely related to the level of economic development (Figure 13). Correlation coefficients between the indices and purchasing power parity adjusted GNP per capita range from –0.64 for CCI to –0.68 to ECI. To

---

[69]Grilli and Milesi-Ferretti (1995) find a similar result in a sample of 61 countries.

Figure 11. Index of Exchange and Capital Controls, 1996

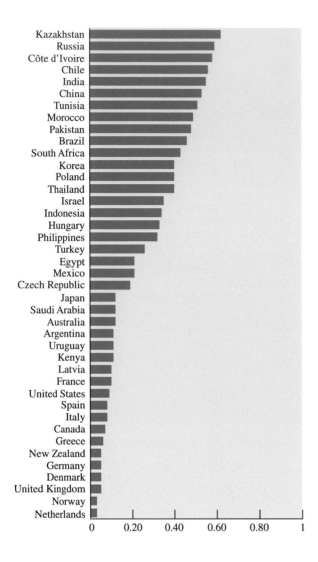

the extent that cross-country results can be interpreted as time series for a representative country, they would imply that, on average, exchange and capital controls tend to be liberalized as the economy develops over time. Figure 13, in addition, suggests that the extent of exchange and capital controls varies across countries with relatively low levels of development. Countries with relatively high levels of development and liberal capital account regimes continue to maintain a number of measures for prudential reasons, for example, open foreign exchange position limits that, as already noted, are covered in the *AREAER* database for completeness.

The direction of causality between the level of economic development and the extent of exchange and capital controls is ambiguous. On one hand, by helping to preserve domestic savings, exchange and capi-

tal controls might promote domestic investment and thus growth—although the evidence that exchange and capital controls have been effective in protecting the balance of payments is weak.[70] On the other hand, extensive government intervention is likely to distort prices and thus reduce efficiency and economic growth.

Furthermore, the extent of exchange and capital controls may depend on the level of economic development, partly because tax and financial systems tend to be more developed in countries with higher per capita income. An extensive system of exchange and capital controls is often part and parcel of more general financial repression and weak budgetary and tax systems.

Exchange and capital controls tend to act as a trade barrier.[71] Specifically, the indices are inversely related to exports and imports with correlation coefficients ranging from −0.32 to −0.41. The extent of exchange and capital controls is also negatively, albeit weakly, correlated with the openness of the economy, defined as the ratio of exports plus imports to GDP. These results may reflect both the size and openness of the economy: smaller and more open economic countries are more prone to external shocks and thus are more likely to impose exchange and capital controls to try to mitigate such shocks. However, the effectiveness of exchange and capital controls tends to be lower in a more open economy, implying an inverse relationship between openness and exchange and capital controls.

As policy measures, exchange and capital controls tend to complement trade policy instruments, particularly tariff barriers. Correlation between the indices and mean tariff rates ranges from 0.52 to 0.54 (Figure 14). A positive relationship between the indices and nontariff measures is weaker with correlation coefficients 0.19–0.21.[72] Weaker correlation may be due to lower reliability of data on nontariff barriers, which are less transparent than tariff ones.

Exchange and capital controls are negatively correlated with different types of capital flows: inflows and outflows of direct, portfolio, and other investment. As a share of GDP, capital flows are also negatively related to the extent of exchange and capital controls. Exchange and capital controls have a relatively high negative correlation with direct foreign investment abroad (the respective correlation coefficient for ECI is −0.49), and portfolio investment liabilities and assets (−0.43 and −0.35, respectively), but less so on other private investment assets (−0.28). In contrast, the impact on the inflow of direct foreign investment

---

[70]See Johnston and Ryan (1994).

[71]See the appendix to Section V for results of an empirical analysis of the role of exchange and capital controls as a barrier to trade.

[72]Although exchange and capital controls are sometimes defined as nontariff barriers, the measures of nontariff barriers here exclude exchange and capital controls.

Table 36. Correlations

Indicators	Current Payment and Transfers (CCI)	Capital Controls (KCI)	Exchange and Capital Controls (ECI)
Exchange system			
CCI (1996)	1.00	0.84	0.91
KCI (1996)	0.84	1.00	0.99
ECI (1996)	0.91	0.99	1.00
Monthly percentage change in U.S. dollar exchange rate (1996)	0.25	0.33	0.32
Monthly percentage change in U.S. dollar exchange rate (1992–96 average)	–0.03	–0.02	–0.02
Parallel, black, or free market premium (c.f. official or interbank market exchange rate) (1996)	–0.15	–0.02	–0.06
Economic development			
Purchasing-power-parity-adjusted GNP per capita (in U.S. dollars) (1995)	–0.01	–0.07	–0.05
Trade	0.03	0.02	0.02
Exports (in million U.S. dollars) (1996)	0.10	0.11	0.11
Imports (in million U.S. dollars) (1996)	0.14	0.10	0.12
Trade/GDP (in percent) (1996)	–0.09	0.06	0.03
Mean tariff rate (in percent) (1995)	0.07	0.21	0.18
Coverage of tariff lines by nontariff barriers (in percent) (1995)			
Capital flows			
Direct foreign investment abroad (in million U.S. dollars) (1995)	0.25	0.24	0.25
Direct foreign investment abroad/GDP (in percent) (1995)	0.13	0.08	0.10
Direct foreign investment in the country (in million U.S. dollars) (1995)	0.07	0.10	0.10
Direct foreign investment in the country/GDP (in percent) (1995)	–0.20	–0.22	–0.22
Portfolio investment assets (in million U.S. dollars) (1995)	0.23	0.22	0.23
Portfolio investment assets/GDP (in percent) (1995)	0.15	0.19	0.19
Portfolio investment liabilities (in million U.S. dollars) (1995)	0.21	0.23	0.24
Portfolio investment liabilities/GDP (in percent) (1995)	0.08	0.04	0.05
Other investment assets (in million U.S. dollars) (1995)	0.12	0.13	0.13
Other investment assets/GDP (in percent) (1995)	0.07	0.08	0.08
Other investment liabilities (in million U.S. dollars) (1995)	0.19	0.17	0.18
Other investment liabilities/GDP (in percent) (1995)	0.25	0.19	0.21
Other private investment assets (1995)	0.11	0.18	0.17
Other private investment assets/GDP (in percent) (1995)	–0.16	0.01	–0.03
Other private investment liabilities (in million U.S. dollars) (1995)	0.20	0.14	0.16
Other private investment liabilities/GDP (in percent) (1995)	0.31	0.21	0.24
Financial sector			
Intermediation spread (lending minus deposit rate) (in percent) (1996)	0.45	0.32	0.37
Spread over LIBOR (deposit rate minus LIBOR) (in percent) (1996)	0.31	0.35	0.35
Domestic credit provided by banks/GDP (in percent) (1996)	–0.04	–0.04	–0.04

(–0.08) and other private investment liabilities (–0.05) is relatively small. The level of trade and investment flows is affected by many factors other than exchange and capital controls, for example, the terms of trade or the relative rates of return. This may partly explain why some countries with relatively restrictive systems of exchange and capital controls could still attract large capital inflows and experience rapid trade growth. The statistical analysis, however, indicates that on average, more extensive exchange and capital controls are associated with lower levels of trade and investment.

Exchange and capital controls tend to be associated with low efficiency and depth of the financial sector, as evidenced by positive correlation coefficients of 0.27–0.28 between the indices and the intermediation spread (i.e., the difference between the lending and deposit rates), and negative correlation coefficients of 0.43–0.46 between the indices and the domestic credit provided by banks as a share of GDP. Exchange and capital controls are also typical in economies with a large spread between the deposit rate and London interbank offered rate (LIBOR) for U.S. dollars; the respective correlation coefficients are 0.38–0.40. One possible interpretation of the result is that exchange and capital controls tend to discourage capital inflows and are associated with higher nominal interest rates due to larger interest payments on government debt or higher inflation, or both.

The extent of exchange and capital controls is positively related to the size of the parallel, black, or free market premium, as compared with official or interbank market exchange rate (correlation coefficients range from 0.46 to 0.53). Information on the black market premium is not always reliable. Nevertheless, the black market premium often indicates the circumvention of restrictive exchange regulations. The relatively high correlation between the size of the

Table 37. Data and Sources for Correlation Analysis

Data	Period	Source
Purchasing-power-parity-adjusted GNP per capita (in U.S. dollars)	1995	World Bank, 1997, *World Development Indicators* (Oxford University Press for The World Bank)
Exports (in million U.S. dollars) Imports (in million U.S. dollars)	1996	International Monetary Fund, 1996, *Direction of Trade Statistics Yearbook* (Washington: International Monetary Fund)
Exports plus imports as a ratio to GDP (in percent)	1996	Calculated on the basis of International Monetary Fund, 1996, *Balance of Payments Statistics* (Washington: International Monetary Fund)
Mean tariff rate (in percent)	1990–93	World Bank, 1997, *World Development Indicators* (Oxford University Press for The World Bank)
Percentage of tariff lines covered by nontariff barriers (in percent)[1]	1990–93	World Bank, 1997, *World Development Indicators* (Oxford University Press for The World Bank)
Domestic credit provided by banks/GDP (in percent)	1996	Calculated on the basis of International Monetary Fund, 1996, *International Financial Statistics Yearbook* (Washington: International Monetary Fund)
Intermediation spread (lending minus deposit rate) (in percent)	1996	Calculated on the basis of International Monetary Fund, 1996, *International Financial Statistics Yearbook* (Washington: International Monetary Fund)
Spread over London Interbank Organization (LIBOR) (deposit rate minus LIBOR) (in percent)	1996	Calculated on the basis of International Monetary Fund, 1996, *International Financial Statistics Yearbook* (Washington: International Monetary Fund)
Parallel, black, or free (c.f. official or interbank market exchange rate) market premium (in percent)	1996	Calculated on the basis of International Monetary Fund, 1996, *International Financial Statistics Yearbook* (Washington: International Monetary Fund) and the *Global Currency Report* (Currency Data and Intelligence, Inc.) (various issues)
Average monthly percentage change in the U.S. dollar exchange rate (in percent)	1996	Calculated on the basis of International Monetary Fund, 1996, *International Financial Statistics Yearbook* (Washington: International Monetary Fund)
Direct, portfolio, and other investment (in million of U.S. dollars)	1995	International Monetary Fund, 1996, *International Financial Statistics Yearbook* (Washington: International Monetary Fund)
Direct foreign investment/GDP (in percent) Portfolio investment/GDP (in percent) Other investment/GDP (in percent)	1995	Calculated on the basis of International Monetary Fund, 1996, *International Financial Statistics Yearbook* (Washington: International Monetary Fund)

[1]Nontariff barriers here cover mostly licensing schemes, quotas, prohibitions, and export restraint arrangements.

black market premium and the indices would confirm this.

The indices are positively related to volatility in exchange rates (correlation coefficients of 0.37–0.49). One interpretation may be that countries with more volatile exchange rates have more incentives to introduce exchange and capital controls. In practice, the success of exchange and capital controls in stabilizing the exchange rate is likely to be limited, particularly in the medium term, because of imperfect enforcement, avoidance, and evasion. Thus, another interpretation is that volatility in exchange rates and reliance on exchange and capital controls are both evidence of poor economic performance and structural weakness in the economy and financial system.

Sensitivity Analysis

Sensitivity analysis examines robustness of the indices to various factors. This analysis indicates that the results are robust with respect to the intensity (severity) of controls and are not seriously affected by different treatment of such measures as international security restrictions, controls on inward and outward direct foreign investment, controls on liquidation of foreign direct investment, and provisions specific to commercial banks and other credit institutions. The indices are also robust to alternative assumptions about missing data.

Intensity of Controls

Welfare effects of different exchange and capital controls tend to vary. For example, price-based measures are likely to be less restrictive than quantity-based measures, and an outright prohibition is likely to be more distortionary than a bona fide test. To assess the significance of various types of measures for the indices, the individual types of control were classified into three groups—mildly restrictive, restrictive, and highly restrictive—on the basis of a survey of ten IMF staff experts on exchange systems. To minimize subjectivity, the survey was organized ac-

Figure 12. Controls on Current Payments and Transfers and Capital Movements

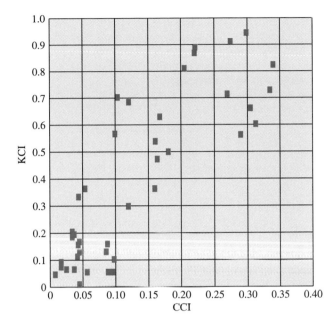

Figure 13. Exchange and Capital Controls and GNP Per Capita

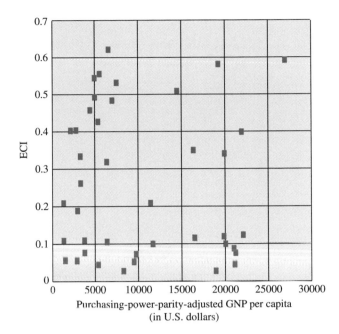

cording to the conventional Delphi method. This method was developed in 1948 to deal with communication distortions typically found in groups: inter alia, domination of the group by one or several individuals, pressures to conform to peer group opinion, and so on. During the survey, the anonymity of experts should be preserved. Individual expert judgments from the first round are aggregated in the form of summary statistical measures and comments and are communicated back to the participants during the second round, thus allowing for feedback, social learning, and modification of prior judgments. The objective of the subsequent rounds is to develop a consensus among experts.

In the first round, experts classified exchange and capital controls by their intensity, assuming perfect enforcement and effectiveness of exchange and capital controls. The qualitative judgments were converted into quantitative measures of intensity: intensity was set equal to ⅓ wherever the measure was classified as mildly restrictive, ⅔ as restrictive, and 1 as highly restrictive. The indices were calculated as an arithmetic weighted mean of the intensity measures and dummy variables reflecting the presence of individual types of control.

Aggregated results of the first round and index estimates were communicated to experts in the second round of the survey. Experts had an option of modifying their earlier judgments and were requested to check whether index estimates complied with their

knowledge of the exchange systems in the selected countries. The final round of the survey led to a reasonable consensus among experts' judgments. Consensus was defined as the mean estimate, mean plus the standard deviation, and mean minus the standard deviation corresponding to the same class of intensity. Consensus did not emerge for the following 5 out of 142 measures: international security restrictions in accordance with UN sanctions, prohibition of foreign exchange accounts, barter agreements and open accounts, open foreign exchange position limits, and the purchase of money market instruments in the country by nonresidents. Because consensus was reached for about 97 percent of individual types of control, the number of the survey rounds was limited to two, and mean estimates of intensity were used in the sensitivity analysis for all types of control.

A comparison of these indices with ones calculated without intensity measures demonstrates their robustness with respect to intensity (the Spearman's rank correlation coefficients are above 0.95). Thus, even without allowing explicitly for the intensity of the measures, the indices tend to reflect the intensity of exchange controls. This is because the indices aggregate information about exchange and capital controls in a hierarchical way—from individual controls to categories to indices—and are based on *AREAER*'s classification, which already implicitly incorporates information about the intensity of exchange and capital controls in the classification.

Figure 14. Exchange and Capital Controls and Tariff Barriers

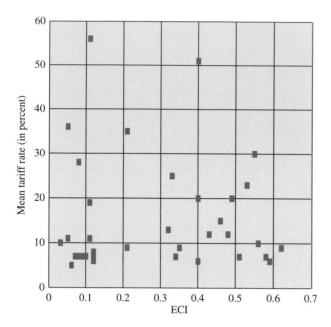

The indices were also recalculated excluding controls on international security restrictions, controls on direct foreign investment, and controls on commercial banks and other credit institutions, to examine whether the indices are sensitive to controls for national interest or prudential reasons, or both. Sensitivity analysis demonstrates robustness of results with respect to the above-mentioned changes in the indices' structure (the Spearman's rank correlation is above 0.95). The above measures are included in the structure of the baseline indices for completeness, since the indices focus on exchange and capital controls in general, that is, independently of the motivation for controls.

Conclusion

The study presents aggregate indices of controls on current payments and transfers and capital movements. The indices reflect the incidence of 142 individual types of exchange and capital control, as classified in the IMF's 1997 *Annual Report on Exchange Arrangements and Exchange Restrictions*. In a cross-country sample of 41 countries, capital controls are found to be more prevalent on average and to have a higher cross-country variation than controls on current payments and transfers. More extensive exchange and capital controls are associated with larger parallel, black, or free market premium; more volatile exchange rate, higher trade barriers, and more inefficient financial sector. Negative correlation is found with the level of economic development, and trade and investment flows measured in absolute terms and as a ratio to GDP. The indices are robust to weighting by the intensity of controls and certain changes in specification.

VIII

Recent Technical Assistance on Exchange Systems, 1994–97

This section reviews the IMF's recent technical assistance on exchange systems and the main elements emphasized during such assistance.

Main Focus of Recent Technical Assistance

Fifty-four countries received IMF technical assistance missions on exchange systems during 1994–97 (see the appendix to this section). The geographical allocation of the recipient countries is as follows: 13 each in European II Department and African Department, 9 in Asia and Pacific Department, 8 in Middle Eastern Department, 6 in Western Hemisphere Department, and 5 in European I Department. Of these, 25 were using IMF resources, and in 19 cases the programs included conditionality on the reform of the exchange system (see Table 38). In a number of cases, including Cambodia, Liberia, Madagascar, Rwanda, Sudan, Tajikistan, Turkmenistan, and Uzbekistan, technical assistance on the exchange system was a critical component of broader efforts to prepare the ground for the programs of macroeconomic adjustment and structural reform, and to pave the way for the recipients to enter into IMF arrangements.

Technical assistance on exchange systems has focused on three main areas: (1) assisting member countries to liberalize their regulatory framework, including for acceptance of the obligations of Article VIII, Sections 2, 3, and 4 of the IMF's Articles of Agreement, and for the liberalization of capital account transactions; (2) developing the interbank foreign exchange market; and (3) strengthening central bank's reserve management.

In providing technical assistance, the IMF draws on the experience of its staff, central banks, and foreign exchange market participants. In the case of the countries of the Baltics, Russia, and the other countries of the former Soviet Union (BRO), 23 central banks have been cooperating with the IMF in an intensive multilateral program for providing technical assistance. In the area of foreign exchange systems, this has focused on establishing the institutional setup for an efficient market-based allocation of foreign exchange; payment

and transfers for current account transactions; unification of exchange rates; capital account liberalization; foreign exchange reserve management; and central bank organization and operations. The cooperating central banks are those of Australia, Austria, Belgium, Canada, Denmark, Finland, France, Germany, Iceland, Ireland, Israel, Italy, Japan, the Netherlands, New Zealand, Norway, Portugal, Spain, Sweden, Switzerland, Turkey, the United Kingdom, and the United States. Progress in reforms on the exchange system was reviewed in central bank reforms in the Baltics, Russia, and other countries of the former Soviet Union,[73] and in the report prepared for the Eleventh Coordination Meeting of Cooperating Central Banks and International Institutions (Basle, Switzerland, May 1998). A number of other central banks have provided assistance to other countries and regions. For example, Tunisia assisted Rwanda in establishing a market-based system; Korea and Chile assisted China on capital account liberalization; the Czech Republic assisted several BRO countries, and Ghana assisted Ethiopia and Malawi in foreign exchange market development.

Liberalization of the Regulatory Framework

Technical assistance has assisted with reviewing and reforming regulatory framework for current international transactions and capital movements.

Assistance in Acceptance of the Obligations of Article VIII, Sections 2, 3, and 4

Substantial assistance was provided in assisting member countries to accept the obligations of Article VIII. Twenty-six countries receiving IMF technical assistance accepted the obligations of Article VIII, Sections 2, 3, and 4 during the period, including Algeria, Armenia, China, Croatia, Georgia, India, Kazakhstan, the Kyrgyz Republic, Kenya, Latvia, Lithuania, Madagascar, Malawi, Malta, Moldova, Mongolia, Pakistan, Paraguay, Poland, Russia, Slovenia, Sri Lanka, Tanzania, Uganda, Ukraine, and the

---

Note: This section was prepared mainly by Bernard Laurens.

[73]Knight and others (1997).

Table 38. Conditionality in IMF Programs and Technical Assistance in Exchange System, 1994–97[1]

Country	Measures
Algeria	*Regulatory framework:* Adopt obligations of Article VIII. Delegate to authorized dealers specific transactions. *Market development:* Establishment of exchange bureaus. Introduction of interbank foreign exchange market, with the commercial banks as authorized intermediaries.
Armenia	*Regulatory framework:* Eliminate multiple currency practices and restrictions arising from correspondent accounts with central banks of the Commonwealth of Independent States. Review and revise existing foreign investment law. *Market development:* Central bank to withdraw from regular participation in foreign exchange market. Set official rate based on market rate of previous day.
Azerbaijan	*Regulatory framework:* Remove all quotas or licensing requirements for imports and exports. Eliminate current account restrictions. Allow nonresidents to participate in treasury bill market. *Market development:* Allow interbank trading in foreign exchange for all banks, and foreign banks to participate in the Azerbaijan National Bank credit auctions market. Increase frequency of foreign exchange auctions.
Ethiopia	*Regulatory framework:* Eliminate negative list at foreign exchange auction; reduce surrender requirements. *Market development:* Allow opening of exchange bureaus, permit commercial banks to bid in foreign exchange auctions on their own account, to hold resident foreign exchange deposits; increase frequency of auctions; eliminate the 25 percent cover requirement for auctions.
Georgia	*Regulatory framework:* Eliminate surrender requirement. *Market development:* Establish interbank credit auction. Widen scope of transactions on the Tbilisi Interbank Foreign Exchange (TICEX) to include noncash sales/purchases. Increase frequency of TICEX auctions. *Reserve management:* Centralize international reserves at the central bank.
Guyana	*Regulatory framework:* Phase out surrender requirement. Review the Exchange Control Act.
Kazakhstan	*Regulatory framework:* Remove remaining restrictions and accept obligations of IMF Article VIII status. *Market development:* Establish formal arrangements for interbank foreign exchange market, including code of conduct.
Madagascar	*Regulatory framework:* Accept obligations of Article VIII. Maintain floating exchange rate system. *Market development:* Authorize banks to lend in foreign currencies. Reduce minimum capital for exchange bureaus.
Malawi	*Regulatory framework:* Establish new limits on open positions. *Market development:* Introduce interbank foreign exchange market.
Mauritania	*Regulatory framework:* Eliminate surrender requirement for nonmineral export proceeds. Enforce limits on open positions. Unify exchange rate. Eliminate current account restrictions, and agree on calendar for moving to acceptance of Article VIII. *Market development:* Introduce interbank foreign exchange market. Allow establishment of exchange bureaus. Central bank to intervene in the interbank market.
Mongolia	*Regulatory framework:* Maintain unified exchange rate system. Introduce limits on open positions with daily reporting. *Market development:* Develop interbank money market, in line with bank restructuring, so that it can serve as a basis for setting of official exchange rate. Refrain from intervening in foreign exchange market except for smoothing operations.
Pakistan	*Market development:* Liberalize and develop interbank foreign exchange market to increase market determination of the exchange rate and promote the development of private forward cover.
Romania	*Regulatory framework:* Amend foreign investment law to facilitate foreign portfolio investment. *Market development:* Liberalize the foreign exchange market and ensure a market-determined exchange rate. Eliminate auction market and ensure reliance on fully fledged interbank foreign exchange market.
Russia	*Regulatory framework:* Maintain market-determined exchange rate.
Tanzania	*Market development:* Establish an interbank foreign exchange market.
Uganda	*Regulatory framework:* Facilitate liberalization of capital account. Improve monitoring and enforcement of foreign exchange exposure limits of commercial banks. Submit new Foreign Exchange Law to Parliament. *Market development:* Unify interbank foreign exchange market.
Ukraine	*Regulatory framework:* Eliminate restrictions inconsistent with Article VIII. Eliminate surrender requirement. *Market development:* Move to daily operations of the foreign exchange market. Allow all licensed banks to participate in the foreign exchange market.
Vietnam	*Regulatory framework:* Issue foreign exchange guidelines to commercial banks. Increase transparency of regulatory framework. *Market development:* Limit official intervention in foreign exchange market. Formalize interbank foreign exchange market with regulatory framework. *Reserve management:* Centralize international reserves at the central bank.
Yemen Republic	*Regulatory framework:* Unify exchange rate and adopt free floating regime. Eliminate multiple currency practices. *Market development:* Allow all commercial banks to participate in interbank foreign exchange market. Achieve full exchange market unification by moving all government and central bank transactions to the freely floating rate.

[1]Reference to the Acceptance of Article VIII means acceptance of the obligations of Article VIII, Sections 2, 3, and 4 of the IMF's Articles of Agreement.

Republic of Yemen.[74] In addition, assistance from headquarters in reviewing legislation was provided to the 13 member countries of the African CFA franc zone, which accepted the obligations of Article VIII, Sections 2, 3, and 4 on June 1, 1996.

Assistance in Capital Account Liberalization

The substantial progress achieved in current account convertibility encouraged increased emphasis on capital account liberalization. IMF advice is typically structured within the context of a broader program of macroeconomic adjustment and structural reform, especially financial regulatory reforms and operational procedures. For example, the liberalization of capital account transactions has been linked to the reform of the foreign exchange system (e.g., Bangladesh, Guyana, India, and the Republic of Yemen), to improvements in monetary control, including the introduction of indirect monetary policy instruments (e.g., Bangladesh, Fiji, Guyana, Russia, the Slovak Republic, and the Republic of Yemen), and to the strengthening of domestic financial systems and markets (e.g., Bangladesh, India, Russia, and the Slovak Republic).

Also, while stopping short of recommending full convertibility, the IMF staff noted in its assessment of India's regulatory framework that capital account liberalization would be important for the development of the interbank foreign exchange market, as banks' foreign exchange transactions were hampered by existing capital controls. In Bangladesh, the staff noted that it seemed to be relatively easy to circumvent existing capital controls through the unofficial market and suggested that capital account liberalization should be undertaken concurrent with the strengthening of indirect monetary controls. In the Slovak Republic, it was emphasized that there were no particular impediments preventing a relatively rapid pace of liberalization. In discussing the liberalization of China's exchange system, the staff emphasized the importance of anticipating the future liberalization of the capital account in preparing new foreign exchange legislation and of coordinating reforms with the strengthening of the banking sector, and the introduction of indirect monetary instruments. Initially, technical assistance to China had been directed at assisting the authorities in unifying its exchange rate (January 1994) and liberalizing current account transactions. China accepted the obligations of Article VIII, Sections 2, 3, and 4 in December 1996. In 1998, discussions focused on the development of the foreign ex-

change market and the orderly liberalization of the capital account. In Fiji, it was recommended that further capital account liberalization be viewed as an integral part of the authorities' overall economic reform program: liberalization of foreign direct investment should go hand in hand with reforms aimed at strengthening the real sector, and liberalization of portfolio flows should be coordinated with reforms in the domestic financial sector.

Interbank Foreign Exchange Market Development

With respect to interbank foreign exchange market development, official policies have been emphasized as having an important role in this process. In particular, the authorities need to eliminate barriers that may hinder foreign exchange dealings and exchange controls arising from official regulations and practices. Below, the core issues relating to the establishment of an interbank foreign exchange market are discussed (Box 8 lists the key institutional and operational reforms involved).

Exchange Control Laws and Regulations

To foster development of the interbank foreign exchange market, authorities need to identify and remove barriers that prohibit authorized dealers from providing foreign exchange to their customers. For example, dealers may not be allowed to maintain open foreign currency positions overnight. Foreign exchange receipts may have to be surrendered to the central bank. Foreign exchange transactions may have to be conducted through the central bank or exchange transactions at an official exchange rate. This restriction would have to be modified as part of the development of the foreign exchange market.

Furthermore, to be able to operate in the interbank exchange market, banks need to be able to deal in the international currency markets for the purpose of converting customers' demands for third currencies into the intervention currency, and vice versa. To engage in hedging forward operations banks should be able to borrow and lend, subject to prudential limits, both domestically and internationally. Where capital controls restrict this activity, forward transactions may be limited to matching purchases and sales of foreign exchange between customers, hindering the development of a liquid forward foreign exchange market. The experiences among IMF member countries show that it takes some time to develop a well-functioning forward market, partly because this requires a liquid and relatively free market for spot transactions and a functioning interbank market for domestic currency.

To ensure efficient foreign exchange allocation in the customer market, foreign exchange should be

---

[74]It is noteworthy that among the countries of the Baltics, Russia, and the other countries of the former Soviet Union, only five, Azerbaijan, Belarus, Tajikistan, Turkmenistan, and Uzbekistan, have not yet accepted the obligations of Article VIII, Sections 2, 3, and 4.

> ## Box 8. List of Key Institutional and Operational Reforms for Foreign Exchange Market Development
>
> Some of the key international and operational reforms in the development of a foreign exchange market are outlined below.
>
> Exchange System and Market Arrangements
>
> - Modify exchange control laws and regulations.
> - Delegate exchange control authority to the authorized dealers.
> - Establish a code of conduct.
> - Improve information technology to facilitate interbank dealings.
> - Use market exchange rates for all foreign exchange transactions.
> - Transfer all private transactions to the interbank market.
> - Facilitate the market-making role of authorized dealers.
> - Establish transparent criteria for licensing dealers.
> - Strengthen payments and clearing arrangements.
>
> Central Bank's Own Operations
>
> - Develop dealing and back-office arrangements.
> - Establish adequate internal controls for foreign exchange operations.
> - Streamline central bank's organization and operations.
> - Establish foreign exchange cash-flow projections.
> - Improve central bank's information technology.
> - Strengthen central bank's supervisory capacity.
> - Increase dialogue with the market and disseminate information.
> - Improve central bank's external reserve management operations.
>
> Supporting Measures
>
> - Introduce prudential guidelines for banks' currency exposure.
> - Establish reporting arrangements for authorized dealers.

ket forces in determining the allocation and pricing of foreign exchange in the market; regulations that apply to foreign exchange trading between dealers should not unduly limit dealers' operations in the interbank foreign exchange market and their access to exchange transactions at any exchange rate they quote. However, prudential controls may be imposed on dealer banks' foreign currency open positions to safeguard the soundness of the banking system.

In the interbank foreign exchange market, foreign exchange proceeds are sold directly to authorized dealers at freely negotiable exchange rates while the central bank typically acquires foreign exchange from the dealers. If capital controls are retained, the requirement to repatriate foreign exchange proceeds to the local interbank market is normally also retained, while the central bank could require that foreign exchange be surrendered to the interbank market (rather than to the central bank) or allow it to be retained in foreign currency accounts with local banks.

The IMF has also recommended that the provision of foreign exchange by the central bank directly to the nonbank private sector should be terminated and these transactions should be transferred to the interbank market; this will both enhance the transparency of foreign exchange allocation and improve liquidity in the interbank market.

Finally, the IMF has recommended that market-determined exchange rates should be used for all foreign currency transactions, including official transactions, so that distortions are avoided. In the case of a fixed exchange rate regime, a "market-determined" rate is one that clears the market, even if it is directly set by the authorities. In other words, a fixed rate is considered to be market-determined when the central bank absorbs excess market supply or demand through its own transactions, without recourse to rationing, and when such excesses sum to zero over some time horizon. All taxes and surcharges related to foreign currency transactions should be abolished. The central bank may, nevertheless, calculate a reference exchange rate based on a weighted average exchange rate of transactions in the interbank market, usually for customs and statistical valuation purposes.

freely available for various external transactions. Therefore, the IMF has emphasized that the introduction of interbank foreign exchange markets has often gone hand in hand with a move toward convertibility of the currency. This may necessitate that exchange control laws and regulations be liberalized, and that the authority to provide foreign exchange and verify the compliance with exchange controls, where these are still relevant, be delegated to authorized dealers.

When the interbank foreign exchange market is introduced, exchange controls and regulations guiding foreign exchange dealings in the market should be modified so that they do not impede the role of mar-

Buying and Selling Quotations

In the interbank foreign exchange market, dealers need to be free to establish their buying and selling exchange rates for transactions between themselves and with their customers. Brokerage fees and prices for customer services should be negotiated between dealers and their customers competitively. The IMF staff's recommendation has been that to foster competition, the spread between buying and selling exchange rates in the interbank market should not be limited. Maximum spreads—although nonbinding—often become a norm in the market, while free competition tends to drive the spreads down. Nevertheless, information about the spreads should be monitored by the central bank to help detect the emergence of noncompetitive behavior, as well as to potentially provide information about market sentiment and uncertainty. Publishing information about spreads would also help improve the transparency of the market.

Mutual Trust

An essential element that facilitates the smooth operation of an interbank foreign exchange market is the mutual trust among market participants. This forms the critical basis for interdealer transactions. To facilitate the building of trust, dealers would need to be able to evaluate the credit risks of their counterparties, based, for example, on published balance sheets and reports on profits and losses. In countries where lack of mutual trust is likely to hinder direct dealings between banks, an interbank fixing arrangement may facilitate interdealer transactions; however, participation in the fixing sessions should be optional, and no limits should be imposed on dealings taking place outside these fixings. Collateral could be introduced to safeguard against possible payments defaults.

In addition to counterparty risk, settlement risk due to inadequate clearing and payments systems can impede interdealer transactions. Improvements in the domestic payments and clearing systems would help eliminate the settlement risk due to insufficient funds in the local currency leg of the transaction.

Code of Conduct

To facilitate the development of an interbank market for foreign exchange, a code of conduct for foreign exchange trading should be adopted, which would be established as a form of self-regulation and would therefore need to be fully accepted by market participants. It would provide participants with a set of rules and guidelines that would govern their dealings in the interbank market, but it would also educate them on issues related to accepted trading practices, such as instruments and procedures that are typically used in foreign exchange dealings, and market terminology. The sample code of conduct provided by the Association Cambiste Internationale would be a basis to develop local codes.

Market Making

To enhance market liquidity, the IMF has advised that some dealers be permitted to assume the leading role in "making the market." The market-making process creates liquidity in the foreign exchange market as the dealers constantly adjust their portfolios on the basis of the flows of market orders and their expectations about the market, while competition forces

exchange rate quotations to converge to a narrow range.

Experience suggests that in emerging markets there may be significant obstacles that prevent the emergence of continuous two-way quotations, associated with instability in foreign exchange flows, lack of trust, inefficiencies in the payments systems, and lack of adequate communication technology and computer systems. In the early stages of market development, the number and the size of currency transactions in the interbank market may be limited. However, the experience also suggests that the initial problems are likely to dissipate as market reforms take hold and market participants become more comfortable in dealing among themselves.

In an emerging interbank foreign exchange market, the nature of the central bank's participation in the market may be critical since this can both facilitate market making and provide liquidity to the market. The IMF staff has recommended that the central bank should avoid undermining the market-making role of banks by exchange control regulations or by providing services that can and should be provided by market participants. However, it could encourage the banks to become market makers by limiting its dealings to banks that provide firm two-way quotations for a set minimum amount; it can also assist by undertaking transactions through broader market operations (where there can be some variations in prices, even under a fixed or pegged regime), as opposed to an on-demand window for individual banks. Such methods can have a strong enforcement effect, particularly when transactions with the central bank are significant. The IMF has also sometimes recommended that a requirement to provide two-way quotations be imposed as part of the licensing process.

Concerning technological requirements for establishing and operating the interbank foreign exchange market, these need not be extensive. If a functioning telephone network exists and dealers have access to telex or fax machines, then it is possible to conduct interbank dealings. Sometimes it is feasible to establish a computer network linking authorized dealers together in the market; this network system may be used as a bulletin board to give information about bids and offers to other dealers while trading is still conducted by phone.

Payment and Communication Systems

In view of the critical importance of effective domestic payments and clearing systems to allow for smooth operation of the interbank foreign exchange market, an adequate domestic payments system is an essential element of a functioning interbank market arrangement. In the early stages of market development a separate clearing facility for the domestic leg of the transactions may be required.

To ensure the dissemination of information—an essential element for efficient pricing of foreign exchange—a suitable information network is needed. While actual dealings may be conducted via telephone lines and confirmed through secured telex or other arrangements (such as SWIFT),[75] bids and offers can be provided via a computer system where information is displayed on screens accessed by dealers. In addition, such an information system will effectively spread information on exchange rate quotations and enhance competition between the dealers in the market.

Market Participants

To enhance market liquidity and competitions, the IMF has recommended licensing a wide range of authorized dealers to trade in the interbank foreign exchange market, including additional banks, domestic and foreign, as well as entities other than deposit-taking banks, such as merchant banks and nonbank dealers. Also, allowing the participation of exchange bureaus has been advocated in countries where collusion between banks has led to nonmarket pricing or allocation of foreign exchange.

Role of the Central Bank

As already noted, when the central bank participates in the interbank foreign exchange market, it should not become a market maker. To avoid doing so, it can buy and sell foreign currency at its own discretion by contacting one or more market participants, usually banks, and requesting firm buying and selling quotations for amounts of foreign exchange that it is willing to deal. This does not mean the central bank should deal with large numbers of banks in countries where there are many of them. For greater effectiveness, it may be preferable to limit the number of institutions with which the central bank has transactions. These banks would assume "primary dealer" status and become agents of the central bank in intervening in the foreign exchange market. Brokers may also be used for interventions. These transactions are then effected at rates agreed by the central bank and the participating dealer(s). These same principles should be applied whether the central bank transacts in the foreign exchange market on its own behalf, for example, to accumulate foreign exchange reserves, as an intervention in the market in accordance with exchange rate policy objectives, or on behalf of a customer, normally the government. The central bank should cease all other commercial activities.

The central bank should also discontinue the provision of exchange rate guarantees, and in particular forward cover. The role of the central bank in this area should be one of assisting indirectly in the development of a forward interbank market by helping to educate market participants, through seminars and the like, about the technology associated with forward market trading and especially about management of the risks involved. It may also have a role in developing appropriate information technology.

Dealers in the interbank foreign exchange market must learn how to manage their foreign currency positions and ensure that their end-of-day open positions conform with prudential standards. In principle, the central bank should not participate in settling the excess end-of-day balances of dealer banks; sometimes, however, it may need to use its discretion to support the market when sales or purchases of foreign exchange by commercial banks make it difficult for the banks to comply with the prudential open position limits, or could result in sharp exchange rate fluctuations. Experience suggests that the need for such intervention may decrease as the regulatory framework for exchange transactions is liberalized.

More important, intervention policy must have a clearly defined goal, whether to maintain a fixed exchange rate or to smooth out short-run exchange rate fluctuations in a more flexible regime. Otherwise, the central bank's interventions can confuse and destabilize the market. In any event, interventions by the central bank are likely to have a major impact on the emerging interbank market; therefore, the interventions should not be used to undermine the market's role in pricing foreign exchange. An assessment of daily foreign exchange cash flows can be helpful in indicating the likely volume of central bank intervention that may be needed, or alternatively the movement that may be needed in the exchange rate.

The central bank's own dealing operations should be properly organized. In particular a clear separation between the back-office and front-office functions is needed. Also, the central bank's top management should provide written guidelines to its dealers to control risks involved in foreign exchange dealings. These guidelines should, at a minimum, include the list of traded currencies and the counterparties with whom the central bank dealers are allowed to deal, and the procedures for reporting and recording executed transactions; the responsibilities of dealers, what they can do and to whom they must report daily, monthly, or periodically; authorized dealing limits; the amounts above which approval of the senior management is required; and the procedures for proper internal supervision.

It is important for the central bank to maintain a continuous dialogue with the market through its trading desk. This would include contacts between the central bank and the dealers in the interbank market,

---

[75]SWIFT is a nonprofit, cooperative organization that facilitates the exchange of payment messages between financial institutions worldwide; it is not a payment system.

Box 9. Decision-Making Hierarchy in Reserve Management

This box lists the main elements in a decision-making hierarchy for international reserve management.

Level of Decision: Governor, Board of Directors

- Defines overall objectives and principles of reserve management.
- Approves principles of currency distribution.
- Approves optimal currency distribution, range of permissible deviation.
- Approves benchmark portfolio durations, permissible range of deviation.
- Approves principles for assets selection.
- Approves principles for managing credit exposure and for establishing limits for banks.
- Sets maximum limit on credit exposure of total reserves.
- Defines nature of liquidity requirement.
- Reviews (annually) reserve management performance.

Level of Decision: Investment Committee

- Defines investment strategy to be pursued within framework determined by board's decision.
- Sets operational guidelines for managing currency exposure.
- Approves principles for determining composition and maintenance of benchmarks.
- Reviews bank limits and credit exposure regularly (semiannually, quarterly).

- Approves dealing counterparties.
- Sets limits for individual bank counterparties, approves increases in limits, approves new bank counterparties.
- Defines and approves assets categories.
- Approves custodian agreements and arrangements.
- Approves other needed contracts and agreements.
- Evaluates liquidity of assets.
- Reviews investment performance (monthly).

Level of Decision: Manager, Reserve Management Unit

- Decides on operational strategy to be followed.
- Responsible for monitoring and reporting on observance of all risk limits.
- Approves individual securities within framework of approved asset categories.
- Responsible for maintaining liquidity of assets.

Level of Decision: Chief Dealer/Dealers

- Responsible for ensuring that dealing takes place within approved framework and with accepted counterparties.
- Make individual investment decisions in line with approved investment strategy.
- Responsible for ensuring that all information needed for settlement of deals is made available to settlement/back office unit.

---

regular meetings between the senior representatives of the central bank and market participants, and so on. The aim would be to prevent any misunderstandings about economic policies that could result in increased uncertainty, and thus volatility of the exchange rate, and to increase market transparency.

Foreign Exchange Risk Regulations

In the area of foreign exchange risk regulations, controlling these risks is the primary responsibility of the management of each bank. The management must identify the types and the amounts of unhedged risks it is willing to assume and put in place appropriate procedures for monitoring individual risk exposures and for detecting any deficiencies in compliance with management's directives. The role of the supervisory authority is to assess the adequacy of the internal procedures set up by banks, while establishing uniform minimum standards to monitor the banks' risk taking. While banks should be allowed to maintain adequate foreign exchange reserves—otherwise the interbank market may not develop—prudential limits on banks' foreign exchange positions are intended to contain banks' risk taking in foreign currencies, not to limit their activities in the interbank market.

To enable the supervisory authority to monitor banks' risk taking and enforce compliance with the established prudential limits, the IMF has recommended implementing the prudential regulations put forward by the Basle Committee of Banking Supervision. These include reporting arrangements to the central bank and limits on the ratio of the net open position to the bank's capital base.

Reserve Management

In a number of countries, assistance was provided to help central banks strengthen their reserve management. It is the task of the top management of the central bank to define the overall objectives and principles of reserve management. On the basis of these guidelines, an Investment Committee may be established to define the investment strategy, and the manager of the reserve management unit would decide on the operational investment strategy, to be followed. Box 9 summarizes a model decision-making hierarchy in reserve management for a central bank.

No investment alternative is available to the central bank that would simultaneously negate all types of risks to which it is exposed to (i.e., liquidity risk, credit risk, and market risk). Thus, the central bank has to determine the appropriate trade-offs between the different types of risks, reflecting the central bank's relative aversion to them. However, as a matter of principle, the IMF staff has advised against investing the international reserves with domestic banks and emphasized that the central bank should not play a lender-of-last-resort role in foreign exchange. Reserves should be invested in marketable government securities or short-term deposit accounts with overseas central banks and, sometimes, the most creditworthy commercial banks.

Concerning the organization of the reserve management function, a clear separation between front office (those who deal) and back office (those who make and authorize settlements on the basis of the deals) is needed. The division would minimize fraudulent collusion to embezzle funds. No transaction type or instrument should be approved for investment purposes unless the back office can handle the settlement and accounting for it.

Appendix. Main Instances of Technical Assistance on Exchange Systems, 1994–97

The table below provides a summary of technical assistance presented by the IMF to its members in the period 1994–97.

Appendix. Main Instances of Technical Assistance on Exchange Systems, 1994–97

Country	Summary of Technical Assistance
Algeria	Follow-up assistance to implement a comprehensive reform of the foreign exchange system, including a floating rate regime in the context of an interbank market and liberal exchange system. Technical assistance was also provided to strengthen the intervention policy of the central bank. Algeria is using IMF resources.
Armenia	Follow-up assistance to further develop the foreign exchange interbank market, the capacity of the central bank to intervene in the market, and to coordinate intervention with monetary operations. Interbank trading is expanding while the role of the foreign exchange auctions is decreasing. Assistance in reserve management and internal controls. Armenia is using IMF resources.
Azerbaijan	Follow-up assistance to further develop foreign exchange auctions and introduce an interbank foreign exchange market; enhanced coordination of monetary and foreign exchange operations; reserve management; and liberalization of exchange system. Azerbaijan is using IMF resources.
Bangladesh	Visit of a short-term expert to advise on the establishment of a foreign exchange dealing room; also remaining foreign exchange restrictions were reviewed in view of acceptance of Article VIII on April 11, 1994.
Bolivia	Design of a plan to phase out surrender requirements; review of intervention policy and procedures, including a phasing out of current auction arrangement. Bolivia is using IMF resources.
Cambodia	Mission and long-term expert to develop a comprehensive reform program to enhance effectiveness of the foreign exchange market, including auctions of foreign exchange, and develop expertise at the central bank.
Cape Verde	Advice to reform the foreign exchange regime and move toward current account convertibility.
China	Follow-up assistance to unify the exchange rate, achieve current account convertibility, develop an interbank foreign exchange market, strengthen payment and settlement systems, and better coordinate monetary and foreign exchange operations. Discussions on the liberalization of the capital account have already started. The exchange rate was unified in January 1994.
Croatia	Assistance on foreign exchange market development, strengthen reserves management, enhance coordination of monetary and exchange policies. Croatia is using IMF resources.
Dominican Republic	Review operations of the foreign exchange market and advise on coordination of intervention with monetary operations.
Ethiopia	Assistance in foreign exchange market development (unification of the auction market and official exchange rate; establishment of foreign exchange bureaus; liberalization of restrictions on payments for invisible transactions; reduction of surrender requirement; and establishment of limits to open foreign exchange positions for commercial banks). Ethiopia used IMF resources (the first annual enhanced structural adjustment facility (ESAF) arrangement under a three-year ESAF lapsed in October 1997 without completion of the midterm review).
Fiji	Review appropriateness of Fiji's exchange rate arrangement and discuss possible alternatives; assess scope for further easing of capital controls.
Gambia, The	Review foreign exchange market and operations and advise to enhance market liquidity.
Georgia	Follow-up assistance for coordination of monetary and exchange policies, improve the operations of the foreign exchange auctions, strengthen reserves management. Georgia is using IMF resources.
Guatemala	Review of regulatory framework for foreign exchange operations and implications for supervisory oversight.
Guyana	Review progress in foreign exchange market development; design strategy for intervention in the interbank market; review remaining exchange controls on capital transactions. Guyana is using IMF resources.
Honduras	Review foreign exchange market and central bank intervention, including coordination between intervention and monetary operations.

Appendix (*continued*)

Country	Summary of Technical Assistance
India	Review foreign exchange market operations, intervention policy, and regulatory framework for capital account transactions.
Iran, Islamic Republic of	Review reserve management policy in view of enhancing market risk monitoring, strengthen internal controls, and propose guidelines for investments.
Kazakhstan	Follow-up assistance for interbank foreign exchange market development; enhance intervention policy; coordinate monetary and exchange operations; strengthen reserves management. Kazakhstan is using IMF resources.
Kenya	Advise on coordination of monetary and foreign operations, to increase reliance on indirect monetary policy instruments. Kenya is using IMF resources.
Kyrgyz Republic	Follow-up assistance to further develop interbank foreign exchange market; enhance intervention capacity; coordinate monetary and foreign exchange operations; strengthen reserves management. The capital account is also free of restrictions. The Kyrgyz Republic is using IMF resources.
Latvia	Review foreign exchange market and operations, reserves management policy and operations. The capital account is free of restrictions.
Lesotho	Broad efforts to develop foreign exchange market and enhance reserves management (benchmark portfolio).
Liberia	Comprehensive reform of the foreign exchange system, including unification of exchange rate, phasing out exchange controls, developing foreign exchange market, and enhancing intervention policy.
Lithuania	Review foreign exchange system, design exit strategy in view of integration into the European Union. The capital account is free of restrictions.
Madagascar	Review interbank foreign exchange market, advise on intervention policy and coordination of monetary and foreign exchange operations.
Malawi	Follow-up assistance to develop interbank foreign exchange market, exchange bureaus, review restrictions on current account transactions. Malawi is using IMF resources.
Maldives	Review foreign exchange operations, trading band for authorized dealers, introduce limits on open position, establish dealers' association, strengthen reserves management, establish dealing room at the central bank.
Malta	Review development of interbank foreign exchange market, widen trading band for authorized dealers, liberalize forward market, establish limits on open positions, adopt code of conduct for foreign exchange market.
Mauritania	Follow-up assistance to further liberalize current account transactions, develop interbank foreign exchange market, introduce exchange bureaus, limit open position for authorized dealers, develop intervention capacity in the market, establish code of conduct for authorized dealers. Mauritania is using IMF resources.
Moldova	Follow-up assistance to develop interbank foreign exchange market, intervention capacity in the market, strengthen reserves management and internal controls. Moldova is using IMF resources.
Mongolia	Follow-up assistance to enhance interbank foreign exchange market, intervention capacity in the market, strengthen reserves management, and liberalize current account transactions. Mongolia is using IMF resources.
Oman	Review current exchange system with the view of assessing the pros and cons of a peg to a single currency versus a peg to a basket of currencies.
Pakistan	Review foreign exchange operations in view of designing a strategy to reduce Pakistan's reliance on short-term capital inflows and enhancing market determination of the exchange rate in the context of a gradual liberalization of exchange controls. Pakistan is using IMF resources.
Paraguay	Review of foreign exchange reserves management (enhance risks controls, internal controls including a separation of front office and back office).
Poland	Review exchange arrangements, recommendations to the effect of introducing crawling peg arrangement. Also review of restrictions on current account transactions.
Romania	Follow-up assistance to enhance the foreign interbank market, establish exchange bureaus, enhance coordination of intervention with monetary operations. Romania is using IMF resources.
Russia	Follow-up assistance to enhance the interbank foreign exchange market, and develop intervention in the interbank market. Review of restrictions on current account transactions. Russia is using IMF resources.
Rwanda	Comprehensive reform of foreign exchange system: establish interbank foreign exchange market, develop intervention capacity in the market, establish exchange bureaus, establish limits on open positions, coordinate intervention and monetary operations, and liberalize current account transactions.
São Tomé and Príncipe	Short-term expert assisted the authorities in improving monitoring and supervision of authorized dealers and formulating policies and regulations to strengthen the foreign exchange market and unify the exchange rate.
Slovenia	Broad effort to strengthen foreign exchange system with the view of developing the interbank foreign exchange market, developing intervention policy supportive of market development.
Sri Lanka	Review of strategy for achieving capital account convertibility, including enhancing coordination of monetary and exchange policies.
Sudan	Comprehensive reform of foreign exchange system and development of a strategy to unify the exchange rate, reform intervention policy, develop limits to open positions for authorized dealers, and liberalize current account.

Appendix (*concluded*)

Country	Summary of Technical Assistance
Tajikistan	Follow-up assistance to improve operations of foreign exchange auction, and enhance reserve management.
Tanzania	Review foreign exchange market reform, reserve management, and payment systems issues, including clarification of the role of exchange bureaus, and strengthening intervention policy in the interbank market. Tanzania is using IMF resources.
Turkmenistan	Follow-up assistance to further liberalize current account transactions, unify the exchange rate, improve the operations of auction mechanism, reduce surrender requirements, centralize reserve management and strengthen internal controls at the central bank, and establish limits on open position for authorized dealers.
Uganda	Follow-up assistance to design a strategy for moving to full convertibilty. Uganda is using IMF resources
Ukraine	Follow-up assistance to develop interbank foreign exchange market; remove remaining restrictions on current account transactions. Ukraine is using IMF resources
Uzbekistan	Follow-up assistance to amend current regulations with a view to liberalizing the current exchange regime, unifying the exchange rate, and paving the way for acceptance of Article VIII. Also strengthen reserve management, including centralization of international reserves at the central bank.
Vietnam	Comprehensive reform of foreign exchange system to establish an interbank foreign exchange market within the context of managed floating, liberalize current account transactions in view of acceptance of Article VIII, and enhance reserves management at the central bank. Vietnam is using IMF resources.
West Bank and Gaza	Develop the capacity of the Monetary Authority to implement a sound reserves management policy.
Yemen, Republic of	Comprehensive reform of foreign exchange system to establish an interbank foreign exchange market, develop intervention capacity in the market, establish exchange bureaus, establish limits on open positions by authorized dealers, coordinate intervention and monetary operations, and liberalize current account transactions. Yemen is using IMF resources.
Zambia	Review foreign exchange system with a view to strengthening the interbank foreign exchange market and intervention capacity in the market, and remove multiple currency practices. Zambia is using IMF resources.

IX

An Operational View of the Foreign Exchange Market

This section discusses the characteristics and typical practices of the foreign exchange market and the interactions with regulatory or market-based policy interventions. Written from an operational perspective, it explains something of the pressures that motivate a dealer when buying and selling currency and relates these to the conceptual issues that lie at the core of questions about the appropriate role of public policy in the foreign exchange market. The main focus is on reasonably advanced foreign currency markets, and especially on the role of banks as dealers and market-makers in the interbank market, as the center of the currency markets in general. Nevertheless, the principles not only apply to industrial countries but also to a fairly wide range of emerging market economies.

The second part of the section provides background on the structure of the market and its constituent parts and considers the environment in which dealing takes place and the effect this has on dealing decisions. The third part deals with the management of exchange transactions and markets. It discusses what is needed for an effective interbank market and what a central bank can do to help bring this about, examining, in particular, the nature of market making, pricing behavior, arbitrage and speculation, and profit seeking or loss avoidance. A concluding section links the preceding discussion to models of exchange market behavior.

Market Structure and Trends

The Agents

Although this section mainly concerns banks and the role they play in the wholesale foreign exchange markets, it is necessary to see how their role relates to that of other actors in the foreign currency markets. The major market participants may be conveniently grouped as follows:

First are the commercial and investment banks that make up the interbank market at the core of the currency exchange system. Some banks elect to make markets—that is, they quote firm bid and offer rates at which they stand ready to deal, in either direction, in all but the most severe market conditions. Other banks confine themselves to servicing customer needs. They account for the largest share of market turnover by far and perform a vital economic function of mediating currency flows. Most take positions at one time or another, and to one degree or another, on future exchange rates. Indeed, taking a view on likely future exchange rates is an inseparable aspect of the market-making role. As such, banks normally have to be willing to accept a significant amount of currency risk but must also be able to manage that risk or find ways of laying it off substantially. The net position banks take, at least beyond very short-term (within a day) time frames, are typically limited by either internal controls or supervisory requirements linked to their capital.

Second are the central banks. Aside from servicing the exchange requirements of government and sometimes other central banks, they generally do not provide market-making services, in more advanced markets at least. Charged with the broader responsibility to maintain reasonable market order, they may stand ready, as a residual supplier of domestic or local currency, to ensure that the foreign exchange market clears at a given exchange rate (depending on the exchange regime), but they are most conspicuous in the market when intervening to manage the exchange rate to absorb market pressures, when these are judged to be excessive. Central banks generally restrict dealing to the local market (reserves management transactions aside). Although at times they may deal overseas, or through nonbanks (e.g., when wishing to conceal their hand), active speculation by central banks on exchange rates is rare and frowned on by the central banking community, as it would involve taking a position against other central banks.

Third are large corporations, including transnational enterprises. They account for the largest *net* flow of funds across the exchanges and therefore have the greatest overall impact on currency values. Moreover, when they alter their hedging policy, accelerating or delaying cover for example, the market disturbance that can be caused is significant. Transnationals and other large corporations generally have little appetite for currency risk and creating exposures for the sole purpose of active speculation (as opposed to hedging) would be unusual for them.

Note: This section was prepared mainly by David Mitchem and Mark Swinburne.

107

Fourth are the derivative dealers, including the derivatives desks of banks. Although controlling relatively small business volumes, they can cause major, if short term, currency unrest when hedging positions in the cash markets. This is especially so when computer programs signal that an option book should be hedged in the cash markets, after the spot rate moves through a strike price. Most derivative dealing is based on arbitrage, where risk in one part of the market is hedged elsewhere. Although futures are used more widely now as a tool for speculation, a derivative dealer's appetite for open risk is generally modest.

The last category of agents is the nonbank financial institutions, including fund managers and the currency hedge funds. To the extent that they invest in longer-term analysis and forecasting, they may be among the first to see upcoming currency pressures and realignments, which they can be quick to hedge against or exploit with large deals that may be temporarily destabilizing. This characterization is often seen to apply to the currency hedge funds, in particular, who can take exchange rate bets of a medium- to longer-term duration, especially in the forward or derivative markets. They are seldom tempted to trade positions but rather retain them, once opened, until an objective is realized or until the decision is taken to cut them. Apart from the high-risk appetite of the currency hedge funds, the interest of other financial institutions tends to be tied to the protection of underlying investment portfolios. As the recent IMF study of hedge funds concluded, however, these organizations are not always "first," nor are their expectations always accurate, let alone "self-fulfilling."[76] The study noted that, while fairly prominent, hedge funds were not conspicuously ahead of other important market players in Thailand's recent currency crisis; that, if anything, they may have lagged behind other players in the speculation against other Asian currencies; and that while they earned their reputation to a large extent in the attacks on EMS currencies in 1992, they appear to have been caught largely unaware by the international bond market turbulence in 1994. Moreover, individual hedge fund deals may be large because of leverage possibilities and may cause market disturbance, as they can often obtain leverage of up to 20 times on an overnight basis, and even 50 times intraday, on their underlying investor resources. Also the cash they receive from investors can itself run in to hundreds of millions of dollars. Nevertheless, they are usually small in the overall scheme of things, when set against longer-term corporate and investment sector position taking or against the transaction sizes involved if banks switch their net positions, within established prudential limits.

Market Turnover and Products

According to the 1995 triennial BIS survey of foreign exchange activity in the 26 largest centers, turnover in all foreign exchange products amounted to some $1.26 trillion a day. Allowing for exchange rate adjustments, this was an increase of 30 percent from the previous triennial survey, more or less the same growth rate shown in the previous three-year period. Activity between banks was 64 percent of 1995 turnover, between banks and other financial institutions, 20 percent, while the balance of 16 percent represented business between banks and their nonfinancial customers. Daily turnover of traditional products averaged $1.19 trillion, of which 44 percent was spot, 7 percent outright forwards, and 49 percent swaps. Currency futures and options contributed an added $70 billion of turnover, which, although small by comparison, was still significant in absolute terms. Of the outright forwards and swaps, 53 and 71 percent, respectively, was concentrated in maturities up to one week (used by banks to manage liquidity), while business over one year was "rare." The dominant form of trading in such derivative products has been the "over-the-counter" (OTC) interbank market, rather than the exchange-traded alternative that requires more standardized products. Not large enough to be mentioned in the BIS survey, a recent and innovative product that is of growing importance in the trading of emerging market currencies is the "nondeliverable forward." This product is settled for a cash consideration on a net basis—that is, only the net gains or losses are settled on maturity, with no exchange of principle sums. Turnover is estimated at $500 million to $1 billion a day, and it is understood that they have been actively used in recent trading of the Asian currencies, both in onshore and offshore currency markets.

Unfortunately, the BIS survey does not directly cover activity *within* emerging markets, (South Africa excepted), although $87.8 billion, or 7.7 percent of daily turnover, was a "residual" figure representing activity in the currencies of countries that did not participate in the survey. Nevertheless, there has been an unmistakable shift in dealing emphasis toward emerging markets in recent years. Deutsche Morgan Grenfell, for example, estimated in 1997 that 25–30 percent of its worldwide foreign exchange revenues came from exotic currencies, while Bank of America reported 25 percent of its activity was emerging-markets driven, up from only 5 percent in 1992. Exotic is market terminology for currencies that do not yet benefit from the large volumes, market liquidity, and well-developed infrastructure of most industrial country currencies and that may be prone to greater volatility. Meanwhile, even before the Asian crisis, HSBC Midland calculated its turnover in exotics had doubled in the preceding three years, and in the last few months Société Générale, Parisbas, and Standard Chartered

---

[76]See Eichengreen, Masson, and others, 1998.

have all announced the creation of new trading desks for emerging markets.

There are several reasons for this shift. The first is the underlying business need, with banks responding to their customers' growing cross-border investment and trading needs, as local economies open to the outside world. The second is that banks are drawn by the fatter margins in markets where the arbitrage community is not yet present in great numbers—in so doing, of course, their own actions tend to drive down those margins as additional suppliers compete. A third reason is that EMU convergence has released dealing capacity in many banks, which has allowed them to bring forward their expansion plans for exotic currencies. It is estimated, for instance, that 20 percent of European foreign exchange business, and up to 40 percent in some countries, will be eroded by EMU. For example, the BIS survey showed almost a fourth of the daily $58 billion turnover in Paris was deutsche mark–French franc, all of which becomes redundant, post-EMU. Part of the capacity released will be absorbed by trading the new euros, but this still leaves a considerable surplus of manpower, capital, and credit resources for deployment elsewhere. Coinciding as it has done with the plans by banks to increase coverage of emerging markets, this EMU contraction has allowed those plans to be accelerated. The final reason for the increase in emerging market interest is the more general developmental phenomenon whereby markets grow vigorously once a certain critical threshold of liquidity is reached. As currency markets deepen and broaden for underlying business and other reasons, as above, this in itself encourages further entry. Liquidity creates confidence, which encourages more banks to do more business, which then creates more liquidity, and so on, at an accelerating pace. A not-too-distant historical example of this same phenomenon is the growth in the financial futures markets in London and Chicago. Doubtless, a number of the emerging markets are in the midst of this sort of process, notwithstanding periods of uncertainty like that associated with Asia recently.

A further noteworthy point here is that the rapid advances in global communications have rendered the concept of locally domiciled trading a thing of the past for many of the world's currencies. Instead, they are today traded continuously and freely across national borders and time zones. At the same time, banks have established global networks of dealing offices to service their clients and to spearhead moves into new markets, but these offices also serve as havens to rehouse dealing books when regulatory constraints in any particular market become onerous. When economies begin opening to the outside world, there is an inevitable erosion of central control that goes with it, because governments have no direct jurisdiction over the free trading of their currencies in offshore centers. Nowadays, dealing quickly migrates when the business climate turns adverse, as a trading book requires little more than good communications and a good address to be operational, both of which can be readily found elsewhere in the global networks of dealing banks. The BIS survey underscored the fact that it is now commonplace for significant volumes of foreign exchange dealing to take place outside the country concerned. It reported that more dollar, deutsche mark, and French franc business was handled in London than in their respective countries, while only 30 percent of Swiss franc turnover actually occurred in Switzerland.

With the rapid growth in foreign exchange turnover, an increasingly recognized issue is the additional risks involved during settlement of both legs of a foreign currency transaction. Bank management and regulators have been concerned at the costs and credit risk issues in foreign exchange settlement for many years. Yet despite many high-level meetings, no one has come up with a solution that enjoys widespread support. A number of the main trading banks have acted on their own, however. For some time they have netted their deals bilaterally, combining all settlements due for the same value date into a single exchange of payments. To automate the bilateral netting process, several systems have been set up, including FXNET, which was established in 1986 by the dealing management of 14 active banks. It now nets the bilateral dealing of 61 participants, which account between them for 10–13 percent of global foreign exchange turnover. In so doing, around $100 billion of daily clearing is now eliminated. More recently, the Exchange Clearing House (ECHO), owned by 36 major banks, finally went live, offering the advantages of a full multilateral clearing facility. According to an internal Echo study, if multilateral netting were accepted universally, global settlements would be reduced by up to 95 percent. To date, the volumes handled by ECHO have been modest, around 1 percent of the market, and the take-up has been slow. Indeed, it has been far from clear that ECHO per se would be very actively supported, because the big dealing banks have already eliminated a major part of their settlement problem through FXNET at a charge of $1.50 a transaction, while ECHO, charging $5 a transaction, seems an expensive and rather marginal alternative. Partly reflecting such doubts, Echo, along with Multinet (another multilateral netting service), has just been merged into a new organization, Continuous Linked Settlement Services (CLSS). CLSS was established by the "G-20 banks," and the previous shareholders of ECHO and Multinet are becoming shareholders in CLSS. CLSS will continue to provide netting facilities but is also planning to establish a bank to handle foreign exchange settlements among member banks. It will be linked with members' own domestic, real-time gross settlement systems to provide simultaneous settlement of both legs of a foreign exchange transaction.

Mechanisms for Dealing

Currency dealers seldom now meet on a trading floor to transact their business, except in markets that have yet to progress beyond central bank auctions. Instead, they trade through terminals or voice brokers. The reason is that floors do not have the capacity to accommodate the often large numbers of banks that raise many deals with each other each day; nor can they accommodate the many screen-based services that banks need, to manage their portfolios. But in addition, the costs of a trading floor tend to be prohibitive—witness the current debate on the floor-based London International Financial Futures Exchange (LIFFE) exchange moving to cheaper screen-based dealing.

The major portion of interbank foreign exchange dealing is still negotiated bilaterally between banks following the traditional pattern of price inquiry followed by a deal, although the former use of telephone and telex has now been largely superseded by systems such as Reuter Dealing 2000–2001. The latter is a screen-based communication system, which is commonly used around the globe. The advantages of Reuter Dealing 2000–2001 in particular are its speed, integrity and reliability, and its facility for making multiple calls (up to four) simultaneously. In addition, its audit trail and electronic data feed to banks' mainframes greatly reduce the scope for costly dealer and processing error, and for fraud. Nevertheless, voice brokers continue to negotiate important volumes of business for the banks, especially in foreign exchange swaps.

Beyond the regular dealing systems like Reuter Dealing 2000–2001, newer electronic systems are changing the nature of market trading in a deeper way. In particular, within the last few years, an electronic alternative to the price inquiry and deal systems has finally overcome dealer prejudice and been successfully introduced to the market. The automated deal matching systems of Electronic Brokering System (EBS)—owned by 14 major banks—and Reuter Dealing 2000–2002, are now estimated to handle around 60 percent of all the brokered business in London, while they have virtually replaced the voice brokers in Asia.[77] These deal-matching systems function through desktop terminals, with the amounts and rates to be dealt keyed in by the dealer. It is not possible to offer different terms for counterparties of different credit standing, but each dealer's terminal is preprogrammed with the names and limits for acceptable counterparties. Only when there is a match with an acceptable counterparty are the names of the counterparts exchanged, but revealed to no one else.

The systems particularly suit the market's middle order transactions of a few million dollars each, which they match smoothly and uneventfully—although larger deals still need to be negotiated directly between banks (the EBS average deal is just under $3 million). But the systems trade on such fine dealing spreads—typically between 1 to 3 basis points compared with the 5 points previously common—that market makers find the systems are making serious inroads into their traditional business. It is a trend that seems likely to continue. Indeed, there is a clear prospect that electronic order matching could become the dominant dealing medium in future. With the loss of a significant part of their business, voice brokering is going through a significant retrenchment. Yet, the voice broker's skill at securing prices under even difficult market conditions means they will probably remain important in many less liquid markets that do not have the turnover to support electronic matching.

Both EBS and Reuter see significant growth ahead. EBS already publishes its worldwide turnover figures. A recent report showed over 32,000 EBS transactions a day, totaling $94.3 billion. With 760–770 clients, compared with Reuter's 1,200 or so but with smaller turnover, EBS claims 46 percent of all brokered business in London, and as much as 80–90 percent in Asia. Reuter has around 15 percent of the London market, according to EBS. Reuter Dealing 2000–2002, meanwhile, covers 35 currency pairs in 33 countries, and is in the course of extending its coverage to emerging markets. Their current move to cover the Mexican and Russian markets is the forerunner of this. Until recently, the two providers handled only spot dealing, but Reuter has just launched a service in forwards for 16 currency pairs in 21 countries—Reuter Dealing 2000–2002 Forwards. EBS is expected to follow shortly, while the brokers are marketing their own automated forwards systems. Conscious of the fundamental change in the way the market does it business, the BIS is to collate data on automated brokering for inclusion in its next triennial survey.

The virtue of electronic matching for regulators and administrators is its relative ease of surveillance and price discovery, and the heightened efficiency it brings from reduced spreads. The operating costs for the banks are not particularly large either. For example, the initiator of a transaction on Reuter Dealing 2000–2002 pays $25, which is insignificant when set against the $326 benefit from improving, say the dollar–deutsche mark rate by 2 basis points on a $3 million deal (e.g., from 1.8400 to 1.8402). The monthly charge for a Reuter Dealing 2000–2002 communication terminal varies between $2,000 and $4,000. A disadvantage that some see, however, is the possibility that such automated systems may not do as good a job in preserving liquidity as voice brokers do, at times when markets are especially turbulent (see below).

---

[77]For a more detailed description of the operation of the Reuters Dealing 2000–2002 system, see Chapter 4 of Frankel and others (1996).

Table 39. Foreign Exchange Trading Revenues
(In millions of U.S. dollars)

	1996	1995	Percent Change
Citibank	932.0	1,124.0	−17
HSBC Midland	597.0	609.0	−2
Swiss Bk Warburg	594.0	422.6	+41
Chase Manhattan	444.0	584.0	−24
UBS	374.0	397.0	−6
NatWest	368.9	370.5	−0.4
JP Morgan	320.0	253.0	+26
Bank of America	316.0	303.0	+4
Standard Chartered	261.9	303.4	−14
State Street	126.0	141.0	−11
Lloyds	113.0	194.8	−7
Barclays BZW	107.0	145.3	−14
Republic Nat Bk	98.0	113.0	−13
American Express	72.0	79.0	−9
Bank of New York	67.0	60.0	+12
Total	4,790.8	5,099.6	−6

Sources: *FX Week* and Deutsche Morgan Grenfell from *Financial Times Survey,* April 18, 1997.

Profitability and Competition Trends

Foreign exchange business is an important source of income for the banking community. Even with the EMU-related stability in Europe, the competition of electronic dealing, and the growing relative importance of nonbank financial institutions, revenues for the major banks listed in Table 39, as a group, were only slightly lower in 1996 (a relatively quiet year) than in the previous years. Meanwhile, early results for 1997 suggest a strong resurgence of revenues. Citibank posted record foreign exchange income of $1,225 billion for 1997, while Chase Manhattan Bank nearly doubled its revenues. In the United Kingdom, foreign exchange earnings at HSBC Holdings were up 72 percent to $1,004 billion and at Standard Chartered up 84 percent to $498 million. One important reason for this is that banks have been shifting the focus of their business away from traditional market making and proprietary trading, where margins are relatively thin, to client-related business (selling more profitable complex derivatives, for example) and to emerging markets (where profit margins are better).

Another related factor has been a continuing trend toward bank consolidation, affecting foreign exchange business and other areas of banking. The BIS survey notes the continuing trend for foreign exchange business to be concentrated in the hands of fewer banks, with the top 10 banks controlling 44 percent of 1995 turnover in London, 47 percent in the United States, and 51 percent in Tokyo. Seen another way, 75 percent of 1995 turnover in the six largest centers was accounted for by 11 percent or less of banks. Yet this trend does not appear to represent a diminution of competition in major foreign exchange markets— more the opposite, in fact. It reflects the intense competitive pressures in the financial sector more broadly, which are encouraging rationalizations, mergers, and acquisitions, as previously distinct—if not protected— market segments are breaking down internationally.

Market Behavior and Policy Interactions

This section examines major foreign exchange dealing considerations and how dealing behavior can affect the movements in the exchange rate.

Nature of Market Making

Whether or not banks operating in the foreign exchange market engage in market making depends on the level of their in-house trading skills and their appetite for risk. Those with limited ambitions confine themselves to servicing customer needs alone and immediately lay off positions with market makers. But banks that elect to be market makers additionally offer two-way dealing services to the interbank market—which places them in a strong position to bid for larger customer deals—while they also establish reciprocal facilities with each other to lay off their own excess risk. In all but exceptional circumstances, market makers stand ready to make firm dealing prices, where the spread and dealable sum are "understood" and consistent—for example, in major markets not more than a 5 point spread and good for a minimum $3 million. There are different tiers of these understandings allowing, for instance, for more ambitious banks to trade with each other for bigger amounts and on closer spreads. The bid-offer spread quoted by a market maker is determined by the competition both of other market makers and the electronic matching systems. Thus, for a large trade,

111

Box 10. A Day of Spot Market Making

The first concern of a dealer approaching a new business day is to discover the price. For the major currencies traded continuously around the globe this is easy: a London dealer, for example, checks the sterling price in Hong Kong SAR that may then be used as the first dealing quotation or the dealer may shade it up or down according to his preference. Alternatively, if the Hong Kong SAR price does not seem to reflect fully the latest news, the dealer could deal on it and open his first speculative position of the day. In the case of a local currency that floats but is not traded internationally, the opening price is more difficult to assess as there is no open market to check. So the dealer has to calculate its theoretical value and then adjust it according to his instincts. The basis is always the previous evening's closing level, but this normally needs adjusting to reflect factors such as international market developments (e.g., a generally firmer dollar), local financial and economic developments, and less tangibly, political developments. Making the first price of the day is then something of a step into the unknown—so it is usually quoted with a wider spread to give some protection.

There is something of a race to be the first to make a call to another dealer because the estimation of the rate can then be checked. The dealer called, however, has had no opportunity to confirm his own assessment of the price but is obligated, nonetheless, to make a two-way dealing price. A dealer is only interested in firm prices—ideas or indications are of little value to him. So if the price quoted broadly agrees with the caller's view there is unlikely to be a deal. But if this is not the case, two things can happen: first the caller could deal and open a position if confident his view was correct and the price quoted was wrong; or second, the dealer could amend his own view of the rate. By this process of calling and dealing, a broad consensus on the rate emerges.

An example of dealing could be the following. When a caller sells dollars to a market maker, the market maker encourages an offsetting deal to close the position and take his profit. The market maker does this by lowering his price (while maintaining the spread) to make the best dollar offer in the market. The next wholesale buyer of dollars ought then to deal with the dealer. But if having dropped the rate to encourage the offsetting deal, the next few callers did the opposite and sold dollars again—possibly the dealer had failed to realize the rate was even lower—the dealer might decide the position had become too large and that proactive action was called for to deal with it. Although dealers have a strong preference for dealing on their own price to conserve the spread, which is often the difference between profit and loss, they would in these circumstances call other banks and sell them dollars to reduce or close the position completely. And if they believed the price would fall further they could even sell more dollars than needed and take an opposite short position. Doubtless, at this point dealers would have made a loss, far from uncommon for market makers; but they would hope to make it up from the short dollar position they had taken and from the day's later market making. As market makers can only control the prices they quote and not the deals that others do with them, it is impossible for a dealer to guarantee a square position at all times.

Yet a dealer must have broad control of the dealing book, the objective being that it is no larger than is consistent with the depth of the market—for example, that the position can always be closed with not more than four calls to other market makers. So it follows that market unrest that reduces the tradable amounts between market makers, dictates smaller positions. Equally, a spell of poor dealing normally calls for a lower risk profile. As the close of the day's business approaches, a dealer will begin fine-tuning his book to ensure he can meet overnight limits. As all banks are doing the same, liquidity begins to contract. The dealer is then less accommodating to callers and will make wider spreads and deal for smaller amounts. Finally, when the position is as the dealer wishes it to be, the dealer will announce to callers that he is closed for business for the day.

---

a bank might expect to be quoted a 5-point spread (say 1.8400–1.8405 on U.S. dollar–deutsche mark, equivalent to 0.027 percent); as noted earlier, the electronic systems usually deal off lower spreads, possibly as little as 1 point, albeit for smaller transactions.

Since a market maker is under a virtual obligation to quote dealing prices on demand, it is difficult for him to regulate his residual position with any precision, given that a counterpart's deal may not always suit the book. But with markets unpredictable and potentially dangerous, it is most important that the broad shape of the book is controlled. There are two techniques dealers use for this. First, they vary the rates they quote, moving them higher or lower and possibly widening the spread, to encourage or discourage counterparties. Second, there are times when they must aggressively lay off risk on the prices of other market makers, whether at a profit or a loss. In fact, knowing when to deal on the prices of others, and having the courage to do so, is generally held to be the key to a dealer's survival (see Box 10 for more specifics on market makers' typical activities).

An active market maker trading one of the major currencies could easily handle many hundreds, or in some cases thousands, of deals each day with turnover running to several billion dollars. With such magnitudes transacted, even quite small price movements can make a significant difference to profits and losses. This leads to a culture of instant decisions. Prices require an immediate response and, even then, may be changed several times on the same call. Indeed, to allow for this, the electronic systems have been designed so that dealing prices may be placed under immediate reference by means of a single key stroke. Against a background of continual exchange rate uncertainty there is an inherent tension in dealing rooms that is fanned by loudspeakers disseminating constant news and rumors from around the world. Hence, perhaps, the common image of frenetic and very short-term oriented decision making. Yet this popular image misses important parts of the story, as discussed further below.

Importance of Liquidity

Like other asset markets, foreign exchange markets need high levels of liquidity to function most efficiently. Liquidity may be described as a market's capacity and readiness to accommodate deals at fine prices without undue disturbance—that is, its ability to absorb even large transactions, without moving the market price unduly against those transactions. Beyond the benefits for the ultimate end users, liquidity is the lifeline that allows market makers to lay off risk and control exposures; allows an exit when dealing decisions go wrong; and exerts a constant downward pressure on transaction costs. As already noted, liquidity emerges only slowly in a market at first, but then, once it reaches some critical mass, tends to become self-perpetuating, growing more rapidly as confidence in the market begins to takes hold. In conceptual terms, market liquidity can be seen as a form of positive externality or public good, providing benefits to all actual or potential users of the market.

Liquidity is produced in several ways. First, liquidity is produced when continuous and natural two-way business permits deals to be absorbed uneventfully, as with electronic deal matching. Second, it is the product of banks agreeing to make markets to each other, for even without an immediate deal to offset an inward transaction, a market maker has to be prepared to accept uncovered risk on his book, at least temporarily. Third, the act of speculation generates liquidity by allowing imbalances in supply and demand to be carried forward to a later time, in anticipation of a reversal of the market. In this regard, the intraday and overnight speculation of the banks play a key role. Indeed, no financial asset market could operate efficiently without speculators to provide liquidity.

To a large extent then, liquidity is the result of banks being ready to accept risk on their books; but before this can happen, it is first essential that management is confident that their dealers possess the necessary skills to do so. However, the skill of dealing is less a question of mathematical competence than of learning to understand market "psychology"—how others are likely to react to developments in a changing and uncertain environment. But these are not skills that are acquired from books; they must be learned from experience, through sitting at the dealing desk and actually dealing, and this may entail some interim costs in the form of dealing losses. Exchange rate quotations are a sensitive and revealing barometer of currency value that is constantly adjusted to reflect current and expected order flows and prevailing sentiment. As such, it is the key indicator to help market makers manage risk and it is therefore imperative that they be able to interpret its ever-changing message. They must, for instance, understand the significance of competing bids and offers, how banks respond when prices are quoted to them and how they react when a deal is made on their price, whether dealing spreads change, and so on. The result is that management is most unlikely to invest in training and expose its bank to the prospect of losses, unless it is clearly in its interest to do so—and the abstract cause of market liquidity on its own will not be a sufficient motive. In short, without a profit motivation, no skills will be developed; and with no skills, there will be no market making and no meaningful liquidity.

The large currency markets have high liquidity and routinely accommodate large deals without stress. However, some commentators feel that the growth of anonymous electronic matching systems may erode this, especially, in future episodes of serious currency unrest. Before automated deal matching became a force, market making was a well-oiled practice that allowed risk to be laid off through direct contacts between dealers and with minimal market disturbance. Voice brokers, too, played a part in this through generating a regular stream of competitive bids and offers in all but the most difficult conditions. The direct human challenge, dealer to dealer and broker to dealer, was an important element in the process. But although the electronic systems have worked admirably so far, confidently handling a growing share of middle and smaller market business, the fear of some is that these orders could be withheld at a time of future turbulence. And since electronic matching provides no facility to challenge a market maker directly for a price, they can, as it were, hide anonymously behind their terminals. Meanwhile, on this view, the old market-making skills are being lost as a new generation of dealers is brought up on electronic dealing, and the "understandings" between banks are being allowed to fall into disuse. Still, even if the above concern is valid in principle, it remains to be seen whether electronic matching systems will in fact largely replace the price inquiry and deal process—especially if markets recognize and value the advantages of more direct contact. As noted earlier, larger transactions are still usually negotiated directly between banks, while smaller markets may not have the turnover to support electronic matching.

Position Taking, Risk Management, and Supervision

Foreign exchange is one of the few areas of banking where large sums of money can be lost very quickly—which is why both management and supervisors impose strict controls on the operations of dealers. The precise requirements of the two are different, however, since management seeks to prevent any erosion of shareholder value, while supervisors concern themselves with the sort of catastrophic loss that places depositors' funds at risk and possibly threatens systemic failure. Well-managed banks scrutinize every aspect of dealing that could give rise to losses and usually impose a comprehensive range of mandatory internal controls that tightly circumscribe the exercise of any dealer discretion. These will include limits on market and counterparty risk and would normally require that positions are regularly marked to market (revalued), with both realized and unrealized profits and losses accounted for. Supervisors, on the other hand, are generally more concerned with overnight and longer-lasting currency positions. Beyond exposure limitations per se, they typically require bank management to demonstrate that they have a proper understanding of the hazards in foreign exchange and that they have installed effective monitoring, measurement, and control systems so that the risks of significant loss are reduced to the barest minimum. Intraday currency exposures, though larger than those held overnight, are not generally subject to supervisory limits (although they may well be curtailed by management). Supervisors consider them to be less dangerous in general, in that they can still be closed in a working market if things go wrong, which is not the case overnight when the dealing room is closed. Yet this perhaps gives a misleading notion of overnight risk, because banks frequently protect their overnight exposures by leaving stop-loss orders with centers that are open.

In the course of a day's dealing, banks may accumulate or initiate substantial open currency positions—especially when acting as market makers. These actions may have a noticeable impact effect on the rate, but, because they must be largely squared before the end of the day, their long-term consequences are seldom significant. Positions carried overnight or for a longer term, on the other hand, can be of greater consequence since they cause a net movement of funds across the exchanges until closed. If banks use their limits to the full, and simultaneously change from an overbought to an oversold position, or vice versa, the impact on the rate could be clearly felt. Yet, this power is frequently exaggerated, because in practice banks never act in unison and to the full extent of their limits. Moreover, supervisory limits are usually highly restrictive. For example, in the past, at least, industrial country supervisors typically set such limits at around 20 percent of a bank's capital, which would only expose a bank to a direct loss of about 5 percent of shareholders' funds, even for an exchange rate movement of 25 percent. Levels of 15–20 percent have been common in industrial countries, though comparability is made more difficult by different calculation methods. A number of industrial countries have already moved away from direct open position limits or are in the process of doing so, on the view that a more holistic view of banks' risk exposure and risk management is desirable. The apparent latitude now afforded some banks to decide their own levels of overnight risk under broader market risk-based capital requirements, in theory, opens the possibility of greater influence on currency values. But it seems unlikely that this will lead to any pronounced change in banks' behavior because, by aggregating the limits for their branches and subsidiaries, the banks concerned have probably not been short of facilities anyway, while U.S. banks have been free of a direct regulatory constraint on open positions for many years.

A dealer will open and close many different and perhaps alternating long and short positions during the day to exploit anomalies. Thus, a currency that has risen suddenly and sharply could be due for a correction, and a short position would be opened. But because markets are unpredictable, a position could be rapidly closed or even reversed if an expected move did not soon occur, even if it meant taking a loss. Indeed, the final tally of the day's performance for an active dealer would be the product of many individual profits and losses during the session. An overnight position taker may also exploit market inconsistencies. Thus an exposure could be taken against the closing trend in the expectation that an end-of-day imbalance was temporary and likely to reverse the following morning. Yet, at other times a position in line with the closing trend could be justified on the basis that trends frequently perpetuate themselves.

Dealing Behavior and Fundamentals

It is often assumed that a dealer's overwhelming preoccupation is with matters of profit. Although that is important, the greater preoccupation is likely to be the fear of loss, since losses arise all too easily in a tense trading environment where time horizons are very short and positions must be closed each day to satisfy internal and supervisory limits. This is compounded by the uncomfortable reality of dealing that the worst losses invariably exceed the best profits—the reason being, first, that human nature being what it is, profits tend to be taken too soon and losses run for too long; and second, when the consensus expectation of dealers is wrong, competition among them to cut positions may drive the rate further away from their previous expectation and increases losses. Conversely, when the market has correctly anticipated a trend, the action of taking profits arrests the trend and reduces additional profit opportunities.

Spot dealers are not primarily concerned whether their decisions are rational or not, in the sense of being consistent with economic fundamentals. In the end, the only logic that makes sense, in this context, is to be long of a currency appreciating and short of one depreciating. Observed price and volume movements, in other words, are the dealers' main short-term indicators of market sentiment, and most of the time no amount of economic analysis and forecasting is likely to provide much additional help in picking movements in the very short term. The result is that, up to a point at least, a dealer may follow a trend on the simple premise that trends tend to perpetuate themselves. In fact the momentum of trends is often so powerful that it may take a brave dealer to be the first to oppose one, even though many may believe a trend has gone too far.

Short-term dealers are, therefore, often influenced by the forecasts of technical analysts (chartists). Extrapolating from trends, technical analysis is widely used to endorse or even initiate trading decisions, so much so in fact that it can cause bouts of short-term price instability when signaling price thresholds that, when breached, trigger additional self-fulfilling movements. Charts may also be used to support longer-term dealing decisions although, naturally, with the passage of time the study of past trends is less relevant.

The value of broader "fundamental" analysis is more important in dealing, however, if the time scale is long enough to allow for short-term market wrinkles to be ironed out, or when there is a need to interpret significant news releases. Even here, however, the dealer's own knowledge of how markets react to news may be just as helpful in the very short term. In support of longer-term or proprietary trading, banks make extensive use of the services of external as well as in-house economic analysts. Thus, it can be quite misleading to think of foreign exchange markets as excessively driven by "short termism" based on an extrapolation of the behavior of spot interbank dealers. This point is discussed in the conclusion of this section and linked to some conceptual analyses of exchange market behavior.

A different facet of exchange market behavior is the view that major banks may be able to manipulate markets for their own gain. The view has some validity, up to a point, but again it is important not to overstate the importance of, or understate the constraints on, such behavior. Specifically, a prominent bank can leverage a strong position and make exchange rates move profitably by inducing the market to draw the wrong conclusions about its business. It could do this in the following way. The customer orders that banks handle are confidential and when large enough, they can move the exchange rate. As a result there is continual guessing about what a bank is doing when it deals aggressively: is it operating for a customer or is it dealing on its own account? The distinction is important. Customer orders can have a lasting effect on the rate, whereas own-account dealing is more neutral because it must generally be unwound at the end of the day. A bank can exploit this uncertainty. It might, for instance, secure a large commercial deal at a price that, in isolation, produces a loss for the dealer. The attraction of the deal, however, is the opportunity it provides for leverage. If the dealer covers twice the amount of the customer deal in the market, and the market is left with a larger imbalance, the rate is more likely to change. Fearing the customer order was larger than it actually was, and that the price would move even more, other banks may then decide to cut their positions and take their losses. This may then cause the rate to fall sufficiently for the original bank to take a profit on its excess position, which more than covers the loss on the underlying commercial deal. From beginning to end, the exercise would typically take not more than 10 minutes. Once successfully accomplished a few times, the instigating bank might even establish a reputation for itself, not for its market leverage, which the banks would remain unaware of, but for its dealing skills—that is, the fact that the market always seemed to follow the direction of its dealing. At that point, the other banks would be inclined to follow whatever the bank did. This would increase the initiating bank's short-term powers even more, for without an underlying order, it could *make* the rate move just by dealing with several banks. As long as it is not too ambitious, a bank operating in the market this way can fairly easily cover its tracks by channeling deals through different market makers, so that no one knows for sure who is behind the activity.

For these tactics to be successful, however, it requires a background of currency instability and uncertainty, with the exchange rate fluctuating relatively sharply in both directions. In such conditions, a market might offer little resistance to a new trend started by a leveraging bank that concealed its hand. And the sums needed to start a market moving depend very much on circumstances. If, in one of the large markets, sentiment were to be fragile, $100 million might be enough; whereas in a more confident and deeper market, $500 million could be readily absorbed with little effect on the rate. As a percentage of market turnover these may not be large sums, but the danger for a leveraging bank is that larger positions carry higher risks if the stratagem fails, which can easily happen. Meanwhile, although exotic currencies can be moved with smaller volumes, positions must still remain consistent with market liquidity to allow for a ready exit. Of course, the added consideration in exotic currency dealing is that smaller liquidity permits a defense to be mounted more easily by the central bank.

If a bank tried leveraging its position in an orderly market, however, it is much more likely to encounter stiff resistance as confident banks willingly absorbed the pressure without disturbance to the rate. They would look upon the attempted manipulation simply as an opportunity to obtain cheap currency. Even in quiet and relatively stable markets, a single bank could impose its will if it has a particularly dominant competitive position, perhaps with privileged access to major clients. Nevertheless, leveraging is seen by most market practitioners as a legitimate tactic in a market of professionals, one they would like to engage in themselves given the opportunity. Few in the market consider it to be improper or unethical, as a bank that leverages its book does not deliberately deceive the market in the sense of spreading misleading or false information, which would be quite a different issue. Rather, it realizes its objectives by doing the opposite and saying nothing, instead allowing other banks to draw their own conclusion about its business. In fact, it would be most unusual that a bank attempted to deceive the market willfully. Were it to do so, it would be dealt with severely by the market itself (through ostracism) and quite likely by official sanction too (possibly withdrawal of a foreign exchange license).

Policy Interventions in the Foreign Exchange Markets

Policy interventions in currency markets take several forms, ranging from market-based operations to regulatory measures that aim to restrict market behavior. The most basic policy intervention, however, is the choice of exchange rate regime, which can have a great deal to do with the incentives for foreign exchange market development, and more particularly for the active management of currency risk. When central bank currency transactions are conducted at rates that are predetermined, and excessively rigid—under fixed or pegged regimes within very narrow bands for example, or when a "floating" rate is never actually allowed to move—there is little or no uncertainty and the banks have no risk to concern themselves with, at least not unless or until the regime collapses. Customer deals are covered directly with the central bank (or matched in-house), which is little more than a clerical exercise that develops no risk awareness. But if instead banks are given no guarantee of direct access to the central bank at "known" prices, and if intervention is channeled at varying rates through broader market operations, rather than made available to individual banks, on demand, at an open window, then the element of uncertainty produced would compel the banks to acquire risk management expertise and train their dealers in such aspects. The point is valid even under a fixed or pegged regime, provided it allows at least some movement in market rates around a central rate. Individual banks would not know for sure where, when, and at what price the central bank would next appear. The better incentives for risk management by

banks would tend to stimulate currency market trading and growing liquidity, while also encouraging nonbanks to pay more attention to exchange rate risk. The Asian crisis amply demonstrated the costs that can be involved if excessively rigid exchange rates encourage either banks or nonbanks, or both, to ignore exchange rate risk.

The recent events in Asia and elsewhere have also reconfirmed old lessons about how to defend and how not to defend specific exchange rate levels. In a nutshell, exchange rates that are clearly unrealistic will probably not be defensible and the many examples of central banks attempting to defend unrealistic exchange rates over the past few decades have provided currency markets with a rich source of income. Yet, there is a significant gray area here, as to what is "unrealistic," and examples of fixed or targeted rates that have been successfully defended against substantial speculative attacks abound. The most important factors appear to be twofold.

First, the authorities need to display a strong commitment. Specifically, they need to be clearly willing to bear the costs of a defense, particularly in terms of higher interest rates, but also in terms of fiscal retrenchment and determined financial sector and other structural policy changes, as required. For several reasons, interest rate defenses are often seen as controversial (and certainly they can be painful). Interest rate defenses may not always work, and even if they do work, they may involve high interest rates, at least for a time. For example, Sweden's interest rate defense in 1992 was unsuccessful, even though short-term interest rates rose to over 500 percent. (Short rates, on an annual basis, are required if a depreciation is widely expected to be imminent: as a simple illustration, if a 10 percent depreciation is expected within a month, an annual interest rate of some 214 percent would be required on one-month domestic currency investments, just to compensate for the expected exchange rate loss.) Moreover, more sophisticated speculators will have already locked in domestic currency liquidity and credit at lower interest rates, as they opened speculative positions against the local currency. But neither of these concerns is an argument against increasing interest rates if the policy objective is to defend the existing exchange rate. The point of interest rate responses is primarily to affect the behavior of those who have not yet committed themselves to speculative positions against the local currency, so that the market is not one-sided. If those who have already taken speculative positions are thereby forced to close out their positions at a loss, so much the better. But that is a side benefit. Overall, interest rate increases may not be sufficient to avert a currency collapse, but they are typically necessary.

Second, the authorities need to act early. Often, authorities have allowed speculative pressures to build up, absorbing these through continued direct intervention in the currency markets but not allowing these to spill over into higher domestic interest rates (let alone contemplating preemptive interest rate increases). The temptation to delay a strong defense, and simply absorb speculative pressures initially, helps explain the often observed phenomenon of an apparently sudden eruption of a currency crisis, even if an underlying fragility had been clear for some time. In many instances, authorities may have also delayed the buildup of full-blown speculation by successfully massaging opinion, convincing the markets for a time that the exchange rate is credible and sustainable. But when the official will and capacity to continue a defense, and broaden it beyond sterilized foreign currency intervention, begins to be questioned, then speculation begins in earnest. Central banks need to be willing to act quickly to restrict the domestic currency credit they themselves are supplying, through one means or another, that is, fueling a speculative attack and holding down short-term interest rates. The need for policies that, to the extent possible, are preemptive is valid for both interest rate and other defensive measures. If extremely high short-term interest rates are needed because speculation has been allowed to build up too far, the market has to take account of the political, if not economic, sustainability of the rates. In other words, the interest rate defense may not be credible. The same general point applies to other defense measures as well, such as fiscal and structural policy changes. Markets look for determined, credible, and timely decision making in these areas, and undue delays or half measures raise doubts about the authorities' commitment. In short then, "too little, too late" is the recipe for an unsuccessful defense.

Sometimes, central banks have conducted their foreign currency interventions in nonspot markets—forwards, futures, and derivatives, for example. Intervention in these forms has often turned out to be quite problematic, however, because there can be a significant temptation to overuse the intervention in the hope the speculative pressures will abate. These points do not relate to the use of such transactions for purely reserves management ends, rather than currency intervention; nor to the use of foreign exchange swaps as an instrument of domestic monetary management. This temptation arises from two factors that are often perceived, somewhat ironically, as the main advantages of such operations as compared with simple spot market or money market intervention. First, intervention in forwards, futures, or derivatives markets appears to offer the ability to defend an exchange rate while economizing on the use of official foreign currency reserves. The spot exchange rate can be influenced quite strongly by such operations, but without the immediate use of the same volume of official reserves and, correspondingly, without the same need to sterilize the foreign exchange intervention to leave domestic monetary conditions unchanged (if that is the policy). Thus,

there may be no obvious limit to the intervention, or at least the limit is less obvious.[78] If the pressures continue, however, the day of reckoning for the spot rate, and the central bank's balance sheet, is not avoided.

Second, the use of nonspot interventions can be less transparent, especially when central banks' publicly reported holdings of foreign exchange reserves do not take account of the actual or potential commitments under forwards, futures, or derivatives contracts. This was a substantive issue in both Thailand and Korea where, even though there were market suspicions that the central banks had a substantial amount of such commitments, their actual volume proved to be an additional unpleasant surprise when it became known. Authorities sometimes see nontransparency as a means of leading market participants to believe that there is underlying market (rather than official) support, presumably because, once there is a perceived lack of market support, it is inevitable that market participants will question how seriously the authorities are willing to defend a given exchange rate. Therefore, if there is a reluctance on the authorities' part to take more fundamental actions to defend an exchange rate (such as allowing or initiating a monetary tightening, and making determined adjustments to fiscal and structural policies), the temptation to overuse less transparent intervention methods may be strong.

In any event, it is doubtful that nontransparent intervention methods are in fact superior to a clear official policy reaction function, as part of a transparent monetary and exchange management framework, with a single, clear, medium-term objective. A clearly oriented and relatively independent central bank may well help in this regard. In the case of a currency board arrangement, a credibility benefit arises instead from the fact that domestic interest rates adjust automatically to foreign currency flows, without the need for specific monetary policy decisions that might delay the interest rate response. Certainly, markets will start to suspect the existence of nontransparent interventions as soon as they begin to become sizable. At that point, nontransparent interventions are more likely to be counterproductive, since they send a negative signal about the willingness of the authorities to bear the costs of a serious defense of the exchange rate.

The other type of policy intervention is to endeavor to reassert direct regulatory controls on markets. Apart from direct capital controls, examples sometimes advocated include measures like circuit breakers and market closure, aimed at the operation of the market; credit controls; a turnover tax to increase costs for speculators or taxes on short-term inflows; the reduction or withdrawal of supervisory limits and prohibitions on banks accepting "speculative" deals; and so on. Yet for countries integrating into the global econ-

---

[78]Freedman (1991) makes the same point.

omy, experience has shown that controls are seldom effective for very long, unless perhaps they are very repressive indeed. Such controls seek to combat economic incentives for capital flight, but in general they do not remove those incentives: rather they serve to convert them into incentives for circumvention of regulatory or tax-like constraints. Credit controls, for example, are complex to implement and difficult to reimpose once lifted. They are often the instrument of their own undoing, since they entice domestic liquidity to seek the higher returns that then become available in the offshore black market. Thus, even if effective in the local market, circuit breakers, market closure, turnover taxes, and constraints on the freedom of local banks all tend to drive business to free trading offshore markets. Corporate treasurers and their advisers are adept at finding ways to actually or in effect get money out of the country through such techniques as leading and lagging, creative intragroup invoicing, and—increasingly important these days—specially structured derivative products such as those with the payoff tied to an exchange rate. When the rewards are high enough, offshore demand will always be satisfied. Foreign exchange knows few boundaries, and in the absence of a strict regulatory body with a global reach, it will migrate and leak overseas to avoid the imposition of controls. It is, meanwhile, a moot point whether the imposition of controls might actually hasten capital flight by undermining investor confidence even further.

Yet it would be misleading to suggest that controls never work, because they certainly catch some agents. But the sophisticated operators are seldom among them, because they anticipate and cover themselves ahead of controls being introduced. Rather, those affected tend to be the domestic enterprises carrying unhedged currency exposures, with neither a proper appreciation of the risks involved nor the financial connections to do much about them, once they realize the predicament they are in.

Meanwhile, formal institutional controls on the structure and organization of the interbank market in the main dealing centers are mostly minimal, if indeed they exist at all. It is widely accepted, among industrial country regulators, at least, that markets perform best if they are allowed to evolve naturally within an appropriate broad incentive structure, free of burdensome overregulation. Freedom from overregulation safeguards the interests of the market's end users by encouraging competition between banks, and this is reflected in finer prices and better service. Equally, when a market can adapt organically to changing external circumstances, the informal understandings governing relations between banks—bid-offer spread, deal size, and so on—are able to evolve smoothly. On the other hand, the general standards of behavior expected of practitioners are normally promulgated in an officially approved (but not usually officially designed) code of conduct, the object of which is to cre-

ate a professional and ethical framework to foster good market practice and confidence. Most dealing centers have produced their own codes, all of which follow the same broad lines, and the international association of dealers has also issued a document with universal application, adopted and modified as appropriate in many less developed currency markets.

Conclusion

From time to time questions are raised about the "efficiency" or "rationality" of foreign exchange markets, particularly at times of currency crisis, and more generally whenever policymakers perceive that exchange rates are substantially "misaligned." Sometimes, these questions seem to mainly reflect discomfort on the part of policymakers about the judgment on economic policies and fundamentals that markets are revealing through their actions. At other times, there may be deeper underlying concerns that markets are "failing" in some important sense. A critical issue in such cases, which however is often not very well-defined, is exactly in what sense markets are thought to be failing—that is, relative to what standards, and why? The "why" is particularly important because any public policy response to a perceived market failure is not likely to resolve the problem—and tends to create additional, unintended distortions instead—if the reason for the failure is not clearly identified and addressed as directly as possible. It should also be remembered that political and other pressures on policymakers can often lead to a strong temptation to find "quick fixes" that address symptoms rather than causes. In turn, both the "why" of the failure, and the definition of the standards against which failure is defined need to be based on an appropriate analytical framework that adequately takes into account how exchange markets actually behave. Defining "failure" relative to a model that bears insufficient resemblance to how exchange markets actually work would not be a sound basis for public policy formulation. With such a model, what appears to a "market failure" could very well be a case of "model failure" instead. For a general discussion of this issue, see, for example, Taumanoff (1984). In this regard, it seems fair to say that there is still a good way to go before generally accepted, sufficiently rich economic models are developed to adequately explain important aspects of exchange market behavior and the exchange rate formulation process, especially for shorter time frames. This section has sought to contribute to richer analysis by providing a more operational perspective on these issues.

The need for a richer analysis of foreign exchange market behavior can be illustrated in two specific respects highlighted in this section. One is the fact that interbank market dealers in particular often take short-term actions in the foreign exchange markets with scant apparent regard to analysis of "fundamentals." In doing so, they often seem to rely on their own intuition about the behavior of clients and other dealers, and to varying extents also on "technical analysis" methods, such as charting. Such "noise trading" behavior is often at the core of models of speculative bubbles or attacks in foreign exchange markets, and of analyses taking the view that the exchange markets "fail." Evidence for this view is often based on a survey of market practitioners presented in Taylor and Allen (1992). This point often seems to be extrapolated, however, to serve as a more general description of both interbank dealer behavior beyond the day-to-day time frame and the behavior of market participants other than the dealers themselves. More formally, the efficiency of the foreign exchange market as a whole may be seen to be compromised by the interreaction of "chartist" and "fundamentalist" behavior.[79] But such an extrapolation beyond short-term dealer behavior is problematic for a number of reasons. First, since economic models of exchange rate behavior are well recognized as particularly weak over shorter-term horizons, dealers can hardly be accused of irrationality and inefficiency if they do not rely much on analysis based on them. In the absence of strong guidance from that direction, the most efficient response for dealers over very short horizons is to focus on the movements in market prices and volumes as summary indicators of market trends. Second, short-term dealer behavior is constrained by internal dealing strategies, position limits, and the like that are set on a somewhat less frequent basis but that are more likely to be influenced by "fundamentals analysis" (even if often not in terms of fully specified, quantitative exchange rate models). Indeed, the Taylor and Allen survey results are quite consistent with this, showing the relative importance of technical analysis falling off substantially as the time frame lengthens, and showing too that a substantial majority of survey respondents perceived that fundamentals and technical analysis were seen as complementary rather than mutually exclusive. Third, the balance between the use of fundamentals and technical analysis may well change according to circumstances, and in a way that, though relatively complex, may be quite consistent with rationality.[80]

The second aspect relates to nonbank end users in the foreign exchange market. While the dealers can be influential and may indulge in various strategies aimed at securing very short-term gains, in the final analysis, the positions they can take on their own behalf are relatively limited at day's end, compared with the volumes that large clients can move. Given the quasi-public good nature of services provided by currency market makers, it is perhaps reasonable to view the scope to make such short-term gains as an indirect return to production of that public good. And furthermore, the signals and sentiments to which they are responding are for the most part derived from the actions of those large nonbank customers. The recent questions some have raised about the role of hedge funds in leading exchange markets demonstrate the point—such organizations are sometimes thought to be market movers who precipitate "herd behavior" on the part of other market participants. As pointed out in Eichengreen, Mathieson, and others (1998), it is not at all clear that this is actually the case for those institutions, more than others. But even if it were, the more important question is whether such behavior is irrational or inefficient given the environment in which markets operate, and in particular whether it is as divorced from fundamentals as the day-to-day activity of dealers appears (on the surface) to be.

In general, uncertainty and limited, costly, or heterogeneous information are all inherent in the real world, and aversion to loss is a major driving force in the short term. Models that assume these factors away are fundamentally incomplete, while models that attempt to explicitly take this into account produce complex interactions. But these more complex models demonstrate that there can be a number of reasons why short-term dealer behavior may, to a large extent, reflect a quite reasonable approach to acquiring information on more fundamental market trends, in a decentralized market where different views on the future are held. They also demonstrate why apparently observed behavior such as herding, speculative bubbles, and the like may be quite rational.[81] These considerations also seem to provide some shorter-term, and more micro, foundation for the view in some recent empirical work that exchange rates do seem to revert to fundamental (e.g., purchasing power parity) equilibria over time, and that they do not seem to be "excessively volatile."[82]

Once one moves toward an understanding of why certain types of market behavior occur, it tends to become more difficult to draw simple conclusions

---

[79]See, among others, De Long and others (1990).

[80]An interesting recent attempt to empirically model the simultaneous existence of chartists and fundamentalists is found in Vigfusson (1997). This paper finds that, though chartists seem to dominate foreign exchange market trading for much of the time, this is typically in periods that are relatively tranquil or smoothly trending. In contrast, fundamentalists dominate in the less frequent periods of greater turbulence, but this turbulence is associated with reequilibration rather than the opposite. The result has some intuitive appeal—fundamentalists dominate when views of the fundamentals have changed, or where the exchange rate has drifted sufficiently far from what seems justified by the fundamentals that arbitrage and speculation to correct the discrepancy will be profitable.

[81]Some recent attempts to model behavior of exchange market participants along these lines include Lyons (1991); and Peiers (1997). Also, Eichengreen, Mathieson, and others (1998) note several reasons why herd behavior, for example, may be quite rational.

[82]On these points, see respectively, for example, MacDonald (1995); and Bartolini and Bodnar (1996).

about market failure. If key aspects of market behavior are in fact rational and efficient given the constraints under which markets inevitably operate, the issue for public policy then becomes more one of whether and how policy measures can improve the environment in which markets work, rather than directly intervening in market behavior. Central in this regard is the promotion of greater certainty about economic and financial conditions, and especially about the nature of current and future public policy, both at the macroeconomic and the microeconomic/structural levels.

Part III

Table A1. Restrictions Maintained by Countries with Article XIV Status, 1997[1]

Country	Under	Description
Afghanistan, Islamic State of[2]	Article XIV	Binding foreign exchange allowances for current invisibles (approved).
	Article VIII	Multiple Currency Practices (MCPs) arising from (1) surrender requirements; and (2) limits on sales of foreign exchange at the commercial rate to only five essential commodities; and bilateral payment arrangements (BPAs).
Albania	Article VIII	Bilateral payment arrangements.
Angola	Article XIV	Binding foreign exchange allowances for current invisibles: education, travel, remittances, and other transfers. Also, limits on the availability of foreign exchange for payment of imports of goods that have been excluded from the positive list.
	Article VIII	External payments arrears to commercial banks, foreign exchange budgets or allocation systems, and limits on the availability of foreign exchange for certain nonessential imports.
Azerbaijan	Article XIV	Binding foreign exchange allowances for current invisibles: education, medical, remittances, and travel; special requests are dealt with on a case-by-case basis.
	Article VIII	Advance import deposits and restrictions on banks' access to the BICEX for payments for current international transactions on behalf of resident individuals.
Belarus	Article XIV	MCP arising from the tax imposed on the repatriation of profits by nonresidents. Also restrictions on the administrative requirements applied to payments for certain categories of imports.
	Article VIII	Binding foreign exchange allowances for current invisibles: remittances.
Bhutan	Article XIV	Foreign exchange budgets or allocation systems arising from restrictions on availability of foreign exchange for certain import payments. Also, binding foreign exchange allowances for current invisibles: travel.
Bosnia	Article VIII	Binding foreign exchange allowances for current invisibles: travel as well as on other transfers. Limitations on availability of foreign exchange for merchandise imports, and for payments or transfers for services by physical persons.
Brazil	Article VIII	MCPs arising from applying dual exchange rates for different activities, and the application of various taxes up to 25 percent on the selling side and taxes of 5–7 percent on the buying side on different transactions.
Bulgaria[3]	Article XIV	Binding foreign exchange allocation for current invisibles: travel.
Cape Verde	Article XIV	Binding foreign exchange allowances for current invisibles: limitations on family allowance, unilateral transfers, transport, insurance, other commercial services, unilateral transfers of the public sector, including diplomatic and military services and technical assistance.
Colombia	Article VIII	MCPs resulting from the tax on remittances of profits from direct investments and the withholding tax on inflows of foreign earnings from personal services and transfers, as well as the issuance of tax credit certificates for exports.
Congo, Democratic Rep. of the (formerly Zaïre)	Article VIII	External payments arrears. Binding foreign exchange allowances for current invisibles: remittances. MCP arising from the segmentation of the exchange market, which is expected to disappear as foreign exchange transactions gradually return to the interbank market.
Egypt	Article VIII	BPA. MCP arising from a special exchange rate for liquidation accounts under terminated BPA.
Eritrea	Article XIV	Binding foreign exchange allowances for current invisibles: education, medical reasons, and travel.
Ethiopia	Article XIV	Binding foreign exchange allowances for current invisibles: education, medical, remittances, and travel.
	Article VIII	MCP that may arise from the operation of "Dutch" foreign exchange auction system; binding foreign exchange allowances for current invisibles arising from limitations imposed on transferability of balances maintained in the nonconvertible birr accounts of nonresidents; other restrictions arising from the unremunerated bid bond requirement imposed on the purchase of foreign exchange in the exchange auctions.
Iran, Islamic Republic of	Article VIII	Binding foreign exchange allowances for current invisibles: travel. MCP arising from dual official exchange rates.
Iraq[4]		
Liberia[5]	Article VIII	External payments arrears. Foreign exchange budgets. MCP arising from dual market.
Libya	Article XIV	Binding foreign exchange allowances for current invisibles: education and transfers of dividends, technical assistance, and training.
	Article VIII	Advance import deposits. Restrictions on remittances by nonresidents. Foreign exchange allowances for travel. MCP arising from a 10 percent fee on outward foreign exchange transfers.
Mauritania	Article VIII	External payments arrears (approved).

Table A1 (*concluded*)

Country	Under	Description
Mozambique	Article XIV	Binding foreign exchange allowances for current invisibles: education, medical expenses, remittances. and travel.
Myanmar	Article VIII	Binding foreign exchange allowances for current invisibles: not specified. MCP arising from foreign exchange certificates and from sale by exporters of proceeds to private importers at negotiated rates.
Nigeria	Article VIII	Binding foreign exchange allowances for current invisibles: remittances under debt equity conversion scheme and travel. MCP from dual market and from occasional spread exceeding 2 percent within the interbank market.
Romania[6]	Article VIII	Limits imposed on the amount of foreign exchange individuals may purchase for current transactions.
São Tomé and Príncipe	Article XIV	Binding foreign exchange allowances for current invisibles: education, medical expenses, travel, on transfers of savings from earnings under technical cooperation agreements with the government; transfer payments of fares, freight, and costs of communication with foreign countries; and suspension of profits by foreign companies established in the country before independence.
	Article VIII	MCP arising from spreads of more than 2 percent between the official and the free market rates. Foreign exchange budget or allocation systems.
Somalia[7]	Article XIV	MCP (but not clearly stated in report).
	Article VIII	External payments arrears (not clear if official or private).
Sudan	Article VIII	BPA. MCPs arising from spreads of more than 2 percent between the official and the free market rates. External payments arrears (not specified if commercial or official).
Syrian Arab Republic	Article VIII	Advance import deposits by public enterprises. BPAs. MCP arising from different market and official rates. Restrictions arising from the requirement that certain imports are to be financed by workers' remittances and export proceeds.
	Article XIV	Restriction arising from foreign exchange budgets or allocation systems.
Turkmenistan	Article VIII	Foreign exchange budgets or allocation systems. Binding foreign exchange allowances for current invisibles: remittances and travel. MCP arising from the application of commercial banks' cash rate to certain transactions. Restrictions arising from the screening in the weekly auctions of all applications for foreign exchange payments by the Central Bank of Turkmenistan and on limits on transfers of interest.
Uzbekistan	Article VIII	Foreign exchange budgets or allocation systems. MCPs arising from (1) the contemporaneous application of the official rate and the current auction rate; and (2) the segmentation of the exchange market, resulting in deviation in the commercial bank rates of up to an administratively set limit of 12 percent.
Vietnam	Article XIV	Binding foreign exchange allowances for current invisibles: not specified.
	Article VIII	External payments arrears. MCP arising from a tax on profit remittances of 5 percent and 10 percent on foreign-invested firms. Other restrictions arising from limitations on foreign exchange for payments and transfers by foreign-invested firms that do not produce certain import substitutions or are not engaged in certain infrastructure work.

[1]Status as of the latest Article IV staff report issued through December 31, 1997.
[2]The last Article IV Consultation with Afghanistan was held in 1991.
[3]Bulgaria accepted the obligations of Article VIII, Sections 2, 3, and 4 on September 24, 1998.
[4]No information is available.
[5]Last consultation was on 1989.
[6]Romania accepted the obligations of Article VIII, Sections 2, 3, and 4 on March 25, 1998.
[7]The last staff report was in 1991.

Table A2. Restrictions Maintained by Countries with Article VIII Status, 1997[1]

Country	Restrictions
Belize	Ad hoc rationing of foreign exchange sales by the central bank (not approved).
Botswana	Multiple currency practices (MCPs) arising from the Foreign Exchange Risk-Sharing Scheme (FERS) applicable to outstanding external loans obtained by certain public enterprises before December 1, 1990. The FERS was discontinued in 1990, and MCPs would be eliminated by 2006, when the last loan under the FERS will mature (approved until March 1, 1998).
Dominican Republic	MCP arising from the existence of a dual exchange rate system (not approved).
Guinea	Arrears on outstanding obligations under inoperative bilateral payment arrangements (BPA) (approved until January 31, 1998, or the next Article IV Consultation).
Honduras	The foreign exchange Dutch auction system used by the central bank to allocate foreign exchange may give rise to an MCP (not approved).
India	Unsettled balances under inoperative BPA with six European countries (not approved). Binding foreign exchange allowances for current invisibles and transfers: (1) dividend remittances from investments in the consumer goods sectors must be balanced by export proceeds; (2) restrictions are imposed on remittances for overseas television advertising and by nonexporters and exporters without an adequate track record; (3) restrictions related to the nontransferability of balances under the Indo-Russian debt agreement; (4) a restriction on dividend payments on investments by nonresidents in air taxi services; (5) a restriction on transfer of amortization payments on loans by nonresident relatives (not approved); and (6) restrictions on remittances of past investment income. MCP arising from exchange rate guarantees on nonresident deposits, which would be phased out by August 1997 (approved until August 31, 1997).
Jordan	Arrears owed to non-Paris Club creditors (approved until September 30, 1997, or completion of the third review under the Enhanced Structural Adjustment Facility, whichever is earlier).
Kenya	MCP arising from obligations under the Exchange Risk Assumption Fund (now abolished); the MCP would be eliminated by 2003 (approved until May 31, 1998, or next Article IV consultation, whichever is earlier).
Kyrgyz Republic	MCP arising from the National Bank of the Kyrgyz Republic foreign currency auction system (approved through December 31, 1998).
Malta	MCP arising from a forward exchange rate guarantee scheme for U.K. and Irish tour operators; the scheme was to be ended with the winter tourist season (not approved, but eliminated in November 1997).
Mongolia	MCP arising from the spreads of more than 2 percent between the official and market exchange rates (not approved).
Philippines	MCP arising from forward cover provided to oil importers (approved until the expiration of contracts by March 1997).
Russia	Binding foreign exchange allowances: limitations on the convertibility of ruble balances held by nonresidents in the "T" accounts and in the ruble accounts of nonresident banks (the remaining restrictions on this particular issue is deemed largely "technical" in nature by the IMF staff and the authorities are in the process of removing the "technicalities." Restriction arising from the requirement that nonresidents who purchase ruble-denominated securities in the government short-term bonds (GKO) market may only repatriate principal and interest earned, if they first enter into a forward exchange contract (eliminated on December 31, 1997).
Seychelles	Arrears owed to commercial creditors (not approved). Foreign exchange budget or allocation system (not approved). Binding foreign exchange allowance for transferring dividends (not approved).
Sierra Leone	Arrears owed to commercial creditors (approved until December 31, 1997). Restriction arising from the requirement of tax clearance certificates for payments and transfers for certain types of current transactions (approved until June 30, 1997).
Suriname	MCPs arising from (1) the mechanism used to determine the intervention exchange rate by the central bank, and (2) the requirement that the commercial banks sell the foreign exchange they acquire from the central bank at the intervention rate plus three cents of Suriname guilder, which might differ from the exchange rate used in other exchange sales (not approved).
Thailand	MCP arising from the remittance tax on the transfer of profits abroad (not approved).
Tunisia	MCP arising from honoring exchange rate guarantees extended prior to August 1988 to development bank; it will expire when existing commitments mature (not approved).
Ukraine	Restrictions arising from (1) the operation of the "loro" accounts of nonresident banks (this restriction was eliminated on May 1, 1997), and (2) limits imposed on the transferability of balances maintained on the hvrynia and foreign exchange settlement, and deposit accounts of nonresident individuals (not approved); these restrictions were eliminated by May 31, 1997.
Zimbabwe	MCPs arising from existing contracts under the discontinued forward foreign exchange scheme of the Reserve Bank of Zimbabwe (approved until May 15, 1997, or the next Article IV consultation, whichever is earlier). Binding foreign exchange allowances arising from the blocking of dividend and profit payments accrued on investments made before May 1993 (approved until May 15, 1997, or the next Article IV consultation, whichever is earlier).

[1]Status as of the latest Article IV staff report issued through December 31, 1997.

Table A3. Total External Payments Arrears, 1993–97

(*In billions of SDRs, end of period*)

	1993	1994	1995	1996	1997
Total outstanding arrears	58.47	63.95	53.01	57.68	58.51
Of which: countries with significant arrears					
Angola	3.05	3.71	3.77	4.24	2.00
Congo, Republic of	1.60	0.89	1.26	0.90	0.99
Congo, Democratic Republic of the	3.34	4.08	4.85	5.64	6.64
Côte d'Ivoire	4.00	4.15	4.32	4.64	4.70
Ecuador	4.44	5.10	0.41	0.40	—
Kyrgyz Republic	—	—	—	—	2.00
Madagascar	0.87	1.16	1.28	1.47	0.72
Myanmar	0.95	1.09	1.16	1.41	1.85
Nicaragua	3.49	4.15	3.14	1.42	1.16
Nigeria	4.44	6.70	8.63	10.36	11.04
Peru	5.89	6.48	6.88	7.33	0.02
Russia	7.49	8.95	—	—	—
Sudan	9.16	9.40	11.00	12.00	13.70
Tanzania	1.16	1.24	1.37	1.55	—
Vietnam[1]	1.67	2.26	—	—	—
Yemen, Republic of	2.62	3.20	3.42	4.04	1.23

Sources: IMF, *World Economic Outlook* (Washington, various issues).

[1]Vietnam eliminated external payment arrears only in convertible currencies.

Table A4. Regional Payment Arrangements, December 1997

Name of Regional Arrangement	Dates	Number of Members	Members	Settlement Period	Modifications to Arrangement/Comments
LAFTA/LAIA—RCPA (Latin American Free Trade Association/ Latin American Integration Association—Reciprocal Payments and Credits Agreement)	1965–80–present	11	Argentina, Bolivia, Brazil, Chile, Colombia, Ecuador, Mexico, Paraguay, Peru, Uruguay, and Venezuela	4 months	The clearing mechanism was modified in 1991 with a two-tier Automatic Payments Program for the transitory financing of balances of multilateral compensation. In 1992, a modification was made for the authorization to channel through the mechanism payments originated in triangular trade.
ACU (Asian Clearing Union)	1974–present	7	Bangladesh, India, Islamic Republic of Iran, Myanmar, Nepal, Pakistan, and Sri Lanka	2 months	Payments between the Islamic Republic of Iran and Pakistan became eligible in 1990. In September 1989, the ACU established a swap facility.
WACH/WAMA (West African Clearing House/West African Monetary Agency)	1976–present	16	Benin, Burkina Faso, Cape Verde, Côte d'Ivoire, The Gambia, Ghana, Guinea, Guinea-Bissau, Liberia, Mali, Mauritania, Niger, Nigeria, Senegal, Sierra Leone, and Togo	1 month	Clearing house for Economic Community of West African States (ECOWAS); 16 members ratified treaty in 1994; WACH was transformed into WAMA on March 8, 1996.
CEPGL (Clearing House of the Economic Community of the Great Lakes Countries)	1976–present	3	Burundi, Rwanda, and Democratic Republic of the Congo	10 days	All countries are also members of the Common market for Eastern and Southern Pacific (COMESA).
ECCASCH (Economic Community of the Central African States Clearing House)	1981–present	10	Burundi, Cameroon, Central African Republic, Chad, Democratic Republic of the Congo, Republic of Congo, Equatorial Guinea, Gabon, Rwanda, and São Tomé and Príncipe	1 month	None.
PTA/COMESA (Preferential Trading Area for Eastern and Southern Africa/ Community of Eastern and Southern African States)	1984–present	20	Angola, Burundi, Comoros, Democratic Republic of the Congo, Eritrea, Ethiopia, Kenya, Lesotho, Madagascar, Mauritius, Mozambique, Namibia, Rwanda, Sudan Swaziland, Tanzania, Uganda, Zambia, and Zimbabwe	2 months	The PTA was transformed in 1994 into the COMESA.
CMEA (Multilateral Clearing System of the former Council for Mutual Economic Assistance)	1949–91	9	Bulgaria, Cuba, Czechoslovakia, Hungary, Mongolia, Poland, Romania, former U.S.S.R., and Vietnam		U.S.S.R., and Vietnam. Terminated.
EPU (European Payments Union)	1950–58	2			Terminated.
CACH/CPS (Central American Clearing House/Central American Payments System)	1961–92	5	Costa Rica, El Salvador, Guatemala, Honduras, and Nicaragua	1 month	Terminated; CACH transformed into CPS in 1990.
RCD/ECO (Regional Cooperation for Development/Economic Cooperation Organization)	1967–90	3	Islamic Republic of Iran, Pakistan, and Turkey		Terminated.
CMCF (Caribbean Multilateral Clearing Facility)	1977–83	13	Antigua and Barbuda, Barbados, Belize, Dominica, Grenada, Guyana, Jamaica, Montserrat, St. Kitts and Nevis, St. Lucia, St. Vincent and the Grenadines, and Trinidad and Tobago		Terminated.

Source: United Nations Conference on Trade and Development Secretariat.

Table A5. Members Accepting Article VIII, Sections 2, 3, and 4 and Nature of Restrictions Maintained, 1994–97

Country	Date of Acceptance	Free of Restrictions	Type of Restriction	Temporary Approval
Grenada	01/24/94	Yes		
Ghana	02/21/94	Yes		
Sri Lanka	03/15/94	Yes		
Uganda	04/05/94	Yes		
Bangladesh	04/11/94	No	Multiple currency practices (MCP) arising from remaining exchange guarantees on interest components under the former Nonresident Foreign Currency Deposits scheme.	Yes
Lithuania	05/03/94	Yes		
Nepal	05/30/94	Yes		
Latvia	06/10/94	Yes		
Kenya	06/30/94	No	MCP arising from the exchange rate guarantees under the Exchange Risk Assumption Fund scheme	Yes
Pakistan	07/01/94	No	MCP arising from preexisting forward foreign exchange cover contracts.	Yes
Estonia	08/15/94	Yes		
India	08/20/94	No	MCP arising from exchange rate guarantees under the Foreign Currency Nonresidents Account scheme.	Yes
			Exchange restriction from limits on foreign exchange allowances for certain current transactions, the nontransferability of balances under a debt agreement with Russia's limitations on dividend remittances by foreign investors in the consumer goods sector, and the restrictions related to the remaining balances under inoperative transferability of current and past investment income by nonresident Indians.	No
Paraguay	08/23/94	Yes		
Western Samoa	10/06/94	Yes		
Malta	11/30/94	No	MCP arising from the forward exchange rate guarantee scheme for United Kingdom and Irish tour operators, and a bilateral payments agreement with the Libyan Arab Republic.	Yes
Zimbabwe	02/03/95	No	Blocked funds relating to profits and dividends accrued on investments; forward foreign exchange cover scheme.	Yes
Jordan	02/20/95	No	Payments arrears.	Yes
Kyrgyz Republic	03/29/95	No	Multiple currency practice arising from the National Bank of the Kyrgyz Republic foreign currency auction system.	Yes
Croatia	05/29/95	No	Payments arrears.	Yes
Poland	06/01/95	Yes		
Moldova	06/30/95	Yes		
Slovenia	09/01/95	Yes		
Philippines	09/08/95	No	MCP arising out of forward cover scheme for oil imports.	Yes
Czech Republic	10/01/95	No	Outstanding balances from the concluded bilateral payment agreement with Slovak Republic were to be settled not later than April 1, 1996.	No

Country	Date	Approval	Description	Approval sought
Slovak Republic	10/01/95	No	Outstanding balances from the concluded bilateral payments agreement with Croatia were to be settled not later than April ?, 1996.	No
Brunei	10/10/95	Yes		
Botswana	11/17/95	No	MCP arising from the discontinued Foreign Exchange Risk Sharing Scheme.	Approval was in effect at the time of acceptance; further approval sought in context of next annual consultation.
Guinea	11/17/95	No	Payments arrears arising from unsettled balances outstanding under inoperative bilateral payment agreements.	Approval sought in context of annual consultation papers issued in November 1995 and discussed in December 1995.
Malawi	12/07/95	Yes		
Sierra Leone	12/14/95	No	Exchange restrictions arising from tax clearance certificate required for certain types of current transactions, and external payment arrears.	Yes
Hungary	01/01/96	Yes		
Mongolia	02/01/96	Yes		
Russia	06/01/96	No	Limitations imposed on the transferability of balances maintained on nonresident "T" accounts and ruble accounts of nonresident banks.	No[1]
CFA countries[2]	06/01/96[3]	Yes		
Tanzania	07/15/96	Yes		
Kazakhstan	07/16/96	Yes		
Madagascar	09/18/96	Yes		
Namibia	09/20/96	Yes		
Ukraine	09/24/96	No	An exchange restriction arising from the rules governing the operation of hryvnia and foreign exchange settlement and deposit accounts of nonresident individuals.	Yes
China	12/01/96	Yes		
Yemen Republic	12/10/96	Yes		
Georgia	12/20/96	Yes		
Guinea-Bissau	01/01/97	Yes		
Lesotho	03/05/97	Yes		
Armenia	05/29/97	Yes		
Algeria	09/15/97	No	An exchange restriction arising from the absence of due notification to the banking system and the public of the central bank's practice of approving all bona fide applications for foreign exchange in excess of de jure limits contained in relevant exchange regulations for business and tourist travel, and for educational and medical reasons.	Yes

[1]No approval was sought as this restriction was to be eliminated on July 1, 1996.

[2]Benin, Burkina Faso, Cameroon, Central African Republic, Chad, Comoros, Republic of Congo, Côte d'Ivoire, Equatorial Guinea, Gabon, Mali, Niger, Senegal, and Togo.

[3]Central African Republic and Comoros accepted later, in July 1996.

Table A6. Country Groupings

Industrial[1]	High Income	Nonindustrial Middle Income	Low Income	Transition
Australia	Aruba	Algeria	Afghanistan, Islamic State of	Albania
Austria	Bahamas, The	Antigua	Angola	Armenia
Belgium	Brunei	Argentina	Bangladesh	Azerbaijan
Canada	Cyprus	Bahrain	Benin	Belarus
Denmark	Hong Kong SAR	Barbados	Bhutan	Bosnia and Herzegovina
Finland	Israel	Belize	Burkina Faso	Bulgaria
France	Korea	Bolivia	Burundi	Croatia
Germany	Kuwait	Botswana	Central African Republic	Czech Republic
Greece	Netherlands Antilles	Brazil	Cambodia	Estonia
Iceland	Qatar	Cape Verde	Cameroon	Georgia
Ireland	Singapore	Chile	Chad	Hungary
Italy	United Arab Emirates	Colombia	China	Kazakhstan
Japan		Costa Rica	Comoros	Kyrgyz Republic
Luxembourg		Djibouti	Congo, Dem. Rep. of the	Latvia
Netherlands		Dominica	Congo, Republic of	Lithuania
New Zealand		Dominican Republic	Côte d'Ivoire	Macedonia
Norway		Ecuador	Equatorial Guinea	Moldova
Portugal		Egypt	Eritrea	Mongolia
San Marino		El Salvador	Ethiopia	Poland
Spain		Fiji	Gambia, The	Romania
Sweden		Gabon	Ghana	Russia
Switzerland		Grenada	Guinea	Slovak Republic
United Kingdom		Guatemala	Guinea Bissau	Slovenia
United States		Indonesia	Guyana	Tajikistan
		Iran, Islamic Republic of	Haiti	Turkmenistan
		Iraq	Honduras	Ukraine
		Jamaica	India	Uzbekistan
		Jordan	Kenya	
		Kiribati	Lao, PDR	
		Lebanon	Liberia	
		Lesotho	Madagascar	
		Libya	Malawi	
		Malaysia	Mali	
		Maldives	Mauritania	
		Malta	Mozambique	
		Marshall Islands	Myanmar	
		Mauritius	Nepal	
		Mexico	Nicaragua	
		Micronesia	Niger	
		Morocco	Nigeria	
		Namibia	Pakistan	
		Oman	Rwanda	
		Panama	Sierra Leone	
		Papua New Guinea	São Tomé and Príncipe	
		Paraguay	Senegal	
		Peru	Solomon Islands	
		Philippines	Somalia	
		Saudi Arabia	Sri Lanka	
		Seychelles	Sudan	
		South Africa	Tanzania	
		St. Kitts and Nevis	Togo	
		St. Lucia	Uganda	
		St. Vincent	Vietnam	
		Suriname	Yemen Republic	
		Swaziland	Zambia	
		Syrian Arab Republic	Zimbabwe	
		Thailand		
		Tonga		
		Trinidad and Tobago		
		Tunisia		
		Turkey		
		Uruguay		
		Vanuatu		
		Venezuela		
		Western Samoa		

[1]For ease of historical comparison, the definition of industrial countries is that used in the IMF's October 1996 *World Economic Outlook* plus San Marino, rather than the updated definition of advance economies used in the October 1997 *World Economic Outlook*. Other groups are defined as in the World Bank's *World Development Report 1997*.

Table A7. Evolution of Exchange Rate Regimes in Transition Economies
(IMF classification)

Country	1990	1991	1992	1993	1994	1995	1996	1997
Baltics, Russia, and other countries of the former Soviet Union								
Armenia	. . .	. . .	Pegged[1]	Free float	Free float	Free float	Free float	Free float
Azerbaijan	. . .	. . .	Pegged[1]	Pegge[1]	Free float	Free float	Free float	Free float
Belarus	. . .	. . .	Pegged[1]	Managed float	Managed float	Managed float	Managed float	Managed float
Estonia	. . .	. . .	Pegged[1]	Pegged[1]	Pegged[1]	Pegged[1]	Pegged[1]	Pegged[1]
Georgia	. . .	. . .	Pegged	Free float	Managed float	Managed float	Managed float	Managed float (Pegged (de facto))[1]
Kazakhstan	. . .	. . .	. . .	Free float	Free float	Free float	Free float	Managed float
Kyrgyz Republic	. . .	. . .	Pegged[1]	Free float	Free float	Managed float	Managed float	Managed float
Latvia	. . .	. . .	Free float	Free float	Free float (Pegged (de facto))[2]	Managed float (Pegged (de facto))[2]	Managed float (Pegged (de facto))[2]	Pegged[2]
Lithuania	. . .	. . .	Free float	Free float	Pegged1	Pegged1	Pegged[1]	Pegged[1]
Moldova	. . .	. . .	Pegged[1]	Free float	Free float	Free float	Free float	Free float
Russia	. . .	. . .	Free float	Free float	Free float	Managed float	Managed float	Managed float
Tajikistan	. . .	. . .	. . .	. . .	Pegged[1]	Free float	Free float	Free float
Turkmenistan	. . .	. . .	. . .	Managed float	Pegged[1]	Managed float	Managed float	Managed float (Pegged (de facto))[1]
Ukraine	. . .	. . .	Free float	Free float	Free float	Managed float	Managed float	Managed float
Uzbekistan	. . .	. . .	. . .	. . .	. . .	Managed float	Managed float	Managed float
Eastern and central Europe								
Albania	. . .	Pegged[2]	Free float	Free float	Free float	Free float	Free float	Free float
Bulgaria	Pegged[2]	Free float	Free float	Free float	Free float	Free float	Free float	Pegged[1]
Croatia	. . .	. . .	. . .	Free float	Managed float	Managed float	Managed float	Managed float
Czech Republic	Pegged[2]	Pegged[2]	Pegged[2]	Pegged[2]	Pegged[2]	Pegged[2]	Pegged[2]	Managed float
Hungary	Pegged[2]	Pegged[2]	Pegged[2]	Pegged[2]	Pegged[2]	Managed float	Managed float	Managed float
Macedonia, former Yugoslav Republic of	. . .	. . .	. . .	Free float	Managed float	Managed float	Managed float	Managed float (Pegged (de facto))[1]
Poland	Pegged[1]	Managed float	Managed float	Managed float	Managed float	Managed float	Managed float	Managed float
Romania	Pegged[2]	Managed float	Free float	Free float	Free float	Free float	Free float	Free float
Slovak Republic	Pegged[2]	Pegged[2]	Pegged[2]	Pegged[2]	Pegged[2]	Pegged[2]	Pegged[2]	Pegged[2]
Slovenia	. . .	. . .	. . .	Managed float	Managed float	Managed float	Managed float	Managed float

[1]Pegged exchange rate vis-à-vis a single currency.
[2]Pegged exchange rate vis-à-vis a currency composite.

Table A8. Changes in Exchange Arrangements, First Quarter 1994–Fourth Quarter 1997[1]

	Official De Jure Arrangement	Of Which: De Facto Pegged Arrangements[2]	Period of Change
A. From Less Flexible to More Flexible Arrangements (33)			
Pegged: Single Currency → Managed Floating (5)	Angola*		1994:Q2
	Nigeria		1995:Q1
	Suriname*		1994:Q3
	Turkmenistan	Venezuela*	1995:Q4
		Venezuela*	1996:Q2
Pegged: Single Currency → Independent Floating (4)	Azerbaijan		1994:Q2
	Tajikistan*		1995:Q2
	Yemen		1996:Q3
	Liberia		1997:Q4
Pegged: Currency Composite → Limited Flexibility (1)	Austria	Austria	1994:Q4
Pegged: Currency Composite → Managed Floating (6)	Czech Republic		1997:Q2
	Algeria		1994:Q4
	Mauritius		1994:Q4
	Hungary	Hungary	1995:Q1
	Solomon Islands	Solomon Islands	1997:Q4
	Thailand		1997:Q3
Pegged: Currency Composite → Independent Floating (5)	Malawi		1994:Q1
	Mauritania*		1995:Q4
	Papua New Guinea		1994:Q4
	Rwanda		1995:Q1
	Zimbabwe		1994:Q2
Managed Floating → Independent Floating (12)	Dominican Republic		1994:Q3
	Guinea		1994:Q4
	Indonesia		1997:Q3
	Lao, PDR*		1995:Q3
	Madagascar		1994:Q2
	Mexico		1994:Q4
	São Tomé and Príncipe		1994:Q4
	Somalia		1994:Q3
	Sudan*	Sudan*	1995:Q4
	Suriname*		1994:Q4
	Eritrea		1997:Q4
	Korea		1997:Q4
B. From More Flexible to Less Flexible Arrangements (35)			
Managed Floating → Pegged: Single Currency (3)	Angola*		1996:Q4
	Guinea Bissau	Guinea Bissau	1997:Q1
	Venezuela*	Venezuela*	1994:Q3
Independent Floating → Pegged: Single Currency (3)	Bulgaria		1997:Q3
	Lithuania		1994:Q1
	Nigeria		1994:Q1
Managed Floating → Pegged: Currency Composite (1)	Latvia*		1997:Q4
Independent Floating → Limited Flexibility (2)	Finland	Finland	1996:Q4
	Italy	Italy	1996:Q4
Independent Floating → Managed Floating (26)	Bolivia*	Bolivia*	1997:Q4
	Brazil	Brazil	1994:Q4
	Costa Rica	Costa Rica	1995:Q4
	Croatia	Croatia	1994:Q3
	Dominican Republic		1994:Q2
	El Salvador	El Salvador	1995:Q4
	Ethiopia		1997:Q4
	Georgia	Georgia	1994:Q2
	Honduras	Honduras	1994:Q2
	Iran, Islamic Republic of	Iran, Islamic Rep. of	1995:Q4
	Kazakhstan		1997:Q4
	Kenya		1997:Q4
	Kyrgyz Republic		1995:Q4
	Lao, PDR*		1997:Q1
	Latvia	Latvia	1995:Q1

Table A8 (*concluded*)

	Official De Jure Arrangement	Of Which: De Facto Pegged Arrangements[2]	Period of Change
	Macedonia, former Yugoslav Republic of	Macedonia, former Yugoslav Republic of	1994:Q3
	Malawi*		1997:Q3
	Mauritania*		1997:Q4
	Norway		1995:Q2
	Romania		1997:Q4
	Russia	Russia	1995:Q2
	Sudan*	Sudan*	1996:Q3
	Suriname*		1995:Q4
	Tajikistan*		1997:Q4
	Ukraine	Ukraine	1995:Q4
	Uzbekistan		1995:Q4

[1]Those countries that switched back and forth between regimes are indicated by an asterisk, *.

[2]Indicates that the arrangement to which the country shifted to bears the features of a pegged system, including de facto fixed pegs, formal/informal horizontal bands, crawling pegs, or crawling bands.

Table A9. Changes in Exchange Rate Arrangements Affecting the Official Classification and Other Currency Adjustments, 1994–December 31, 1997[1]

Country	Reclassified	Date[1]	Remarks	Changes Within the Existing Classification
Algeria		1994:Q2		*Devaluation:* The dinar was devalued in two stages, by 37.5% and 7.3%, at the outset of the program in 1994 and in October 1994, respectively.
	Pegged: Currency Composite: Other	1994:Q4	Foreign exchange auctions for the dinar were introduced.	
Angola		1994:Q1		*Devaluation and unification of exchange rate:* The exchange rate was devalued in two stages (from Nkz16,500 to Nkz16,830 to Nkz35,000), reflecting a cumulative devaluation of 81.4% and effectively unifying the dual exchange rate system.
	More Flexible: Other Managed Floating	1994:Q2	Angola adopted a single official exchange rate determined in foreign exchange auctions conducted by the central bank three times a week.	
	Pegged: Single Currency: U.S. dollar	1995:Q3		*New currency:* A new currency, the readjusted kwanza, was introduced replacing the new kwanza. The readjusted kwanza was equivalent to 1,000 new kwanzas.
		1996:Q1		*Devaluation:* The central bank devalued the readjusted kwanza in the secondary official exchange market twice to a total cumulative devaluation of 85%.
		1996:Q3		*Devaluation:* The readjusted kwanza was devalued from KZR161,386 per US$1 to KZR202,000 per US$1, close to the rate prevailing in the parallel market.
	More Flexible: Other Managed Floating	1996:Q4	The authorities pegged the official exchange rate to the U.S. dollar.	*Devaluation:* At the same time as pegging the exchange rate the currency was also devalued from KZR161,386 to KZR202,000 per US$1, close to the rate prevailing in the parallel exchange market.
		1997:S2		*Devaluation:* The readjusted kwanza was devalued by 30%.
Armenia	More Flexible: Independently Floating	1996:Q3		*Change in spread:* The spread between the buying and selling exchange rates was widened in an effort to determine a band for interbank trading to allow more exchange rate flexibility. The spread was less than 2%. The central bank intervenes nearly daily in the market mostly to manage liquidity in the market.
Austria	Pegged: Currency Composite: Other	1994:Q4	The Austrian schilling entered the Exchange Rate Mechanism (ERM) of the European Monetary System	
Azerbaijan	Flexibility Limited vis-à-vis a Single Currency or Group of Currencies	1994:Q1		*Legal tender:* The manat became the sole legal tender and was temporarily pegged to the U.S. dollar and repegged to the Russian ruble later.
	More Flexible: Independently Floating	1994:Q2	The exchange rate is set once a week on the basis of a weighted average of exchange rates quoted by commercial banks.	
	Pegged: Single Currency: Other	1995:Q1		*Unification of exchange rate:* A unified exchange rate was adopted at the market level that applied to both current and capital account transactions.
Bangladesh	Pegged: Currency Composite: Other	1996:Q2		*Devaluation:* The taka was devalued twice in April 1996: from Tk41 to Tk41.50, to Tk41.75.

134

Country	Classification	Date	Description
		1996:Q3	*Devaluation:* The central bank continued to adjust the exchange rate of the taka at frequent intervals. There were six small adjustments in the external value of the taka since April 1996. The taka was last devalued by 0.355% in September.
		1997:S1	*Devaluation:* The taka was devalued by 0.7% in February, and by 1% in March and April, bringing the cumulative depreciation to 4.4% so far in 1996–97.
		1997:S2	*Devaluation:* The taka was devalued by 1%.
Belarus	More Flexible: Other Managed Floating	1994:Q2	*Legal tender:* The Belorussian ruble became the sole legal tender.
		1994:Q4	*New currency:* The ruble replaced the Belorussian ruble. The conversion was carried out at the rate of 10Br to 1 rubel. *Unification of exchange rate:* The exchange rates for cash and noncash foreign currencies were also unified. *Introduction of a band:* An informal exchange rate band of Rbl 11,300–Rbl 13,100 per US$1 was introduced. The upper limit was raised to Rbl 15,000 through end-1996.
		1997:S1 and 1997:S2	*Change in band:* The limits of the exchange rate band were raised to Rbl 15,500 and Rbl 21,000 per US$1 for 1997. *Unification of exchange rate:* The exchange rate was unified and immediately reached the upper limit of Rbl 21,000 with a 5% margin for cash transactions. In the period between end-February 1997 and end-February 1998, the authorities permitted the official rate to depreciate in nominal terms from Rbl 22,800 to Rbl 32,670 per US$1.
Bolivia	More Flexible: Independent Floating	1997:S2	The exchange regime has been reclassified in view of the information that the deviations of the market exchange rate from the official exchange rate (determined in daily anchors of the central bank) are extremely tight due to the very narrow spread between the bank's bid and ask prices, and that the regime is in practice a crawling peg aimed at maintaining the competitiveness of the economy.
Bosnia and Herzegovina	Pegged: Single Currency: deutsche mark	1997:S2	*Introduction of new currency and currency board arrangement:* Previously also maintained peg to deutsche mark.
Brazil		1994:Q1	*New currency:* A new unit of account, the Unit of Real Value, was introduced equivalent to one U.S. dollar.
		1994:Q2	*New currency:* A new currency was introduced, the real. The central bank set a parity for the value of the real in terms of the U.S. dollar.
	More Flexible: Independently Floating	1994:Q4	The authorities intervene occasionally in the foreign exchange market. Within this adjustable exchange rate band mechanism, the central bank in practice has announced periodically a wide exchange rate band, changed about once a year, and induced a monthly depreciation of the real vis-à-vis the U.S. dollar by moving a mini band within the wider band. The width of the outer band has been about 9%, while the width of the inner band has been generally kept below 1%, with the exchange rate determined by interbank market participants within this mini band.
		1995:Q1	*Change in band:* A new exchange rate policy is adopted based on an adjustable exchange rate band, with central bank intervention taking place within the limits of the band. The band was initially set within the range of R$0.86/US$1 to R$0.90/US$1, and later modified to a range of R$0.88/US$1 to R$0.93/US$1, a 5.7% spread.

Table A9 (continued)

Country	Reclassified	Date[1]	Remarks	Changes Within the Existing Classification
		1995:Q2		*Change in band:* The exchange rate band was widened to a range of R$0.91/US$1 to R$0.99/US$1, an 8.8% spread.
		1996:Q1		*Change in band:* The exchange rate band was widened to R$0.97–R$1.06 per U.S. dollar.
		1997:S2		*Change in band:* The central bank widened the exchange rate band from R$0.96–R$1.05 to R$1.05–R$1.14 per US$1, while the currency continued to depreciate within the band (the band was adjusted to R$1.12–1.22 per US$1 on January 18, 1998).
Bulgaria		1997:S1		*Change in exchange rate determination:* The way to determine the central exchange rate was changed to base it on the weighted average of transactions in the interbank exchange market during the previous trading day.
	More Flexible: Independently Floating	1997:S2	The Law on the Bulgarian National Bank was amended and established a currency board arrangement whereby the deutsche mark is the peg currency at the rate of lev 1,000 per DM 1.	
Cambodia	More Flexible: Other Managed Floating	1994:Q1		*Unification of exchange rate:* The dual exchange market was unified by narrowing the spread between the official and parallel market exchange rates to no more than 1% on a daily basis.
		1995:Q1		*New currency:* The authorities issued new coins and bank notes in larger denominations.
CFA franc countries	Pegged: Single Currency: French franc	1994:Q1		*Devaluation:* The parities of the CFA franc and the Comoran franc were changed to 100 CFA francs per 1 French franc and 75 Comoran francs per 1 French franc, respectively. This resulted in a 50% devaluation of the CFA franc and a 33.3% devaluation of the Comoran franc.
Chile	More Flexible: Other Managed Floating	1994:Q4		*Change in basket composition:* The Reference Currency Basket (CRM) was revalued; the dollar, deutsche mark, and yen were given new weights. The "agreement dollar" continued to be calculated on the basis of the CRM and the daily international exchange rates. The central bank continued to allow fluctuations of the actual exchange rate within a range limited to 10% above or below the agreement dollar value.
		1997:S1		*Change in basket composition:* The composition of the currency basket used to calculate the central reference exchange rate of the exchange rate band was adjusted by increasing the weight of the U.S. dollar from 45% to 80%, while reducing that of the deutsche mark and Japanese yen from 30% to 15% and from 15% to 5%, respectively. *Change in band:* Additionally, the width of the exchange rate band was increased from ±10% to ±12.5%. As a result the reference exchange rate was revalued by 4%.
Colombia	More Flexible: Adjusted According to a Set of Indicators	1994:Q1	The exchange rate was managed within a preannounced band set initially at ±7%. The central bank intervenes in the market from time to time.	*Change in band:* The annual rate of depreciation of the exchange rate band against the U.S. dollar was established at 11%.

136

Country	Classification	Date	Description
Costa Rica	More Flexible: Independently Floating	1994:Q4	*Change in band:* The midpoint of the exchange rate band was appreciated by 7.5%. The width of the band was established at ±7% on each side of the midpoint exchange rate. The slope of the band was increased to 13.6%.
		1997:S1	*Change in band:* The annual rate of depreciation of the midpoint of the exchange rate band against the U.S. dollar was increased from 13.6% to 15% while preserving the band width.
	More Flexible: Managed Floating	1995:Q4	The colon is adjusted by the central bank on a daily basis.
		1997:S2	*Change in rate of crawl:* The rate of crawl of the exchange rate was reduced to 9 cents a day (10.5% on an annual basis). The central bank continued with the crawling peg system of daily devaluations based on targeted inflation.
Croatia, Republic of	More Flexible: Independently Floating	1994:Q2	*New currency:* The Croatian dinar was replaced with the kuna at a ratio of 1,000 to 1.
		1994:Q4	The external value of the kuna is determined in an interbank market. The authorities manage the exchange rate of the kuna against the deutsche mark within a narrow band and intervene in the market to smooth undue fluctuations in the exchange rate.
Czech Republic	Pegged: Currency Composite: Other	1996:Q1	*Change in band:* The foreign exchange band was widened from ±0.5% to ±7.5%.
	More Flexible: Managed Floating	1997:S2	The Czech authorities abandoned the ±7.5% fluctuation margins of the Czech koruna and adopted a managed floating exchange rate arrangement. The koruna immediately depreciated 12% below its central parity, before gradually recovering to about 10% below the central parity.
Dominican Republic	More Flexible: Independently Floating	1994:Q3	The official exchange rate began to be adjusted on a weekly basis according to developments in the private interbank market.
		1997:S1	*Devaluation:* The Dominican peso was devalued by 9% bringing it closer in line with the interbank exchange rate.
Ecuador	More Flexible: Managed Floating	1995:Q1	*Change in band:* The central bank devalued the midpoint of the exchange rate by an additional 3% but maintained the width of the band (±2%) and the 12% annual rate of devaluation against the U.S. dollar.
		1995:Q4	*Change in band:* The width of the band was changed from ±3.8% to ±10%, and the midpoint exchange rate was depreciated by 3.1% against the U.S. dollar. Also, the pace of depreciation of the midpoint exchange rate was accelerated from 12% to 16.5%.

Table A9 *(continued)*

Country	Reclassified	Date	Remarks	Changes Within the Existing Classification
		1996:Q3		*Change in band:* The midpoint of the sucre's exchange rate band was depreciated, and its pace of depreciation was accelerated to 18.5% a year.
		1997:S1		*Change in band:* The midpoint of the exchange rate band was depreciated by 3.7%, and the annual rate of depreciation of the midpoint was changed from 18½% to 21%. The central bank also announced it will maintain the market exchange rate within a narrow band (inner band) with a width of 2 sucres on each side of the observed exchange rate of the previous day.
Egypt,	More Flexible: Other Managed Floating	1997:S1		*Change in Spread:* The spread between the buying and selling rates for foreign exchange was increased to 0.3%
El Salvador	More Flexible: Independently Floating	1995:Q2	The central bank adopted a policy of limiting the variation of the colon against the U.S. dollar.	
Eritrea	More Flexible: Other Managed Floating	1995:Q4		*Unification of exchange rate:* The official and the auction exchange rates were unified and the preferential exchange rate was kept. Multiple currency practices emerged from a spread of more than 2% between the auction and preferential exchange rates.
		1997:S2		*Unification of exchange rate:* The official and preferential exchange rates of the birr were unified, fixing the unified rate at Br.7.2 per US$1, which is an administered rate that approximates the parallel market rate.
	More Flexible: Other Managed Floating	1997:S2	In November 1997, Eritrea introduced its national currency, the Nakfa, which is market determined.	*Introduction of new currency:* Eritrea introduced its national currency in November 1997, and the Ethiopian Birr ceased to be legal tender in Eritrea as of November 22, 1997.
Ethiopia	More Flexible: Independently Floating	1994:Q2		*Devaluation:* The official exchange rate was devalued in three stages to a cumulative devaluation of 11.7% from B5.00 to B5.66 per US$1. Later it was revalued to B5.59 per US$1.
		1995:Q4		*Unification of exchange rate:* The official and auction exchange rates were unified, with the official exchange rate set as the marginal rate resulting from the biweekly auction.
	More Flexible: Independently Floating	1997:S2	The official exchange rate of the birr is the marginal rate determined in weekly auctions for announced quantities of foreign exchange as determined by the National Bank of Ethiopia. In view of this information, the exchange rate arrangement has been classified to managed floating.	
Finland	Flexibility Limited vis-à-vis a Single Currency or Group of Currencies: Cooperative Arrangement	1996:Q4	The Finish markka entered the ERM of the European Monetary System. The markka's central rate is Fmk5.85424 as of December 31, 1997 (changed to Fmk6.01125 on March 16, 1998) and is maintained within a margin of ±15% around the bilateral central rates against other participating currencies.	
Georgia	More Flexible: Independently Floating	1994:Q4	The coupon is determined by an auction system whereby the central bank intervenes.	

138

Country	Classification	Date	
		1995:Q3	*New currency:* A new national currency, the lari, was introduced. The conversion from coupon to lari took place at a rate of one million coupons to one lari for both cash and bank accounts in coupons. An official exchange rate of ruble 4,000 per lari was also announced for the conversion of rubles to lari. The lari became the sole legal tender in Georgia.
		1996:Q3	*Exchange rate unification:* The official exchange rate for the lari against the U.S. dollar is set daily at the level of the Tbilisi Interbank Currency Exchange auction rate, thus terminating the multiple currency practice. The spread between the auction rate and the street rate is now less than 1%.
Guinea	More Flexible: Other Managed Floating	1994:Q4	An interbank market for exchange rate determination was introduced.
Guinea-Bissau	More Flexible: Other Managed Floating	1994:Q1	*Change in spread:* The spread between the buying and selling exchange rates was reduced from 3.5% to 2% thus eliminating the multiple currency practice.
	Pegged: Single Currency: French Franc	1997:S1	Guinea-Bissau joined the West African Monetary Union. The currency conversion was made at a rate of PG65 per CFAF 1.
Honduras	More Flexible: Independently Floating	1994:Q2	The interbank market was replaced by an auction system. The reference rate is equal to the weighted average of the prices of successful bids at each auction. The base exchange rate is the arithmetic average of the reference exchange rates of the previous 15 auctions.
		1996:Q2	*Change in band:* The exchange rate band was widened from ±1% to ±5% around the central rate (widened further to ±7% in March 1998).
		1997:S1	*Devaluation:* The first pace of devaluations of the base rate was initiated in April: the base rate was devalued by 2.5% by May. The forward-looking exchange rate crawl was maintained.
Hungary	More Flexible: Other Managed Floating	1994:Q1	*Devaluation:* The forint was devalued twice, by 1% and by 2.6%, against the basket of currencies to which it is pegged.
		1994:Q3	*Devaluation:* The forint was devalued by 8% against the basket of currencies.
		1994:Q4	*Devaluation:* The forint was devalued by 1.1% against the basket of currencies in October, and by 1.0% in November. *Change in band:* The band was widened from ±2.5% to ±4.5% in December.
	Pegged: Currency Composite: Other	1995:Q1	*Devaluation:* The forint was devalued by 1.4% in January, by 2% in February, and by 8.3% in March when Hungary reclassified its exchange rate arrangement. A new preannounced crawling peg exchange rate arrangement was introduced.

139

Table A9 (*continued*)

Country	Reclassified	Date[1]	Remarks	Changes Within the Existing Classification
		1996:Q1		*Change in rate of crawl:* The rate of crawl was reduced from 1.3% to 1.2% per month. Margins around the central rate were maintained at ±2.25%.
		1996:Q4		*Change in basket:* The composition of the basket was changed by replacing the European currency unit (ecu) with the deutsche mark keeping the same weight. In addition, the central bank began to base its official exchange rate on interbank spot rates.
		1997:S1		*Change in rate of crawl:* The monthly depreciation of the crawling peg against a basket of currencies was reduced from 1.2% to 1.1%.
		1997:S2		*Change in rate of crawl:* The monthly rate of devaluation against the basket of currencies was reduced to 1.1% a month in April, and to 1% in August.
Iceland	Pegged: Currency Composite: Other	1995:Q3		*Change in basket:* The official basket of currencies against which the exchange rate of the krona is determined was changed to 16 currencies and replaced the previous basket that constituted the ECU, the U.S. dollar, and the Japanese yen. Also, the band around the central rate was widened from ±2.25% to ±6%.
		1997:S2		*New system of exchange rate determination:* The krona is fixed on the basis of indicative prices quoted by other market participants. The central bank can intervene, and when it does intervene it bases the rate on actual trading prices made at that time.
Indonesia		1995:Q2		*Change in spread:* The spread between Bank Indonesia's buying and selling exchange rates was widened from Rp 30 per US$1 to Rp 44 per US$1.
		1995:Q4		*Change in band:* The exchange rate band within which the rupiah is freely traded was widened from 2% to 3%. A distinction began to be made between the intervention band within which the interbank rate fluctuates, and the conversion rates (with a maximum of 2% spread) that the central bank applies to certain transactions.
		1996:Q2		*Change in band:* The exchange rate band was widened from ±3% to ±5%.
		1996:Q3		*Change in band:* The exchange rate band was widened from ±5% to ±8%.
	More Flexible: Other Managed Floating → More Flexible: Independently Floating	1997:S2	In August, the currency was no longer protected within a set trading exchange rate band and became an independently floating exchange rate system.	*Change in band:* In July, the central bank widened the intervention band to ±12% from ±8%.
Iran, Islamic Republic of		1994:Q2		*Dual exchange system:* A dual exchange system was introduced comprising an export and official floating exchange rates. The new export exchange rate is set daily at Rls 50 per US$1 lower than the midpoint of the buying and selling rates in the free market. The official floating exchange rate continues to be announced daily in terms of the SDR. The official floating exchange rate continues to be used as the representative rate for the Iranian rial.

Country	Classification		Date	Comments
	More Flexible: Independently Floating	More Flexible: Other Managed Floating	1995:Q2	The central bank introduced a 100% repatriation and surrender requirement on non-oil exports; all transactions were required to be effected through the banking system. *Devaluation:* The official export exchange rate was devalued by 21.8%.
Israel	More Flexible: Other Managed Floating		1995:Q2 1997:S2	*Change in band:* The exchange rate band within which the sheqel fluctuates with regard to the currency basket was widened from ±5% to ±7% on either side of the band's central rate. *Change in band:* The authorities announced that the exchange rate would be widened to ±15%. In June 1997, the depreciation limit of the exchange rate was widened to 21% from 7%, while its slope remained at 6% a year. This implied that by May 1998 the range of fluctuation of the new sheqel would be 30%.
Italy	More Flexible: Independently Floating	Flexibility Limited vis-à-vis a Single Currency or Group of Currencies: Cooperative Arrangement	1996:Q4	The Italian lira entered the ERM of the European Monetary System. The lira's central rate was set at Lit 1,906.48 per ECU and is maintained within a fluctuating margin of ±15% around the bilateral central exchange rates against other participating currencies.
Jordan	Pegged: Currency Composite: SDR		1995:Q4	From October 1995, the Jordan dollar has been tightly pegged to the U.S. dollar without a formal change in the regime.
Kazakhstan	More Flexible: Independently Floating	More Flexible: Other Managed Floating	1997:S2	The exchange regime has been reclassified to reflect more accurately the practice followed by the central bank.
Kenya	More Flexible: Independently Floating	More Flexible: Other Managed Floating	1997:S2	The exchange rate regime was reclassified to reflect the actual practice of the authorities to intervene on a frequent basis, and sometimes massively.
Korea	More Flexible: Other Managed Floating	More Flexible: Independently Floating	1995:Q4 1997:S2	*Change in band:* The width for the band within which the exchange rate of the won fluctuates was widened from ±1.5% to ±2.25% around the base exchange rate. *Change in band:* The width of the band was widened several times, most recently in November 1997 to ±10%. Effective December 16, 1997, the exchange rate band was abandoned and the won was floated to be determined by supply and demand.
Kyrgyz Republic	More Flexible: Independently Floating	More Flexible: Other Managed Floating	1995:Q4	The central bank maintains the som within a relatively narrow band with interventions in the foreign exchange market
Lao, People's Democratic Republic of	More Flexible: Independently Floating	More Flexible: Other Managed Floating	1995:Q2 1995:Q3	*Devaluation:* A series of step devaluations were effected during this quarter. The exchange rate was devalued from KN719 to KN785, representing a cumulative devaluation of 8.4%. A unified market-determined exchange rate regime was introduced. In practice, the kip has a de facto peg to the U.S. dollar.

Table A9 (*continued*)

Country	Reclassified	Date[1]	Remarks	Changes Within the Existing Classification
		1997:S1		*Devaluation:* The authorities adjusted the exchange rate quoted by a major state-owned commercial bank and completed the two-step depreciation of the kip by depreciating it by an additional 2%, completing the total of 5% depreciation.
		1997:S2		*Devaluation:* The exchange rate of the kip was devalued by a total of 42% between June and October in line with the movements in the parallel exchange market.
Latvia	More Flexible: Independently Floating	1995:Q1	Under the formally announced shift to managed float regime, the exchange rate showed a very close relationship to the SDR with the authorities pursuing a de facto peg to the SDR.	
	More Flexible: Other Manage Floating	1997:S2	This reclassification reflects the formalization of the authorities' de facto peg followed since February 1994 under the formally announced floating exchange rate arrangements.	
Liberia	Pegged: Single Currency (the U.S. dollar)	1997:S2	Although the Liberian dollar is pegged to the U.S. dollar at 1:1, the U.S. dollar trades at substantial premium in parallel market transactions, and this market-determined rate was sanctioned for official transactions with passage of an interim budget in October 1997. Accordingly, the regime was classified as Independently Floating.	
Lithuania	More Flexible: Independently Floating	1994:Q1	Under the Litas Stability Law a currency board arrangement was established whereby the litas was pegged to the U.S. dollar.	
Macedonia, former Yugoslav Republic of	More Flexible: Independently Floating	1994:Q4	The central bank intervenes in the foreign exchange market to support the target exchange rate of the denar.	
		1997:S2		*Devaluation:* The denar was devalued to denar 31 per deutsche mark from denar 26.7 per DM 1.
Madagascar	More Flexible: Adjusted According to a Set of Indicators	1994:Q2	An interbank market for foreign exchange is introduced.	
Malawi	Pegged: Currency Composite: Other	1994:Q1	The exchange rate was determined on the basis of supply and demand conditions; in practice, the authorities intervened in the market to maintain the nominal exchange rate under a de facto peg regime against the U.S. dollar.	

Country	Classification (from)	Classification (to)	Date	Description
	More Flexible: Independently Floating	More Flexible: Other Managed Floating	1997:S2	The authorities allowed the kwacha to depreciate significantly starting from July 1997, abandoning the de facto peg against the U.S. dollar, and stated their intention to manage the exchange rate in a flexible manner, with intervention limited to smoothing out fluctuations of the rate and with due regard to consideration for the international reserve targets.
Mauritania	Pegged: Currency Composite: Other	More Flexible: Independently Floating	1995:Q4	The dual exchange rate market was unified and the official exchange rate is market determined.
	More Flexible: Independently Floating	More Flexible: Other Managed Floating	1997:S2	Since 1997, the authorities have been following a more active policy to reverse real appreciation of the currency; the authorities have pursued a nominal depreciation of 2.6% a month against the U.S. dollar compared with an average of 1% during the first half of 1997.
Mauritius	Pegged: Currency Composite: Other	More Flexible: Other Managed Floating	1994:Q4	An interbank market for foreign exchange was introduced.
Mexico	More Flexible: Other Managed Floating	More Flexible: Independently Floating	1994:Q4	*Change in band:* Before the floating of the peso, the fluctuation band within which the peso fluctuated vis-à-vis the U.S. dollar was widened while retaining its current rate of daily depreciation, moving the ceiling of the exchange rate band to N$4.0016 per US$1. The new peso was allowed to float freely.
Nepal	Pegged: Currency Composite: Other	Pegged: Single Currency: Other	1997 S2	The Nepalese rupee is determined by linking it closely to the Indian rupee. This reclassification reflects current information and not the result of a change in policy.
Nicaragua	More Flexible: Other Managed Floating	More Flexible: Other Managed Floating	1995 Q4	*Unification of exchange rate:* The dual exchange rate system was unified and the existing crawling peg system was maintained.
Nigeria	Pegged: Single Currency: U.S. dollar	More Flexible: Other Managed Floating	1995:Q1	*Dual exchange system:* A dual exchange rate system was introduced comprising the pegged official exchange rate and a floating and more depreciated interbank market exchange rate, with periodic central bank intervention by sales to end users through banks.
Norway	More Flexible: Independently Floating	More Flexible: Other Managed Floating	1995:Q2	Monetary policy was aimed at maintaining a stable exchange rate against European currencies, based on the range of the exchange rate maintained since the krone was floated in 1992.
Pakistan	More Flexible: Other Managed Floating		1995:Q4	*Devaluation:* The exchange rate of the rupee was devalued by 7%.
			1996:Q3	*Devaluation:* The rupee was devalued by 3.7%.
			1996:Q4	*Devaluation:* The rupee was devalued by 7.9%.
			1997:S2	*Devaluation:* The rupee was devalued by 8.7%.

Table A9 (*continued*)

Country	Reclassified	Date[1]	Remarks	Changes Within the Existing Classification
Papua New Guinea		1994:Q3		*Devaluation:* The kina was devalued by 12% against the basket of currencies against which it was pegged.
	Pegged: Currency Composite: Other	1994:Q4	The exchange rate was determined by market forces centered on a twice-daily interbank auction with the central bank acting as a broker.	
Philippines	More Flexible: Independently Floating	1997:S2	In July, the authorities announced the floating of the peso. This did not imply a reclassification since Philippines was already classified as Independently Floating even though they had a de facto peg to the U.S. dollar.	*Introduction of a band:* In October, the Bankers' Association of the Philippines introduced a 4% volatility band (comprising the three tiers) in an attempt to stabilize the market. The first band was set at ±2%, the second at ±3%, and the third at ±4%. The band was further widened to ±6% on January 7, 1998 and abandoned on March 6.
Poland	More Flexible: Other Managed Floating	1994:Q3		*Change in rate of crawl:* The zloty's monthly rate of depreciation under the existing crawling peg exchange rate arrangement was reduced from 1.6% to 1.5%.
		1994:Q4		*Change in rate of crawl:* The monthly rate of depreciation of the zloty against the basket of currencies to which it is pegged was reduced to 1.4%.
				Change in rate of crawl: The rate of the monthly depreciation of the zloty against the currency basket was reduced to approximately 1.2% and the central bank temporarily widened the bid-ask spread around its central exchange rate from ±0.5% to ±2%.
		1995:Q1		*Introduction of band:* A system that allows the zloty to fluctuate by ±7% on either side of a predetermined central exchange rate was introduced.
		1995:Q2		*Change in rate of crawl:* The crawling peg arrangement under which the zloty's central exchange rate was devalued by 1.2% a month, and the composition of the currency basket was maintained. The above change removed the multiple currency practice.
		1995:Q4		*Revaluation:* The zloty's central exchange rate was revalued to the prevailing level of the market rate, representing an appreciation of 6.4% against the basket of currencies. The market rate was allowed to appreciate to 2.5% above the new central rate. The zloty continued to be devalued at a rate of 1.2% a month against the basket of currencies, with the ±7% band around the mid-rate also maintained.
		1996:Q1		*Change in Rate of Crawl:* The zloty's monthly rate of depreciation was reduced from 1.2% to 1%.
		1997:S2		*Devaluation:* The exchange rate is adjusted under a crawling peg policy at a preannounced monthly rate of 1% and within the ±7% band (widened to ±10% on February 1998, simultaneously with a reduction in the crawl rate to 0.8%). After the February 1998 action, the authorities allowed the zloty to fluctuate widely within the exchange rate band.
Portugal	Flexibility Limited vis-à-vis a Single Currency or Group of Currencies: Cooperative Arrangements	1995:Q1		*Devaluation:* The bilateral exchange rates of the escudo against other participating currencies in the ERM were adjusted. In this context, the exchange rate of the Portuguese escudo was devalued by 3.5%.

Country	Classification	Date	Description
Romania	More Flexible: Independently Floating	1994:Q2	*Change in spread:* The mechanism of exchange rate determination in the auction market was modified to one based on the principle of market clearing. The spread between the auction rate and the exchange bureau rate was eliminated.
	More Flexible: Independently Floating	1997:S2	Exchange rate regime was reclassified to reflect the central bank's de facto practice of intensified foreign exchange intervention to engineer a depreciation of 2–3% a month.
Russia	More Flexible: Independently Floating	1995:Q2	An exchange rate band regime for the Russian ruble was introduced whereby the ruble can fluctuate between Rub 4,300 and Rub 4,900, implying an exchange rate band spread of ±14%.
		1995:Q4	*Change in band:* The exchange rate band within which the ruble fluctuates was changed from Rub 4,300–4,900 to Rub 4,550–5,150 per US$1.
		1996:Q3	*Change in band:* The central bank adopted a sliding band regime, whereby the lower and upper band were initially set at Rub 5,000–5,600 per US$1. The band was expected to shift to Rub 5,600–6,100 by December. The band is intended to slide at a predetermined rate of 1.5% a month, with a width maintained at Rub 600 per US$1. The central bank will announce the lower and upper bands on this basis each calendar day. The central bank is committed to maintaining the rate within the sliding band, but there is no predetermined rate of crawl for the actual exchange rate.
		1996:Q4	*Change in band:* The authorities changed the band to Rub 5,750–6,350 per US$1. The band is intended to depreciate at just over 4% a year, with the margins around the midpoint maintained around ±5%.
		1997:S2	*Change in band:* Authorities announced on November 10 a new exchange rate policy for 1998–2000, in which the central exchange rate will be set at 6.2 new rubles per US$1, with a margin of ±15% (compared with ±5% at end-1997 under the sliding corridor policy). At the same time, the authorities would seek to maintain the current policy of a gradual crawl within the new horizontal band.
Rwanda	Pegged: Currency Composite: SDR	1995 Q1	A new liberalized exchange rate system was introduced.
São Tomé and Príncipe	More Flexible: Other Managed Floating	1994 Q4	The exchange rate was allowed to be determined by market forces.
Seychelles	Pegged: Currency Composite: SDR	1996 Q2	The peg of the Seychelles rupee to the SDR was replaced with a peg to the Seychelles Trade and Tourism Weighted Basket. The basket includes U.S. dollar, pound sterling, French franc, South African rand, Singapore dollar, deutsche mark, Italian lira, and Japanese yen.
		1997:S2	*Change in basket:* The weights of the eight currencies that make up the Seychelles Trade and Tourism Weighted Basket were revised.

Table A9 (continued)

Country	Reclassified	Date[1]	Remarks	Changes Within the Existing Classification
Slovak Republic	Pegged: Currency Composite: Other	1994:Q3		*Change in basket composition:* The composition of the basket of currencies to which the koruna is pegged was changed to the U.S. dollar and the deutsche mark.
		1996:Q1		*Change in band:* The central bank widened the foreign exchange band within which the koruna fluctuates from ±1.5% to ±3%.
		1997:S1		*Change in band:* The foreign exchange band was widened from ±5% to ±7%.
Socialist People's Libyan Arab Jamahiriya	Pegged: Currency Composite: SDR	1994:Q4		*Change in band:* The margins of the band within which the exchange rate of the dinar fluctuates against the SDR was widened from ±25% to ±47%.
Solomon Islands	Pegged: Currency Composite	1997:S2		*Devaluation:* In December 1997, the Solomon Islands dollar was devalued by 20%.
	Pegged: Currency Composite	1997:S2	Exchange rate arrangement has been reclassified to reflect the actual de facto practice of gearing the exchange rate policy toward maintaining competitiveness with periodic monthly adjustment of the exchange rate based on inflation differentials, terms of trade movements, and overall external position.	
Somalia	More Flexible: Other Managed Floating	1994:Q3	The value of the shilling was freely determined	
South Africa	More Flexible: Independently Floating	1995:Q1		*Unification of exchange rate:* The financial rand scheme was abolished and the dual exchange rate of the South African rand was unified.
Spain	Flexibility Limited vis-à-vis a Single Currency or Group of Currencies: Cooperative Arrangement	1995:Q1		*Devaluation:* The Spanish authorities and the member states of the European Union agreed to adjust the central exchange rate of the peseta and set new central exchange rates in the ERM. As a result the bilateral exchange rates of the peseta against other participating currencies of the ERM were devalued by 7%.
Sudan		1994:Q2		*Unification of exchange rate:* The dual exchange system was abolished and a new unified exchange rate determined in an interbank market composed of Sudan's 27 commercial banks was adopted.
	More Flexible: Other Managed Floating	1995:Q4	A market-determined exchange rate was introduced.	
	More Flexible: Independently Floating	1996:Q1		*Multiple exchange rates:* As a result of strong monetary expansion and the inherent weaknesses in the operation of the exchange rate system the unified market-determined exchange rate system was segmented into various types of exchange rates.
	More Flexible: Other Managed Floating	1996:Q3	The foreign exchange market was reunified.	
	More Flexible: Independently Floating	1997:S1		*Unification of exchange rate:* The multiple exchange rates were unified and the exchange rate system was changed whereby a Joint Committee and the central bank determine daily the exchange rate band, within which each dealer freely trades. In March the spread between the upper limit of the trading band and the accounts-to-accounts rate was reduced from 20% to 16%.

146

Country	Classification	Date	Description
		1997:S2	*Change in band:* The exchange rate band was widened from ±0.3% to ±2%. *Change in spread:* The spread between the accounts-to-accounts market and official dealer exchange rates was reduced in steps, from 23.1% at end-1996 to 14.4% at end-May 1997, to 12.7% at end-June, and to 7.3% at end-1997. The government announced that it would continue to reduce the spread between the joint committee rate and free market rate to a maximum of 6% by end-March 1998.
Suriname	Pegged: Single Currency: U.S. dollar		
	More Flexible: Other Managed Floating	1994:Q3	All multiple exchange rates were unified and the new exchange rate was managed flexibly by the central bank with participation in the unified market from time to time.
	More Flexible: Independently Floating	1994:Q4	The exchange rate system was unified and the exchange rate was allowed to be determined by market forces.
	More Flexible: Other Managed Floating	1995:Q4	The central bank sets a daily exchange rate taking into account the level of the interbank market exchange rate over the previous five days, resulting in the official exchange rate deviating from the closing interbank rate of the previous day by more than 2%. Consequently a multiple currency practice arose as the spread between these two exchange rates varies by more than 2%.
Syrian Arab Republic	Pegged: Single Currency: U.S. dollar		Syria maintains three official and two unofficial exchange rates.
		1996:Q1	*Devaluation:* The budget accounting exchange rate was devalued by 51.3%. All other exchange rates remained unchanged.
		1996:Q3	*Devaluation:* The exchange rate applied to transactions with neighboring countries was devalued by 2.3%.
		1997:S1	*Devaluation:* The budget accounting exchange rate was devalued by 34.3%.
		1997:S2	*Devaluation:* The exchange rate applied to transactions with neighboring countries was devalued by 3.3%.
Tajikistan	Pegged: Single Currency: Other	1995 Q2	The Tajik ruble was introduced and became the sole legal tender. The exchange rate of the Tajik ruble against the U.S. dollar is determined at weekly foreign exchange auctions.
	More Flexible: Independently Floating	1997:S2	Official exchange rate of the central bank is set based on the results of the auctions held at Tajik Interbank Foreign Currency Exchange (TICEX). Interbank and retail market rates are freely determined but generally based on, and close to, the TICEX rate. The reclassification reflects this information.

Table A9 (*continued*)

Country	Reclassified	Date[1]	Remarks	Changes Within the Existing Classification
Thailand	Pegged: Currency Composite: Other → More Flexible: Other Managed Floating	1997:S2	Due to strong pressure in the foreign exchange market the authorities floated the Thai baht.	*Multiple currency practice:* A two-tier currency market was established with separate rates for investors buying baht in domestic markets and investors buying baht in markets overseas.
Turkmenistan	Pegged: Single Currency: U.S. dollar	1994:Q4		*Devaluation:* An exchange rate applied to individual transactions was introduced set at manat 220 per US$1. *Unification of Exchange Rate:* The special exchange rate of manat 10 per US$1 was unified at the commercial exchange rate of manat 75 per US$1, representing a devaluation of 86.7%.
		1995:Q3		*Devaluation:* The two exchange rates for the manat were devalued as follows: the official exchange rate was devalued by 62.5%, and the commercial or cash rate was adjusted by 61%.
	Pegged: Single Currency: U.S. dollar → More Flexible: Other Managed Floating	1995:Q4	The dual exchange rate was unified at the market exchange rate level.	
		1996:Q1		*Devaluation:* In January the official exchange rate was devalued from manat 200 to 2,400 per US$1; in February it was appreciated and fixed at manat 1,000 per US$1; and in April it was devalued to manat 3,000 per US$1 in line with the exchange rate in the bank market.
		1997:S2		*Multiple currency practice:* The unification of the exchange rate carried out in 1996 was reversed when the official rate that applies to the bulk of foreign exchange transactions was fixed at a substantially more appreciated level than the commercial bank rate. The exchange rate regime was a very strictly managed one, with the exchange rate being fixed during May 1997–April 1998. This practice was discontinued in April 1998, but a new gap between the emerged subsequently, widening to more than 30% by the end of the year.
Ukraine		1994:Q4		*Unification of Exchange Rate:* The official exchange rate applied to the surrender requirement was unified with the auction exchange rate. Two other exchange rates remained in effect: the cash market exchange rate and the noncash parallel market exchange rate.
	More Flexible: Independently Floating → More Flexible: Other Managed Floating	1995:Q4	The central bank intervenes periodically to smooth fluctuations of the exchange rate of the karbovanets.	
		1996:Q3		*New currency:* The karbovanets were replaced with the hryvnia as national currency at a rate of Krb100,000 per HRV1. At the same time, the authorities adopted an official exchange rate of HRV1.76 per US$1 and intervened to keep the rate unchanged during the two-week period allowed for the currency conversion.
		1996:Q4		*Adoption of band:* The practice of de facto fixing the exchange rate was abandoned and the authorities let the exchange rate move within the informal band of HRV1.7–HRV1.9 per US$1.
		1997:S2		*Change in band:* The fluctuation band for the hryvnia was formalized at HRV1.7–1.9 per US$1.

148

Country	Classification	Date	Description
Uruguay	More Flexible: Other Managed Floating	1996:Q2	*Change in rate of crawl:* The rate of depreciation of the peso within its exchange rate band was lowered from 2% vis-à-vis the U.S. dollar to 1.8% a month.
		1996:Q4	*Change in rate of crawl:* The rate of depreciation of the peso within its exchange rate band was lowered to 1.4%.
		1997:S2	*Change in rate of crawl:* The rate of depreciation of the exchange rate and reduced to 0.8% a month by end-1997.
Uzbekistan		1994:Q3	*New currency:* A new national currency was introduced, the sum.
		1994:Q4	*Unification of exchange rate:* The official and cash exchange rates were unified at sum 22 per US$1.
	More Flexible: Independently Floating	1995:Q4	The official exchange rate is determined daily, either at the auctions, or based on the weighted average exchange rates at which authorized banks purchase and sell foreign exchange in the interbank market on days without auctions. The central bank manages the official exchange rate of the sum through the amount of foreign exchange supplied to the foreign exchange auctions.
		1996:Q2	*Change in spread:* The spread between the auction-determined official rate and the cash rate at the exchange bureaus was widened from 1½–3% to 8½–19% for buying from customers, and from 2½–4% to 11–21½% for selling to customers.
		1997:S1	*Multiple currency practice:* A system of multiple currency practices was introduced.
Venezuela	More Flexible: Other Managed Floating	1994:Q2	*Pace of depreciation:* The rate of depreciation of the crawling peg exchange rate was accelerated and a dual exchange market emerged.
	Pegged: Single Currency: U.S. dollar	1994:Q3 1995:Q4	*Dual exchange rate system:* The central bank temporarily introduced an exchange rate applicable to tourism and credit transactions. *Devaluation:* Subsequently, the official exchange rate of the bolivar was devalued by 41.38% and made applicable to all transactions, thus effectively unifying the temporary exchange rate system. A parallel exchange rate remained in place.
	More Flexible: Other Managed Floating	1996:Q2	*Introduction of a band:* In July, the central bank introduced a system of exchange rate bands. The initial central rate was set at Bs470 per US$1, and the width of the band at ±7½%. The central rate is adjusted in line with the inflation target for the fourth quarter of 1996 (1½% a month).
	Pegged: Single Currency: U.S. dollar	1997:S1	*Change in band:* The authorities announced the exchange rate band system would be maintained but the central exchange rate was revalued from Bs514 to Bs472 per US$1. The new central exchange rate would depreciate at a monthly rate of 1.32%.
		1997:S2	*Change in band:* The authorities announced that the exchange rate band system would be maintained but the central rate would be revalued from Bs517 to Bs498 per US$1. The new central rate would depreciate at a monthly rate of 1.16%.

Table A9 (*concluded*)

Country	Reclassified	Date[1]	Remarks	Changes Within the Existing Classification
Vietnam	More Flexible: Other Managed Floating	1996:Q4		*Change in band:* The fluctuation band for the dong was widened to ±1% from ±0.5% around the central exchange rate.
		1997:S1		*Change in band:* The band was widened from ±1% to ±5%.
		1997:S2		*Change in band:* The trading band for the dong was widened from ±5% to ±10% in October 1997. (In February 1998, the band width was maintained, but the central rate around which the dong fluctuates was devalued by about 5.3%.)
Yemen, Republic of		1995:Q1		*Change in multiple exchange system:* The number of exchange rates in effect was reduced from 5 to 3.
	Pegged: Single Currency: U.S. dollar	1996:Q1	A two-stage approach to unification of the foreign exchange markets was adopted and the currency was floated.	
	More Flexible: Independently Floating	1996:Q3		*Unification of exchange rate:* The dual exchange rate system comprising the official and the floating exchange rates was unified.
Zimbabwe	Pegged: Currency Composite: Other	1994:Q2	The dual exchange rate system introduced in January 1994 was unified.	
	More Flexible: Independently Floating			

[1]Data for 1994–96 are divided in four quarters, while for 1997 are divided in two semesters, 1997:S1 and 1997:S2.

Table A10. Exchange Rate Bands in Selected Countries

Country	Period	Rate of Crawl	Band Width	Flexibility in the Band	Peg Currency
Chile	Aug. 1984–present	*Backward looking:* The central parity is adjusted with announced daily depreciations for the coming month based on the difference between past domestic and forecast foreign inflation; a real appreciation of 2% was built into the formula to compensate for fast relative productivity growth in November 1995.	Widened from ±0.5% initially to ±12.5% in February 1997 in five steps.	Makes use of the full band width with the exchange rate moving within the band flexibly.	Central rate set vis-à-vis a basket
Colombia	Nov. 1991–present (formally in Jan. 1994)	*Forward looking:* Rate of crawl set at 11% initially and raised to 13.6% at end–1994 and 15% in 1997. Crawl rate is announced 10 days in advance (in practice a year); the rate is chosen so as to hold real exchange rate constant if consistent with official inflation target; crawl has been insensitive to actual inflation.	±7%	Intervention frequent but small, aimed at reducing volatility within the band, also from time to time to defend it; also supported by capital controls.	U.S. dollar
Ecuador	Dec. 1994–present	*Forward looking:* A preannounced crawl rate. The rate of crawl was accelerated from 12% initially to 21% in steps in 1995–97.	Widened in steps from ±2% initially to ±10% in late 1995.	In 1997, it was announced that market rate will be kept within an inner band on each side of previous day's exchange rate. During first half, the rate moved close to band center.	U.S. dollar
Honduras	April 1997–present	*Forward looking:* The base rate is devalued at a preannounced rate.	Widened from ±1% to ±5% (then to ±7% in March 1998).		U.S. dollar
Hungary	Dec. 1994–present	*Forward looking:* Rate of crawl is preannounced. The rate of crawl was reduced from 1.9% a month to 1.0% in four steps in 1995–97.	±2.25%		Central rate set vis-à-vis a basket
Indonesia	Jan. 1994–Aug. 1997	*Backward looking:* Band depreciated gradually, broadly to offset inflation differential vis-à-vis trading partners. The rate of crawl was reduced from 5.6% a year to 3.5% in response to persistent upward pressure on the exchange rate.	Widened from R/$ 30 to R/$ 4 (±2%), then to ±12% in 7 steps.	The rate moved within the band flexibly until mid–1996, and until mid-1997 hit more appreciated edge under upward pressures; the band was abolished under downward pressures.	Band vis-à-vis a basket
Israel	Jan. 1992–present	*Forward looking:* The rate of crawl is chosen to equal the difference between tarige inflation rate and the expected average inflation rate of countries in the basket. The crawl rate was adjusted twice in 1993–94 to consolidate success in reducing inflation and in 1997 (slowdown in the crawl of the lower band with unchanged crawl of the upper band) in response to appreciation pressures.	Widened from ±5% to ±7%, then only the upper band was widened to 21%.	Heavy sterilized intervention directed to defending an unpublished inner band movable at the discretion of the central bank; after mid–1995, greater flexibility has been allowed within the band.	Central rate set vis-à-vis a basket
Mexico	Nov. 1991–Dec. 1994	*Forward looking:* No announced central parity; lower and upper bands were announced daily; the lower band was fixed, while upper band was allowed to depreciate at a preannounced rate based on projected domestic and foreign inflation.	Gradual widening with a fixed lower and crawling upper band.	Fluctuations of the exchange rate were restricted to a narrow inner band through heavy intramarginal intervention.	U.S. dollar
Poland	May 1995–present	*Forward looking:* The central rate is allowed to depreciate at a fixed rate set at a smaller rate than projected inflation differentials; the crawl rate adjusted from 1.2% a month to 1.0% in 1996, and to 0.8 percent in February 1998.	±7% Widened to ±10% in February 1998.	Fluctuations of the zloty were restricted to a narrower band through intramarginal intervention. In 1997, the zloty was allowed to fluctuate fairly widely in the band.	Central rate set vis-à-vis a basket

151

Table A10 *(concluded)*

Country	Period	Rate of Crawl	Band Width	Flexibility in the Band	Peg Currency
Russia	July 1996– Dec. 1997	*Forward looking:* The band is intended to slide at a pre-determined rate of 1.5% a month. The rate of crawl was reduced in end-1996. In November 1997, the central bank announced a new policy for 1998–2000 in which the central rate would be fixed at 6.2 new rubles per $1 with a horizontal band of ±15%.	About ±5%	To stabilize the exchange rate on a short-term basis, the central bank announces each day a narrow band at which it is willing to transact.	U.S. dollar
Sri Lanka	Mar. 1995–present	*Forward looking:* The middle rate of the band is announced daily, with the band shifting periodically at a given rate.	±1%	Generally flexible within the band with intervention at margins.	U.S. dollar
Uruguay	Oct. 1992– present	*Forward looking:* The rate of crawl is set at a forward-looking predetermined rate; the rate was lowered from 2% initially to 1.4% in two steps in 1996.	±3.5%	Little intervention at margins. The exchange rate was allowed to be close to the most appreciated band.	U.S. dollar
Venezuela	July 1996–present	*Forward looking:* The central rate to be adjusted in line with the inflation target for the upcoming quarters; in early 1997 the crawl rate was set at 1.32% a month, reduced to 1.16% in the third quarter of 1997, and increased again to 1.28% in early 1998.	±7.5%	Authorities' intention is to keep the currency close to band center but to allow more flexibility if needed to deal with capital inflows.	U.S. dollar

Sources: Piero Ugolini, "Crawling Exchange Rate Bands Under Moderate Inflation" (unpublished; Washington: International Monetary Fund); John Williamson, *The Crawling Band as an Exchange Rate Regime: Lessons from Chile, Colombia, and Israel* (Washington: Institute for International Economics, October 1996).

152

Table A11. Exchange Rate Regimes and Indices of Exchange and Capital Controls, 1996

Country	Exchange Rate Regime	Current Account	Capital Account	Exchange Regime
Kazakhstan	Managed float	0.30	0.95	0.62
Russia	Managed float (crawling band)	0.27	0.91	0.59
Côte d'Ivoire	Single currency peg (CFA franc)	0.34	0.82	0.58
Chile	Managed float (crawling band)	0.22	0.89	0.56
India	Independent float	0.22	0.87	0.55
China	Managed float (de facto horizontal band)	0.33	0.73	0.53
Tunisia	Managed float (crawling peg)	0.21	0.81	0.51
Morocco	Basket peg	0.27	0.72	0.49
Pakistan	Managed float (de facto peg)	0.31	0.66	0.48
Brazil	Managed float (de facto horizontal band)	0.31	0.60	0.46
South Africa	Independent float	0.29	0.56	0.43
Korea, Rep. of	Managed float (de facto horizontal band)	0.10	0.70	0.40
Poland	Managed float (crawling band)	0.12	0.69	0.40
Thailand	Managed float	0.17	0.63	0.40
Israel	Managed float (crawling band)	0.16	0.54	0.35
Indonesia	Managed float (crawling band)	0.18	0.50	0.34
Hungary	Managed float (crawling band)	0.10	0.57	0.33
Philippines	Independent float (de facto peg)	0.16	0.47	0.32
Turkey	Managed float (crawling peg)	0.16	0.36	0.26
Egypt	Managed float (de facto peg)	0.12	0.30	0.21
Mexico	Independent float	0.05	0.36	0.21
Czech Republic	Managed float	0.04	0.33	0.19
Japan	Independent float	0.09	0.16	0.12
Saudi Arabia	Limited flexibility vis-à-vis single currency	0.03	0.21	0.12
Australia	Independent float	0.04	0.20	0.12
Argentina	Single currency peg (currency board)	0.03	0.19	0.11
Uruguay	Managed float (crawling band)	0.09	0.13	0.11
Kenya	Independent float	0.05	0.17	0.11
Latvia	Managed float (de facto peg)	0.10	0.10	0.10
France	Limited flexibility within a cooperative arrangement	0.04	0.16	0.10
United States	Independent float	0.05	0.13	0.09
Spain	Limited flexibility within a cooperative arrangement	0.04	0.11	0.08
Italy	Limited flexibility within a cooperative arrangement	0.10	0.06	0.08
Canada	Independent float	0.09	0.06	0.07
Greece	Managed float (crawling peg)	0.06	0.06	0.06
New Zealand	Independent float	0.02	0.09	0.05
Germany	Limited flexibility within a cooperative arrangement	0.04	0.07	0.05
Denmark	Limited flexibility within a cooperative arrangement	0.02	0.07	0.05
United Kingdom	Independent float	0.03	0.07	0.05
Norway	Managed float	0.01	0.05	0.03
Netherlands	Limited flexibility within a cooperative arrangement	0.05	0.01	0.03
Memorandum items				
Mean		0.13	0.39	0.26
Standard deviation		0.10	0.30	0.20
Minimum		0.01	0.01	0.03
Maximum		0.34	0.95	0.62

Source: Based on the IMF's *Annual Report of Exchange Arrangements and Exchange Restrictions* (Washington, 1996).

153

Table A12. Foreign Exchange (FX) Market Development, Mid-1997

Country	Exchange Rate Determination	Auction Market	Interbank Market	Bureau Market	Parallel Market	Forward Market
Afghanistan, Islamic State of	Official rate is maintained by the central bank and a commercial rate is set by the government.			Not applicable.	Yes.	No.
Algeria	Determined in the interbank market.		No margin limits are established on buy-sell rates in the interbank market.	Not applicable.	Not available.	Authorized banks are permitted to provide forward cover to residents (not active).
Angola	Determined in fixing sessions conducted by the central bank from time to time.	Dominant market; all transactions must take place at the official fixing rate.		Not active; exchange houses are no longer allowed to deal at market determined rates but at rates set for commercial banks.	Yes.	No.
Armenia	At the midpoint of the previous day's buy-sell rates in interbank and auction markets.	Decreasing role in the total FX market.	Dominant market.	Active.	No.	No restrictions for forward cover against exchange risk operating in official or commercial banking sectors.
Azerbaijan	Set at daily FX auctions.	Dominant market.	Interbank trading is allowed since August 1997.	Used for cash exchange; not very active.	Not available.	No.
Bangladesh	Pegged to a weighted basket of currencies of the main trading partners.		Authorized banks are free to set their own buying/selling rates for the U.S. dollar and the ratio of other currencies based on cross rates in international markets.	Not applicable.	Not available.	Forward contracts are available from authorized banks, covering periods of up to 6 months for export proceeds and import payments and covering up to 3 months of remittances of surplus collection of foreign shipping companies and airlines. Currency swaps and forward exchange transactions are permitted when they are against underlying approved commercial transactions.
Belarus	Set on the basis of the auction rate.	Dominant market, although it is believed that most trade and foreign exchange transactions were carried out at more depreciated rates such as those on the Moscow parallel market and the cash market.	Limit on transactions volume was lifted in end-1996, but activity remains limited due to restrictions on banks' ability to determine the exchange rate.	Serves as a channel for retail transactions; not very active.	Yes.	Yes, regulated by the same rules as the spot market.
Bolivia	Determined at auctions held daily by the central bank.	Dominant market, with the auction rate applying to all FX transactions.		Active.	Not available.	No.

154

Country	Exchange Rate Arrangement		FX Market	Forward Market	Hedging/Forward Cover
Bosnia and Herzegovina	Fixed under the currency board.	No.	Commercial banks are free to buy/sell FX with the central bank communicating exchange rate at least once a day.	Active.	Not available.	No.
Brazil	Determined within a band established by the central bank.	No.	Transactions are carried out by banks, brokers, and tourist agencies authorized to deal in FX.	Active; tourist agencies and brokers deal only in banknotes and traveler's checks.	A small market exists.	Banks are permitted to trade FX without restriction on forward basis but must be settled within 360 days.
Brunei	Fixed under the currency board.	No.	Banks are free to deal in all currencies with no restrictions on the amount, maturity or transactions type.	Not applicable.	No.	No; but FX risk can be hedged in terms of Singapore dollars by resorting to facilities available in that country including currency futures and options in Singapore markets.
Bulgaria	Fixed under the currency board.	No.	Yes, well developed.	Active.	Not available.	No.
Burundi	Pegged to a basket of currencies.	No.	Commercial banks are authorized to buy and sell in their own account and on behalf of their customers within ±1% around the middle rate set by the central bank.	Not applicable.	Not available.	Commercial banks and exporters through their banks or customers can borrow FX to hedge against exchange risk.
Cambodia	Official rate determined by the central bank.	No.	Exchange transactions take place at the market rate, with commercial banks free to buy and sell FX at their own rates.	Active; FX dealers are permitted to buy and sell banknotes and traveler's checks at the market rate.	Yes.	No.
Chile	Determined within the crawling band mechanism.	No.	Formal FX market consists of commercial banks and exchange houses and other entities licensed by the central bank; economic agents are free to negotiate rates in both formal and informal markets.	Active.	Not available.	Yes.
China	Determined in the interbank market with the central bank announcing a reference rate based on the weighted average price of FX in the previous day.	No.	All FX transactions are conducted through a nationally integrated electronic system for interbank FX trading, electronically linked with 25 FX trading centers located in major cities.	Active.	Not available.	No; however, there are proposals with the central bank to introduce forward contracts on the yuan.
Colombia	Determined within the crawling band mechanism.	No.	All FX transactions take place at market-determined exchange rates effected by FX market intermediaries, excluding teller transactions.	Not applicable.	Not available.	Residents may buy forward cover against exchange risk for FX debts in convertible currencies and to deal in over-the-counter forward swaps and options.

Table A12 (*continued*)

Country	Exchange Rate Determination	Auction Market	Interbank Market	Bureau Market	Parallel Market	Forward Market
Congo, Democratic Republic of the	Determined in the weekly fixing sessions, based in part on the exchange rates prevailing in the unofficial market. During most of 1997, there were separate fixing sessions in various provinces, resulting in premiums or discounts relative to the official exchange rate.	Yes; but limited activity.	Yes; but limited activity; a large share of transactions take place on the informal market, or are merely brokered by commercial banks.	Yes.	Yes.	No.
Costa Rica	Exchange rate determined in the interbank market.	No.	FX trading occurs in an organized electronic market where central bank and authorized dealers participate. Also takes place between authorized dealers outside the organized market.	Not applicable.	Not available.	No.
Croatia	Exchange rate is set in the interbank market; the central bank sets intervention rates to smooth undue fluctuations.	Yes. The central bank intervenes through an auction market that it convenes periodically for that purpose.	Dominant market; central bank applies intervention rates to transactions with banks outside the interbank market. Lack of trust between banks due to inadequate procedures to assess counterparty risk hampers interbank market activity.	No.	No.	The central bank has provided on occasion swap facilities at par for banks in a very limited forward market.
Cyprus	Pegged to a basket of currencies within a ±2.25% band.	No.	Subject to certain limitations, including a limit on buy-sell spreads, authorized dealers (banks) are free to determine and quote their own rates.	Not applicable.	Not available.	Authorized dealers may trade in the forward market with their customers, and purchase official forward cover from the central bank for exports and imports. There are limits on forward margins that dealers can change.
Czech Republic	Determined by supply and demand conditions with occasional central bank intervention.	No.	Commercial banks set their in exchange rates that are applied to transactions with their customers.	Not applicable.	Not available.	Yes. Developed over-the-counter forward exchange market.
Dominican Republic	Dual exchange rate system. Since March 1997, the official exchange rate has been held fixed while the market rate has been determined under a managed float.	No.	Dominant market.	Not applicable.	Not available.	No.
Ecuador	Determined within a crawling band mechanism.	No.	Banks and other financial institutions conduct FX transactions within the established band.	Not applicable.	Not available.	Authorized banks and other financial institutions may conduct forward swaps and options and transactions in other financial derivative instruments, subject to supervision and control.

Egypt	Determined in the FX market.	No.	There is a free FX market in which authorized FX dealers are permitted to operate.	Authorized nonbank FX dealers may operate in the free market, buying and selling banknotes, coins, traveler's checks on their own account, in cash or through their accounts with authorized banks: they may broker FX operations with limitations.	Not available.	Authorized banks may conduct forward transactions for their own account at freely determined rates, with no prior approval from the central bank.
El Salvador	Determined as a simple average of exchange rates set by commercial banks and exchange houses on the previous day under de facto peg.	No.		Active.	Not available.	No.
Eritrea	Official rate is the marginal auction rate and preferential rate is fixed by the authorities.			Not applicable.	Yes.	No.
Estonia	Fixed under the currency board.	No.	Competitive.	Not applicable.	Not available.	Yes.
Ethiopia	Determined on the weekly central bank auctions.	Quantities to be sold at weekly auctions are set by the central bank		Foreign exchange bureaus operate only within the commercial banking system and are allowed to engage in transactions related to travel, health, education, and acquisition of publications (within specified limits). The activity in this market, however, is quite insignificant.	Yes; the premium, however, has been reduced significantly and is currently close to zero percent.	No.
Fiji	Pegged against a basket of currencies.	No.	Authorized FX dealers are allowed to transact among themselves within a market band of ±1.2%; however, the market is very small and thin with most banks preferring to deal with the central bank at a risk-free, predetermined rate.	Restricted FX dealers deal only in travel-related transactions, and money changers exchange traveler's checks and FX into Fiji dollars.	No.	Forward exchange facilities are provided by authorized dealers for trade transactions with certain maturities; the activity in this market, however, is quite insignificant.
Gambia, The	Determined in the FX market.	No.	Commercial banks and FX bureaus are free to trade among themselves, with the central bank or their customers at freely negotiated rates.	Active.	Not available.	No.
Georgia	Set on the basis of daily auction rate.	Dominant market.	Relatively small (16% of turnover), but growing.	Used for cash transactions.	Not available.	No.

157

Table A12 (continued)

Country	Exchange Rate Determination	Auction Market	Interbank Market	Bureau Market	Parallel Market	Forward Market
Ghana	Determined in the interbank market.	No.	Dominant market for large scale noncash transactions.	Active.	Yes.	No.
Guatemala	Determined in the interbank market.	No.		Not applicable.	Not available.	No.
Guinea	Determined in the interbank market.		Since 1994:Q4 the exchange rate is freely determined in the interbank market between authorized dealers and their clients or among dealers themselves.	Not applicable.	Not available.	No.
Guinea-Bissau	Pegged against the French franc.	No.	Consists of two commercial banks and FX bureaus.	Active.	Not available.	No.
Guyana	Determined freely in the cambio market.	No.	Average quotations of the three largest dealers in the cambio market determine the exchange rate.	Not applicable.	Not available.	Official FX cover as exchange rate guarantees provided to certain deposits in dormant accounts; no guarantee for deposits made after 1989.
Haiti	Determined in the FX market.	No.	Commercial banks quote buy-sell rates for certain currencies other than the U.S. dollar based on buy-sell rates of the U.S. dollar in world markets. The market is dominated by money changers; banks follow this market.	Active.	Not available.	No.
Honduras	Determined in the FX auctions.	Auction system replaced interbank market in 1994:Q2. Banks and exchange houses must sell their daily FX purchases to the central bank.	Replaced by the auction system in 1994:Q2.	Active; amount that can be obtained from the auctions is subject to limitations.	Not available.	No.
Hong Kong SAR	Fixed under the currency board.	No.	Exchange rate of the HK dollar is set in the FX market at freely negotiated rates for all transactions except for note issuing.	Not applicable.	Not available.	Operated on private sector initiatives.
Hungary	Determined under the crawling band system.	No.	Licensed banks are free to determine their own margins within the established crawling band.	Not applicable.	Not available.	Commercial banks may engage in forward transactions at rates negotiated freely between banks and their customers.

Country						
Iceland	Fixed on the basis of indicative prices quoted by market participants each trading day or on actual trading prices.	Daily fixing meetings used to set the exchange rate was abandoned in July 1997.	Since July 1997, organization of the FX market was changed to abandon daily fixing meetings and to allow market participants to act as market makers and make binding offers.	Not applicable.	No.	There is no organized forward market but forward contracts can be freely negotiated in all currencies.
India	Determined in the interbank market.	No.	The market is transactions driven in part because capital controls limit operations of authorized dealers. Lack of adequate up-to-date information on activities in the FX market reduces transparency.	Not applicable.	Not available.	Authorized dealers may deal forward in certain currencies. Forward deals against rupee with banks abroad are prohibited. Official cover for certain currencies.
Indonesia	Determined under a free floating system based on supply and demand conditions.	No.		Not applicable.	Not available.	Forwards and swaps conducted at rates set bilaterally between the central bank and the banks concerned; official forward cover. In September 1997, forward foreign exchange contracts offered by domestic banks to nonresidents were limited to US$5 million a customer.
Jamaica	Determined in the interbank market.	No.	Foreign exchange market is operated by the commercial banks, other authorized dealers, cambios, and the central bank.	Active.	Not available.	Yes, but currently inactive.
Jordan	Pegged to SDR (de facto to the U.S. dollar).	No.	Not applicable.	Not available.	Not available.	Licenced banks may transact with no limit with their customers on forward basis for imports; official forward facility for very specific projects.
Kazakhstan	Determined at the daily auction and in the interbank market.	Decreasing role in the total FX market.	Dominant market (about two-thirds of total transactions).	Fairly significant (about 2,000 licenced bureaus).	Not available.	Foreign exchange futures are quoted at the foreign exchange auction.
Kenya	Determined in the interbank market.	No.		FX bureaus are authorized to deal in cash and traveler's checks.	Not available.	Commercial banks may engage in forward transactions at market-determined rates in any currency, amount, or period.
Kyrgyz Republic	Determined in the twice-weekly FX auctions (reduced to once a week as of January 1998).	Dominant market, but share is declining.	Developing steadily (39% in first half of 1997, though lack of trust among banks constrained somewhat further development. Interbank market captured about 48% of the total central bank foreign exchange sales in 1998, Q1, compared with 41% in 1997 and 27% in 1996.	Not applicable.	Not available.	No.

ANTANT

ОбÉ

Table A12 (*continued*)

Country	Exchange Rate Determination	Auction Market	Interbank Market	Bureau Market	Parallel Market	Forward Market
Lao People's Democratic Republic	Determined in the interbank market.	No.	In practice a large state owned commercial bank which is the dominant transactor in the official exchange rate market sets the exchange rate.	FX bureaus are free to buy-sell FX at freely determined rates provided the spread between buy-sell rates is below 2%.	Not available.	No.
Latvia	Pegged in terms of SDR.	No.	Dominant market; trade takes place through a telephone system.	Not applicable.	Not available.	No
Lebanon	Determined in the market within upper and lower limits of ±0.1 percent around a central parity on Lebanese pound–U.S. dollar rate, which follows a path that is announced by the central bank. Frequent central bank interventions.	No.	Banks are allowed to engage in spot transactions in any currency except for Israeli currency.	Active.	Not available.	Forward transactions are permitted only for foreign trade.
Liberia	Pegged to the U.S. dollar.	No.	Commercial banks charge high premiums for sales of offshore funds; other nonbank FX dealers are permitted to buy and sell currencies other than the U.S. dollar at market determined rates.	Active.	Yes.	No.
Lithuania	Fixed under the currency board.	No.	Dominant market.	Not applicable.	Not available.	Yes.
Macedonia, former Yugoslav Republic of	Determined under managed floating with a de facto peg to the deutsche mark.	No.	The wholesale market in which the central bank, commercial banks, and enterprises operate.	FX bureaus owned and operated by commercial banks, enterprises, and natural persons. May hold FX positions of 100% of the net FX purchases in preceding 10 days.	Not available.	Forward FX contracts for trade transactions are permitted; the central bank may conclude forward FX contracts.
Madagascar	Determined freely in the official interbank market.	No.	Introduced in 1994:Q2. French franc is the only currency quoted in this market, and the exchange rates of other currencies are determined on the basis of cross rates in the Paris FX market.	Not applicable.	Not available.	Limited arrangements for forward cover against exchange risk; exporters can buy FX 120 days prior to settlement from their banks.
Malawi	Determined on the basis of supply and demand.	No.	Authorized dealer banks may buy-sell foreign currencies at freely determined market rates.	FX bureaus are authorized to conduct spot transactions with general public on the basis of rates negotiated with their clients.	Not available.	No.

160

Country						
Malaysia	Determined on the basis of supply and demand with central bank intervention to maintain orderly conditions.	No.	Commercial banks are free to determine and quote exchange rates, spot or forward, to all customers for all currencies other than those of Israel and Federal Republic of Yugoslavia.	Not applicable.	Not available.	Forward contracts may be effected for both commercial and financial transactions, with prior approval for the latter. In August 1997, Bank Nefara Malaysia imposed controls requiring banks to limit their noncommercial related ringgit-offer side swap transactions (forward order/spot purchases of ringgit by foreign customers) to US$2 million a foreign customer.
Maldives	Authorities maintain a de facto peg against the U.S. dollar under a managed float.	No.	Market not well developed. Daily limits imposed on purchases of FX at the Post Office Exchange Counter (POEC) and the practice of the monetary authority to sell FX to trading firms and individuals through the POEC impeded market development.	Not applicable.	Not available.	No.
Malta	Determined on the basis of a weighted basket of currencies.	No.	Transactions in small amounts are handled through the inter-bank market with no limits on buy-sell rates	Not applicable.	Not available.	The central bank provides forward cover directly to public sector, with rates based on interest rate differentials.
Marshall Islands	Pegged with US$ as legal tender.	No.	FX transactions are handled by 3 commercial banks (authorized FX dealers regulated by a statutory banking board); banks buy-sell at rates quoted in international markets.	Not applicable.	Not available.	Forward transactions may be conducted through commercial banks without restrictions.
Mauritania	Determined in the market.	No.	Intermediary banks and FX bureaus licenced by the central bank are authorized to buy-sell FX; they are free to set their commissions for FX transactions.	Active; in addition to FX bureaus, hotels, shipping firms, and travel agencies may buy (not sell) banknotes, traveler's checks under licenced intermediate banks' control.	Not available.	No.
Mauritius	Determined in the interbank market.	No.	Introduced in the last quarter of 1994.	Yes. Hotels are also willing to buy foreign exchange.	Not available.	Forward transactions can be conducted through commercial banks without restrictions.

161

Table A12 (continued)

Country	Exchange Rate Determination	Auction Market	Interbank Market	Bureau Market	Parallel Market	Forward Market
Mexico	Determined in the interbank market.	Monthly auction of options (giving financial institutions the right to sell $ to the central bank in exchange for pesos) was introduced in August 1996.	Dominant market.	Not applicable.	Not available.	Forward cover available from authorized banks. There is an OTC market in forwards and options in FX and Chicago Mercantile Exchange trades future contracts on the peso.
Micronesia	Pegged with U.S.dollar as legal tender.	No.	FX transactions are handled by 3 commercial banks (authorized FX dealers regulated by a statutory banking board); banks buy-sell at rates quoted in international markets.	Not applicable.	Not available.	Forward transactions may be conducted through commercial banks without restrictions.
Moldova	Determined in daily fixing sessions.	Role of fixing sessions declined significantly.	Has further developed and gained depth (98% of turnover); increase in confidence among banks and establishment of Reuters lines are necessary for further development.	Used for cash transactions; active and functioning well.	Not available.	No.
Mongolia	Determined once a week on the basis of average buy-sell rates in the interbank market.	No.	Market is small and volume of trading is very low, with the exchange rate controlled by the rate fixed by the central bank.	Active.	Yes.	No.
Morocco	Determined in the interbank market within a very narrow band since June 1996.	No.	Interbank market was created in June 1996.	Not applicable.	Not available.	Yes; official forward cover was suspended in June 1996 following the creation of the FX market.
Mozambique	Determined in the interbank market.	No.	Established in July 1996, where central bank, commercial banks, and FX bureaus participate.	Active.	Not available.	No.
Namibia	Pegged to the South African rand at par.	No.	Exchange market has developedas an extension of the exchange market in South Africa.	Not applicable.	Not available.	Authorized dealers may conduct forward FX operations for certain trade and nontrade transactions for a given maturity and currency; official cover is provided for import financing at preferential rates.
Nicaragua	Determined within a crawling peg system.	No.	Financial institutions and FX houses may carry out transactions with the private sector.	Active.	Not available.	No.

Country					
Nigeria	Official rate is pegged against the U.S. dollar; all other transactions (interbank and bureau de change transactions and intervention) take place at a market determined rate.	No.	An autonomous foreign exchange market with interbank dealing and periodic central bank sales to end users was reintroduced in 1995: QI together with a dual exchange rate system as part of a strategy to partly liberalize the FX market.	Yes.	Forward FX transactions in the interbank market are permitted among authorized FX dealers and between dealers and their customers. However, the size of this market is small.
Pakistan	Set by the central bank.		Not applicable.	Not available.	The central bank provides forward FX cover for private FX deposits.
Papua New Guinea	Determined in the interbank market auctions.	Authorized dealer banks participate with the central bank acting as broker.	Not well developed, with commercial banks being the only authorized FX dealers. Banks publish rates for all transactions with their customers within a maximum buy-sell spread of 2%.	Not available.	Commercial banks provide forward cover to exporters and importers at market rates, subject to prudential limits on uncovered forward position.
Paraguay	Determined in the exchange market.	No.	No.	Not available.	Commercial banks may enter into forward contracts for trade transactions on terms freely negotiated with customers.
Peru	Determined freely by supply and demand.	No.	No.	Not available.	Forward transactions take place only in the commercial banking sector.
Philippines	Determined freely in the FX market.	No.	Commercial banks trade in FX through an electronic screen-based network.	Not available.	All forward transactions to purchase FX from nonresidents require clearance by the central bank; BSP met foreign currency needs of foreign banks and banks with maturing nondeliverable forward contracts on a forward basis in July/August/December. Also, corporations with future foreign exchange obligations can enter into a nondeliverable forward facility contract with a bank, which in turn covers the forward contract with BSP.

163

Table A12 (*continued*)

Country	Exchange Rate Determination	Auction Market	Interbank Market	Bureau Market	Parallel Market	Forward Market
Poland	Determined in the interbank market, which is allowed to fluctuate within a band around a crawling central parity.	No.	Developed gradually since 1990, with the central bank having played an active role in its promotion with the provision of the basic regulatory infrastructure.	Active; natural persons may transact freely with the exchange rate determined by supply-demand conditions.	Not available.	No formal forward exchange market, but large commercial banks provide forward contracts if requested.
Qatar	Pegged to SDR within margins of ±7.25%.	No.	Commercial banks set exchange rates for their transactions based on the central bank buy-sell rates with a spread of QR 0.0087 applied to exchange transactions with public.	Not applicable.	Not available.	In the commercial banking sector, importers may purchase FX in the forward market.
Romania	Determined in the interbank market.		Transaction volumes in the FX market have increased significantly, indicating some deepening of the market. There is lack of commitment to market-making by banks.	FX bureaus conduct transactions in foreign banknotes and traveler's checks with natural persons; free to set their rates.	Not available.	No major forward exchange market exists.
Russia	Determined based on bid-ask quotes of large banks in the interbank market.	In the form of fixing sessions. Role of the auction market faded.	Dominant market (about 99% recently); trade is active and accelerated through dealings through phone, brokers, and Reuters screens; the central bank intervenes at its discretion in this market, except when the market exchange rate hits the upper or lower bounds of the daily exchange rate band, in which case it sells/buys foreign exchange at those rates.	Active.	Not available.	There is a futures trading market in Moscow; forward contracts are sold by authorized banks; the central bank provides forward cover to authorized banks for nonresidents to repatriate investment proceeds in government securities. Ruble forward market recently opened at the Chicago Mercantile Exchange.
Rwanda	Determined freely in the exchange market.	No.	Commercial banks and FX bureaus operate in this market with banks permitted to apply variable commission to these operations.	Active.	Not available.	No.
São Tomé and Príncipe	Indicative exchange rate is set as a weighted average of the rates of FX bureaus, banks, and the parallel market previous day.	No.		Active.	Yes.	No.
Saudi Arabia	Pegged to SDR within margins of ±7.25%.	No.	The central rate against the U.S. dollar set by the central bank and its buy-sell rates form the basis for exchange rate quotations in the market; banks may charge commissions up to a given percentage.	Not applicable.	Not available.	The commercial banking sector has an active forward market to cover exchange risks for up to 12 months.

Country						
Seychelles	Pegged to a currency basket.	No.	Commercial banks are authorized to deal in foreign currencies at rates based on the exchange rates circulated daily by the central bank.	Casinos, guest houses, hotels, restaurants, tour operators, travel and shipping agents may buy during their licensed activity; must sell all FX proceeds to commercial banks; all other transactions are forbidden.	Not available.	No.
Sierra Leone	Freely determined in the interbank market.	No.	Commercial banks and licensed FX bureaus may buy and sell FX with customers and trade among themselves or with the central bank freely; the weighted average rate of bank and FX dealer transactions in previous week is used to calculate official rate.	Active; FX bureaus are limited to spot transactions and are not allowed to sell traveler's checks.	Not available.	No.
Singapore	Freely determined in the FX market with the monetary authority monitoring the exchange rate against a trade-weighted basket.	No.	Not applicable.	Not applicable.	Not available.	Trade in foreign currency futures are permitted. Banks can hedge against exchange rate risk through forward FX transactions.
Slovak Republic	Determined in daily fixing sessions.	Daily fixing sessions are used to determine the official exchange rate, but the importance of this market in total FX transactions declined.	Dominant market for FX transactions.	Not applicable.	Not available.	Not applicable.
Slovenia	Determined in the interbank market.		Licensed banks may conduct FX transactions among themselves. The market, however, is undeveloped and segmented and volume of transactions is small due to capital controls, active central bank involvement, and intransparent regulations on banks' positions.	Active; natural persons with banks and FX offices at freely negotiated rates.	Not available.	There is a forward exchange market but the volume trading is not significant.
Solomon Islands	Pegged against a currency basket.	No.	Commercial banks are free to determine their exchange rates for all foreign currencies except the U.S. dollar, which is provided by the central bank; there is a tax on FX sales exceeding a certain amount.	Not applicable.	Not available.	Commercial banks may enter into forward contracts with residents in any currency.

Table A12 (*continued*)

Country	Exchange Rate Determination	Auction Market	Interbank Market	Bureau Market	Parallel Market	Forward Market
Somalia	Determined in the free market by supply and demand.	No.	In the free FX market the exchange rate is freely negotiated between resident holders of FX accounts; there is also an official market with the central bank and 2 commercial banks that operate as authorized dealers.	Not applicable.	Not available.	No.
South Africa	Determined freely in the FX market.	No.			Not available.	Authorized dealers provide cover, including for nonresidents subject to limitations, and for trade and nontrade transactions of residents with nonresidents; there is official cover in U.S. dollars with documentary evidence.
Sudan	A Joint Committee of commercial bank representatives, nonbank dealers and the central bank determine daily the official exchange rate band within which dealers trade freely. Exchange rate in the account-to-account market is determined by market forces.	No.	About 27 commercial banks and other exchange dealers trade freely within the exchange rate band set by the Joint Committee, with fixed margins between buy-sell rates eliminated in early 1997.	Active.	Yes, legal	No.
Suriname	Determined in the interbank market. The central bank determines the exchange rate to be used in official transactions, which is based on the weighted average rate of commercial bank transactions over the last five days.	No.	Commercial banks and licensed FX houses may trade with their customers and among themselves at freely negotiated rates.	Active.	Not available.	No.
Tajikistan	Based on weekly auctions since July 1997.	Weekly auctions resumed in mid-1997 after having ceased; the market is not transparent and is segmented with the curb market.	Permitted but attracts limited interest.	Used for retail transactions, but rates are influenced by, or close to, the auction rate.	Yes.	No.
Tanzania	Determined in the interbank market.	No.	Central bank plays a dominant role in the interbank market. Access to the market limited; all FX bureaus were prohibited from participating the in the interbank market from July 1996.	Large nonbank dealers were upgraded so that they could provide a broad range of services.	Not available.	Authorized dealers may enter into forward contracts for purchases and sales of FX with their customers in export and import transactions.
Thailand	Determined under a managed float.	No.	Commercial banks may transact among themselves and with their customers.	Not applicable.	Not available.	All forward exchange transactions must be related to underlying trade and financial transactions.

166

Country						
Trinidad and Tobago	Determined in the interbank market.	No.	Banks are allowed to conduct spot FX transactions without limitation	Not applicable.	Not available.	Banks are allowed to conduct forward FX transactions with public without limitation.
Tunisia	Determined in the interbank market.	No.	Interbank market was introduced in May 1997, where domestic banks were permitted to trade foreign currencies in the spot market among themselves, with foreign correspondents. and non-resident banks in Tunisia.			Domestic banks are allowed to undertake forward FX operations related to trade and services from end-June 1997; the central bank provides exchange guarantees to certain officially guaranteed loans.
Turkey	Determined in the interbank market under a managed float.	No.		Commercial banks, special financial institutions, post, telephone and telegraph offices and precious metal intermediaries are free to set their exchange rates.	Not available.	Banks and precious metal brokers may enter forward transactions at freely established rates; banks may enter swap transactions with the central bank (not currently active).
Turkmenistan	Established at the weekly auctions.	Dominant market; but access is restricted, certain transactions are excluded, and not transparent.	Permitted but volume of transactions is small and subject to restrictions.	Not applicable.	Yes.	No.
Uganda	Determined in the interbank market.	No.	Authorized banks and FX bureaus licensed to buy and sell FX operate at freely negotiated rates. Market is thin in part due to instability of FX flows. Very few banks have access to Reuters screens for dealing.	Active. Have important role in the FX market.	Not available.	Authorized dealers may deal in the forward exchange market provided there is an underlying approved import/export contract.
Ukraine	Determined by competitive bidding at daily FX auctions.	Role in total transactions is declining.	Trade is allowed to take within a margin of ±0.6% around the official rate; turn over larger than the auction market.	Active.	Not available.	No.
Uruguay	Determined in the exchange market under crawling band mechanism.	No.	Undeveloped.			No.
Uzbekistan	Based on daily FX auctions.	Dominant market; dormant, not transparent.	Small volume of cash transactions take place with buy-sell rates administratively set at a more depreciated rate.		Yes.	No.

Table A12 (concluded)

Country	Exchange Rate Determination	Auction Market	Interbank Market	Bureau Market	Parallel Market	Forward Market
Vietnam	Determined in the interbank market within stipulated ranges.	Activity in the auction market effectively ceased in 1995.	All FX transactions are channeled through the interbank market since 1995 with trading taking place within stipulated ranges determined by the central bank.	Not applicable.	Not available.	Yes.
Zambia	Determined in the daily fixing sessions.	Central bank determines the amount of FX sold or bought through its dealing window. Dominant market.	Exchange rates prevailing in the interbank market follow closely those established at the central bank's dealing window. The market is fairly small due to high seasonality of flows and lack of trust among banks.	Not applicable.	Not available.	No.
Zimbabwe	Determined in the exchange market.	No.	Authorized dealers and FX bureaus base their exchange rates on current international market rates. There is limited competition in the market and insufficient market-making by banks. There is no screen-based information network.	Active.	Not available.	Forward exchange contracts are permitted for trade transactions, with no limit on the size but on the maturity.

Bibliography

Anderson, J.E., 1979, "A Theoretical Foundation of the Gravity Equation," *American Economic Review,* Vol. 69 (March) pp. 106–116.

Baliño, T., C. Enoch, A. Ize, V. Santiprabhob, and P. Stella, 1997, *Currency Board Arrangements: Issues and Experiences,* IMF Occasional Paper No. 151 (Washington: International Monetary Fund).

Bartolini, L., and G.M. Bodnar, 1996, "Are Exchange Rates Excessively Volatile? and What Does 'Excessively Volatile' Mean, Anyway?" *Staff Papers,* International Monetary Fund, Vol. 43, pp. 72–96.

Bartolini, L., and A. Drazen, 1997, "When Liberal Policies Reflect External Shocks, What Do We Learn?" *Journal of International Economics,* Vol. 42 (May), pp. 249–73.

Basle Committee on Banking Supervision, 1997, *Core Principles for Effective Banking Supervision* (Switzerland, April).

Bergstrand, J., 1985, "The Gravity Equation in International Trade: Some Microeconomic Foundations and Empirical Evidence," *The Review of Economics and Statistics,* Vol. 67 (August), pp. 474–81.

——, 1989, "The Generalized Gravity Equation, Monopolistic Competition and the Fact-Proportions Theory in International Trade," *Review of Economics and Statistics,* Vol. 71 (February), pp. 143–53.

——, 1990, "The Heckscher-Ohlin Theorem, the Linder Hypothesis, and the Volume and Pattern of Bilateral Trade," *Economic Journal,* Vol. 100 (December), pp. 1216–29.

Cardoso, Eliana, and Ilan Goldfajn, 1997, "Capital Flows to Brazil: The Endogeneity of Capital Controls," IMF Working Paper 97/115 (Washington: International Monetary Fund).

Cukierman, A., S. Webb, and B. Neyapti, 1992, "Measuring the Independence of Central Banks and Its Effect on Policy Outcomes," *World Bank Economic Review,* Vol. 6, (September), pp. 353–98.

Dean, J., S. Desai, and J. Riedel, 1995, "Trade Policy Reform in Developing Countries Since 1985: A Review of Evidence," *World Bank Discussion Paper No. 267* (Washington: The World Bank).

De Long, J.B., and others, 1990, "Noise Trader Risk in Financial Markets," *Journal of Political Economy,* Vol. 98 (December), pp. 703–38.

Dooley, M., and P. Isard, 1980, "Capital Controls, Political Risk, and Deviations from Interest-Rate Parity," *Journal of Political Economy,* Vol. 88 (April), pp. 370–84.

Edwards, Sebastian, 1998, "Capital Flows, Real Exchange Rates, and Capital Controls: Some Latin American Experiences," paper presented at the Conference on Capital Inflows Emerging Markets held in Cambridge, Massachusetts, February 20–21.

Eichengreen, B., Donald Mathiesen, and others, 1998, *Hedge Funds and Financial Market Dynamics,* IMF Occasional Paper No. 166 (Washington: International Monetary Fund).

Eichengreen, Barry, Paul Masson, and others, 1997, *Exit Strategies. Policy Options for Countries Seeking Greater Exchange Rate Flexibility,* IMF Occasional Paper No. 168 (Washington: International Monetary Fund).

Fischer, S., 1996, "Maintaining Price Stability," *Finance and Development* (December).

Fitzpatrick, G., and M. Modlin, 1986, *Direct-Line Distances: International Edition* (Methuchen, New Jersey and London: The Scarecrow Press).

Frankel, Jeffrey A., and others, eds., 1996, *The Microstructure of Foreign Exchange Markets* (Cambridge, Massachusetts: National Bureau for Economic Research), Chapter 4.

Freedman, C., 1991, "Foreign Exchange Management and Monetary Policy," in *The Evolving Role of Central Banks,* ed. by Patrick Downes and Reza Vaez-Zadeh (Washington: International Monetary Fund).

Greenwood, J., and K. Kimbrough, 1987, "An Investigation in the Theory of Exchange Controls," *Canadian Journal of Economics,* Vol. 20(2), pp. 271–88.

Grilli, V., D. Masciandaro, and G. Tabellini, 1991, "Political and Monetary Institutions and Public Financial Policies in the Industrial Countries," *Economic Policy: A European Forum,* Vol. 6 (October), pp. 342–92.

Grilli, V., and Gian Maria Milesi-Ferretti, 1995, "Economic Effects and Structural Determinants of Capital Controls," *Staff Papers,* International Monetary Fund, Vol. 42 (September) pp. 517–51.

Gwartney, J., and R. Lawson, 1997, *Economic Freedom of the World: 1975–1995* (Vancoover: Frasier Institute).

Helleiner, E., 1994, "Freeing Money: Why Have States Been More Willing to Liberalize Capital Controls Than Trade Barriers?" *Policy Sciences,* Vol. 27, pp. 299–318.

Helpman, E., and P. Krugman, 1985, *Market Structure and Foreign Trade* (Cambridge, Massachusetts: The MIT Press).

Hoakman, B., 1995, "Assessing the General Agreement on Trade in Services," in *The Uruguay Round and the Developing Economies,* ed. by W. Martin and A. Winters, World Bank Discussion Paper 307 (Washington: The World Bank).

International Monetary Fund, 1994, *International Trade Policies: The Uruguay Round and Beyond. Volume II. Background Papers,* World Economic and Financial Surveys (Washington).

_____, 1995a, *Issues in International Exchange and Payments Systems,* World Economic and Financial Surveys (Washington).

_____, 1995b, "Policy Responses to Previous Surges of Capital Inflows," in *International Capital Markets: Developments, Prospects, and Policy Issues,* World Economic and Financial Surveys (Washington), pp. 80–94.

_____, 1997a, *Annual Report on Exchange Arrangements and Exchange Restrictions* (Washington).

_____, 1997b, *International Capital Markets: Developments, Prospects, and Key Policy Issues* (Washington).

_____, 1997c, *Selected Decisions and Selected Documents of the International Monetary Fund* (Washington, 22nd issue).

_____, *Recent Economic Developments,* various issues.

_____, 1998, *Trade Liberalization in IMF-Supported Programs* (Washington).

Johnston, R. Barry, 1983, *The Economies of the Euro Market: History, Theory and Policy* (London: Macmillan).

_____, Salim Darbar, and Claudia Echeverria, 1997, "Sequencing Capital Account Liberalization: Lessons from the Experience in Chile, Indonesia, Korea, and Thailand," IMF Working Paper 97/157 (Washington: International Monetary Fund).

Johnston, R. Barry, and C. Ryan, 1994, "The Impact of Controls on Capital Movements on the Private Capital Accounts of Countries' Balance of Payments: Empirical Estimates and Policy Implications," IMF Working Paper 94/78 (Washington: International Monetary Fund).

Kim, K.S., 1994, "Trade and Industrialization Policies in Korea," in *Trade Policy and Industrialization in Turbulent Times,* ed. by G.K. Helleiner (London; New York: Routledge), pp. 317–63.

Knight, Malcolm, and others, 1997, *Central Bank Reforms in the Baltics, Russia, and Other Countries of the Former Soviet Union,* IMF Occasional Paper No. 157 (Washington: International Monetary Fund).

Krueger, A., 1986, "General Issues in Economic Liberalization" in *Economic Liberalization in Developing Countries,* ed. by A. Choksi and D. Papageorgiou (Oxford: Basil Blackwell).

Krugman, Paul, 1998, "What Happened To Asia?" available at http://web.mit.edu/krugman/www/disinter.html

Lewis, K., 1996, "What Can Explain the Apparent Lack of International Consumption Risk Sharing," *Journal of Political Economy,* Vol. 104(2), pp. 267–97.

_____, 1997, "Are Countries with Official International Restrictions 'Liquidity Constrained'?" *European Economic Review,* Vol. 41 (June), pp. 1079–1109.

Loser, C., and E. Kalter, eds., 1992, *Mexico: The Strategy to Achieve Sustained Economic Growth,* IMF Occasional Paper No. 99 (Washington: International Monetary Fund).

Loungani, P., A. Razin, and C. Yuen, 1997, "Capital Mobility and the Output-Inflation Tradeoff," *International Finance Discussion Paper* No. 577 (Board of Governors of the Federal Reserve System).

Lyons, R.K., 1991, "Private Beliefs and Information Externalities in the Foreign Exchange Market," NBER Working Paper No. 3889 (Cambridge, Massachusetts: National Bureau for Economic Research).

MacDonald, R., 1995, "Long-Run Exchange Rate Modeling: A Survey of the Recent Evidence," IMF Working Paper 95/14 (Washington: International Monetary Fund).

Mathieson, D., and L. Rojas-Suárez, 1993, *Liberalization of Capital Account: Experience and Issues,* IMF Occasional Paper No. 103 (Washington: International Monetary Fund).

McKinnon, R., 1993, *The Order of Economic Liberalization: Financial Control in the Transition to a Market Economy* (Baltimore: Johns Hopkins University Press).

Mehran, H., M. Quintyn, T. Nordman, and B. Laurens, 1996, *Monetary and Exchange System Reforms in China: An Experiment in Gradualism,* IMF Occasional Paper No. 141 (Washington: International Monetary Fund).

Papageorgiou, D., A. Choksi, and M. Michaely, 1990, *Liberalizing Foreign Trade in Developing Countries: The Lessons of Experience* (Washington: World Bank).

Park, Yung Chul, 1998, "Gradual Approach to Capital Account Liberalization: the Korean Experience," a paper prepared for the IMF Seminar on Capital Account Liberalization (held in March in Washington).

Peiers, B., 1997, "Informed Traders, Intervention, and Price Leadership: A Deeper View of the Microstructure of the Foreign Exchange Market," *Journal of Finance,* Vol. 52 (September), pp. 1589–1614.

Pritchett, L., 1993, *Tariff Rates, Tariff Revenue, and Tariff Reform: Some New Facts,* World Bank Policy Research Working Paper, No. 1143 (Washington: The World Bank).

Sachs, J., and A. Warner, 1995, "Economic Reform and the Process of Global Integration," *Brookings Papers on Economic Activity: 25,* Brookings Institution, pp. 1–118.

Sharer, R., P. Sorsa, N. Calika, P. Ross, C. Shiells, and T. Dorsey, 1998, *Trade Liberalization in Fund-Supported Programs,* World Economic and Financial Surveys (Washington: International Monetary Fund).

Soto, Claudio G., 1997, *Control of Capital Flows: An Empirical Assessment of the Case of Chile,* Central Bank of Chile (October).

Stockman, A., and A. Hernandez, 1988, "Exchange Controls, Capital Controls, and International Financial Markets," *American Economic Review,* Vol. 78(3), pp. 362–74.

Tamirisa, N.T., 1998, "Exchange and Capital Controls as a Barrier to Trade," IMF Working Paper 98/81 (Washington: International Monetary Fund).

Taumanoff, Peter G., 1984, "A Positive Analysis of the Theory of Market Failure," *Kyklos,* Vol. 37, No. 4, pp. 529–41.

Taylor, A., 1996, "International Capital Mobility in History: The Saving-Investment Relationship," NBER Working Paper No. 5743 (Cambridge, Massachusetts: National Bureau for Economic Research).

Taylor, Mark P., and Helen Allen, 1992, "The Use of Technical Analysis in the Foreign Exchange Market," *Journal of International Money and Finance,* Vol. 11 (June), pp. 304–14.

Thomas, V., J. Nash, and associates, 1991, *Best Practices in Trade Policy Reform* (Oxford: Oxford University Press).

Vigfusson, Robert, 1997, "Switching Between Chartists and Fundamentalists: A Markov Regime-Switching Approach," in *Exchange Rates and Monetary Policy,* Bank of Canada (Ottawa).

Williamson, J., 1996, *The Crawling Band as an Exchange Rate Regime: Lessons from Chile, Colombia, and Israel* (Washington: Institute for International Economics).

World Bank, 1993, *The East Asian Miracle: Economic Growth and Public Policy* (Oxford University Press for the World Bank).

_____, 1997, *World Development Indicators* (Oxford University Press for the World Bank).

World Economic and Financial Surveys

This series (ISSN 0258-7440) contains biannual, annual, and periodic studies covering monetary and financial issues of importance to the global economy. The core elements of the series are the *World Economic Outlook* report, usually published in May and October, and the annual report on *International Capital Markets*. Other studies assess international trade policy, private market and official financing for developing countries, exchange and payments systems, export credit policies, and issues discussed in the *World Economic Outlook*. Please consult the IMF *Publications Catalog* for a complete listing of currently available World Economic and Financial Surveys.

World Economic Outlook: A Survey by the Staff of the International Monetary Fund

The *World Economic Outlook,* published twice a year in English, French, Spanish, and Arabic, presents IMF staff economists' analyses of global economic developments during the near and medium term. Chapters give an overview of the world economy; consider issues affecting industrial countries, developing countries, and economies in transition to the market; and address topics of pressing current interest.

ISSN 0256-6877.
$36.00 (academic rate: $25.00); paper.
1999 (Oct.). ISBN 1-55775-839-5. **Stock #WEO EA 298.**
1999 (May). ISBN 1-55775-809-3. **Stock #WEO-199.**
1998 (Dec.). ISBN 1-55775-793-3. **Stock #WEO-1799.**

Official Financing for Developing Countries
by a staff team in the IMF's Policy Development and Review Department led by Anthony R. Boote and Doris C. Ross

This study provides information on official financing for developing countries, with the focus on low-income countries. It updates the 1995 edition and reviews developments in direct financing by official and multilateral sources.

$25.00 (academic rate: $20.00); paper.
1998. ISBN 1-55775-702-X. **Stock #WEO-1397.**
1995. ISBN 1-55775-527-2. **Stock #WEO-1395.**

Exchange Rate Arrangements and Currency Convertibility: Developments and Issues
by a staff team led by R. Barry Johnston

A principle force driving the growth in international trade and investment has been the liberalization of financial transactions, including the liberalization of trade and exchange controls. This study reviews the developments and issues in the exchange arrangements and currency convertibility of IMF members.

$20.00 (academic rate: $12.00); paper.
1999. ISBN 1-55775-795-X. **Stock #WEO EA 0191999.**

Staff Studies for the World Economic Outlook
by the IMF's Research Department

These studies, supporting analyses and scenarios of the *World Economic Outlook*, provide a detailed examination of theory and evidence on major issues currently affecting the global economy.

$25.00 (academic rate: $20.00); paper.
1997. ISBN 1-55775-701-1. **Stock #WEO-397.**

International Capital Markets: Developments, Prospects, and Key Policy Issues
by a staff team led by Charles Adams, Donald J. Mathieson, and Garry Schinasi

This year's report provides a comprehensive survey of recent developments and trends in the advanced and emerging capital markets, focusing on private and public policy challenges raised by the global financial turbulence in the fall of 1998, nonstandard responses to external pressure in emerging markets, the role of credit rating agencies in global financial markets, progress with European monetary integration, and corporate restructuring in Japan.

$25.00 (academic rate: $20.00); paper.
1999 (Sep.). ISBN 1-55775-852-2. **Stock #WEO EA 699.**
1998 (Dec.). ISBN 1-55775-793-3. **Stock #WEO-1799.**
1998. ISBN 1-55775-770-4. **Stock #WEO-698**

Private Market Financing for Developing Countries
by a staff team from the IMF's Policy Development and Review Department led by Steven Dunaway

This study surveys recent trends in flows to developing countries through banking and securities markets. It also analyzes the institutional and regulatory framework for developing country finance; institutional investor behavior and pricing of developing country stocks; and progress in commercial bank debt restructuring in low-income countries.

$20.00 (academic rate: $12.00); paper.
1995. ISBN 1-55775-526-4. **Stock #WEO-1595.**

Toward a Framework for Financial Stability
by a staff team led by David Folkerts-Landau and Carl-Johan Lindgren

This study outlines the broad principles and characteristics of stable and sound financial systems, to facilitate IMF surveillance over banking sector issues of macroeconomic significance and to contribute to the general international effort to reduce the likelihood and diminish the intensity of future financial sector crises.

$25.00 (academic rate: $20.00); paper.
1998. ISBN 1-55775-706-2. **Stock #WEO-016.**

Trade Liberalization in IMF-Supported Programs
by a staff team led by Robert Sharer

This study assesses trade liberalization in programs supported by the IMF by reviewing multiyear arrangements in the 1990s and six detailed case studies. It also discusses the main economic factors affecting trade policy targets.

$25.00 (academic rate: $20.00); paper.
1998. ISBN 1-55775-707-0. **Stock #WEO-1897.**

Available by series subscription or single title (including back issues); academic rate available only to full-time university faculty and students. For earlier editions please inquire about prices.

The IMF *Catalog of Publications* is available on-line at the Internet address listed below.

Please send orders and inquiries to:
International Monetary Fund, Publication Services, 700 19th Street, N.W.
Washington, D.C. 20431, U.S.A.
Tel.: (202) 623-7430   Telefax: (202) 623-7201
E-mail: publications@imf.org
Internet: http://www.imf.org